D1601411

★ ★ ★

THE PRESIDENT,
THE CONGRESS,
AND
THE MAKING OF
FOREIGN POLICY

★ ★ ★

THE PRESIDENT, THE CONGRESS, AND THE MAKING OF FOREIGN POLICY

★ ★ ★

Edited by Paul E. Peterson

University of Oklahoma Press : Norman and London

Library of Congress Cataloging-in-Publication Data

The President, the Congress, and the making of foreign policy / edited by Paul E. Peterson.
    p.   cm.
  Includes bibliographical references and index.
  ISBN 0-8061-2654-X (cloth). — ISBN 0-8061-2685-X (paperback)
  1. Presidents—United States. 2. United States. Congress. 3. United States—Foreign
relations. I. Peterson, Paul E.
  JK570.P74 1994
  353.0089—dc20   94-11855
                                                                            CIP

Text design by Cathy Carney Imboden.

1 2 3 4 5 6 7 8 9 10

★ ★ ★
CONTENTS
★ ★ ★

Part IV. The Policy Arenas

TABLES

★ ★ ★

Chapter Five

Chapter Six

Chapter Seven

PREFACE

★ ★ ★

Any reader who suggests that the title of this book alludes to a children's book by C. S. Lewis will be shot. *The Lion, the Witch and the Wardrobe* has nothing to do with the president, the Congress, and the making of foreign policy. Presidents may be fierce, but they are seldom sacrificial lions. If Congress sometimes seems to be a witch, it is usually effective in its craft only when it needs to be. One cannot construct a foreign policy by magically passing through a wardrobe. The international system constitutes a reality that foreign policy-makers cannot escape.

As a matter of fact, too much of the analysis of the foreign policy process has been cast in the moralistic language of lions and witches. Republican presidents have been excoriated, denounced, and threatened with impeachment for ignoring the will of Congress. Democratically controlled Congresses have been censured for intruding on the prerogatives of the executive to a degree that incapacitates effective defense of the national interest. The high dudgeon into which contributors to this debate have been able to work themselves is really quite remarkable.

When recent struggles between the two branches are viewed with the historical perspective provided by the closing of the Cold War, a more tempered view seems appropriate. At the time that the Cold War first began, many in Congress wanted to fight communism fiercely. Presidents were content with the more modest objective of containing its spread. After Vietnam and after the beginnings of detente, Democrats in Congress saw less need for continued vigilance than Republican presidents felt prudent. But however bitter the partisan debate, actual policy differences were marginal, not fundamental. Despite the bickering between the branches, containment remained fundamental to U.S. policy, and presidents never lost the capacity to take the steps necessary to keep containment policy intact.

Old disputes have also been twisted by the arrival in the White House of the first post–Cold War presidency of William Clinton. Democrats are no longer so sure that presidential power must be kept in check. Republicans are no longer so certain that foreign policy expertise is lodged exclusively — or even primarily — within the executive branch.

The roles of President and Congress have been further affected by the rise of the United States to unchallenged superpower status. Although much is to be said for the creation of a Pax Americana, this extraordinary transformation of the international system complicates efforts to define the national interest. To take just one of the most pressing of the issues under debate, exactly when should the world's only superpower intervene in regional conflicts? Most of the time, no overriding national interest is at stake in the same way that it was in Berlin in 1948, Korea in 1950, Afghanistan in 1979, or even Vietnam in 1964. When regional conflicts arise, suffering and death can scarcely be avoided no matter what the United States does. But regardless of the outcome, the United States will remain the world's only superpower. How does one distinguish one situation from the next? Can moral principles substitute for realpolitik?

When the national interest gives little guidance, domestic politics is allowed freer rein. If the recent past is any guide to the near future, the president will decide these questions with a keen eye to the domestic consequences of his actions. Voices in Congress will remain constantly, if not consistently, critical — especially when presidential mistakes are apparent. If presidents intervene in regional conflicts, critics will question the exposure of American soldiers to danger and death. If the president withholds the use of U.S. military power, critics will wonder why dictators remain in power and ethnic hatreds flourish. The debate will be as partisan as ever, perhaps more so. But the separation of powers between the branches will not seriously undermine the capacity of the president and the Congress to make acceptable foreign policy. The lion need not be sacrificed to prevent witches from capturing power. It is time to come back through the wardrobe and let the common sense contained in the following essays replace morality-play interpretations of the foreign-policy-making process.

This study was made possible by a grant from the Lynde and Harry Bradley Foundation to the John M. Olin Institute for Strategic Studies in the Center for the Study of International Affairs at Harvard University. The editor is especially grateful to the director of the Institute, Samuel Huntington, for his perceptive, if skeptical, observations and ever-helpful suggestions throughout all stages of the research. Additional support for the overall project was made available from the Joseph B. Grossman fund in Harvard's Center for American Political Studies. Drafts of the essays were presented at a small conference at the Brookings Institution, which generously made available its conference facilities. Discussants at the conference included

Barry Blechman, Aaron Friedberg, Samuel Huntington, Thomas Mann, Stephen Rosen, Mark Peterson, Alan Platt, Nelson Polsby, and Paul Watanabe.

Assistance for research done in conjunction with one or more chapters was provided by the Central Intelligence Agency, the Dirksen Congressional Center, the Interuniversity Consortium for Political and Social Research (ICPSR), Michigan State University's Research Initiation Grant Program, and, for the chapter by David Rohde, the National Science Foundation. Patrick Wolf provided especially valuable research assistance throughout the project, including organizing the Brookings conference and commenting on all papers presented. Others who assisted in the research for one or more chapters include Paul Baker, Henry Broitman, Michael Busse, Rick Dunn, Amy Fletcher, Amy Jutras, Robert Lieberman, James Meernik, Sarah Peterson, Michael Schmidt, Margaret Schuelke, and Renee Smith. The contributors also thank the following colleagues for comments on one or more chapters: John Ferejohn, Morris Fiorina, Linda Fowler, Stephen Hess, Richard E. Neustadt, H. W. Perry, Jr., J. David Richardson, Steven Roberts, Judith N. Shklar, and Martin Tolchin.

PAUL E. PETERSON

Cambridge, Massachusetts

Part I

THE
INTERNATIONAL AND
CONSTITUTIONAL
CONTEXT

Chapter One

★ ★ ★

THE INTERNATIONAL SYSTEM AND FOREIGN POLICY

★ ★ ★

Paul E. Peterson

In the fall of 1991 George Bush saw his own attorney general defeated in an off-year Pennsylvania senatorial race. Richard Thornburgh, once the state's very popular governor, fell victim to attacks by Harris Wofford, an aging, politically inexperienced, unabashedly liberal college professor. The Democrats succeeded in a state that had rejected their candidates in every Senate election since 1962.

Curiously, the defeat came in the same year that George Bush had (1) won a spectacular victory in the Persian Gulf War, (2) negotiated a breathtaking arms control agreement with the Soviet Union, (3) promised a further unilateral cut in nuclear weapons, (4) supported Gorbachev in his final showdown with conservative forces within the Soviet Union, (5) witnessed the liberation of the Baltic states, (6) arranged the first international peace conference on the Middle East, (7) helped achieve a settlement among contending forces within Cambodia, (8) facilitated a political settlement between blacks and whites in South Africa, and (9) opened negotiations with Mexico and Canada on the North American Free Trade Agreement. If these most recent triumphs were not enough, the president could also point with pride to earlier successes, including the fall of the Berlin Wall, the reunification of Germany, the democratization of Eastern Europe, and the resolution of the conflict in Nicaragua. Admittedly, history had not yet quite come to an end (Fukuyama 1992). Disasters had struck the Philippines, the Croatians were fighting the Serbs in Yugoslavia, and a military coup had reversed democratic tendencies in Haiti. But George Bush could tout foreign policy successes beyond the wildest imagination of his predecessors. Not surprisingly, his standing in the polls reached levels that none of his postwar predecessors could match, achieving a spectacular 87 percent in February 1991 ("Presidential Job Ratings").

Harris Wofford ignored these accomplishments. The president, he said, was spending too much time on world affairs; more attention had to be given to domestic matters. Noting that the recovery from the 1990–91 economic recession had petered out, Wofford emphasized how heartless George Bush had been in refusing to extend benefits to the unemployed. The president had also ignored the fact that health care costs were growing, while many Americans were either unable to secure medical insurance or trapped in unwanted jobs for fear of losing their health coverage. Even some of Bush's foreign policy triumphs were dubious, Wofford claimed, alleging that the free trade negotiations with Mexico would cost Pennsylvania thousands of blue-collar jobs. By the end of the campaign, the president's travel abroad had actually become a political liability; Wofford's campaign workers wore T-shirts celebrating Bush's "Anywhere but America" world tour.

The day after the election the president announced that his Thanksgiving trip to the Far East had been canceled. On the day Americans celebrated their Pilgrim ancestors, Bush put Peking duck and sashimi to one side and ate turkey (and crow) instead. By Thanksgiving Day his popularity rating had fallen to just 51 percent (*New York Times*, 26 Nov. 1991, 1). Quite clearly, George Bush, for all his foreign policy successes, was beginning to discover that the domestic front was quite another matter.

The denouement came within a year. George Bush was unable to transform his foreign policy achievements into a reelection victory. His opponent, Bill Clinton, eschewed foreign policy in favor of domestic and social policy themes. One of his key advisers was Harris Wofford's campaign manager, who placed a sign on his desk reminding him that the issue was "The Economy, Stupid!" Despite the fact that Clinton, a little-known governor of a small southern state, had avoided the draft by studying at Oxford, he defeated a commander-in-chief who could claim credit for having brought the cold war to an end.

Although the differences between the politics of foreign and domestic policy seldom reveal themselves this dramatically, they have been enduring features of American politics. At the same time, certain forces in American society reduced these distinctions in the years following the Vietnam War. The loss of Vietnam and the Watergate scandal subverted executive authority, control of the legislative and executive branches was usually in the hands of opposing political parties, and the parties themselves became internally more homogeneous and increasingly differentiated from one another. Foreign policy issues seemed to be completely absorbed into domestic disputes.

These changes raised key questions concerning the conduct of the nation's foreign policy. Had partisanship become so intense that it no longer stopped at the water's edge? Had a prolonged period of almost continuously divided government handicapped the president's capacity to formulate foreign policy? Had the congressional role in the making of foreign policy been so enhanced that the differences between the making of foreign and domestic policy had been all but obliterated? To answer these questions, I asked specialists in the presidency, the Congress, and foreign policy to examine as systematically as possible the changes that occurred between 1965 and 1990, a period when a government divided between a Republican president and a Democratic Congress became the norm rather than the exception.

METHODOLOGICAL PLURALISM

Ascertaining change in power relations between two branches of government poses numerous methodological problems. Power is a slippery phenomenon that is not easily measured. It can be exercised directly or indirectly. It can be realized through initiating actions or by preventing others from so much as proposing an action. It can vary dramatically from one time period to another and from one topic to the next. It takes place not only when actual pressure activity occurs but also when one political participant anticipates what another might want or do. It may be estimated (more or less accurately) by examining the political resources of individuals, identifying the skill with which they participate in the political game, and determining the extent to which outcomes are consistent with the interests of the participants.

Because of these difficulties, it was decided that the best approach to examining the relative power of the branches was to employ a diversity of methodologies and approaches. Because power is an elusive phenomenon, examining it from only one perspective may lead to biased estimates. But if a diversity of methodologies generates a similar set of findings, then one can have greater confidence in the results. The approach, called triangulation by sociologists as well as by surveyors, is rooted in the assumption that if you study a phenomenon from three perspectives, and if you reach the same point each time, you may be quite confident that you have properly fixed the subject under investigation. If one cannot obtain the same results from three different approaches, then one must either revise one's theory or consider the ways in which findings are shaped by the methodology employed.

The three major approaches used in this study are constitutional, institutional, and issue-oriented. The constitutional chapter (part 1) examines the changes in court doctrine with respect to the power relations between the executive and the legislature. The instutitional chapters (parts 2 and 3) examine the way in which specific components of the legislative and the executive branches have characteristically behaved. These chapters include studies of voting behavior of members of the House of Representatives, the use of public hearings by the intelligence and foreign relations committees, and the activities of the congressional leadership. Third, policy making within certain issue areas—trade, defense, arms control, and Latin America—is examined (part 4) to see whether patterns of influence have changed within specific domains.

The answers to the questions posed are varied but not inconsistent. Many of the studies indicate that foreign policy making became increasingly partisan and that Congress became increasingly involved. At the same time, several of the chapters show that the executive retains considerable leadership capacity. As the listing of George Bush's foreign policy triumphs illustrates, the presidency continues to be the dominant foreign policy-making institution. For all of Capitol Hill's increased involvement, it still remains a secondary political player. Conflict between the branches, moreover, remained more contained than has been generally realized. Congressional criticism does not seem to have been more intense in recent decades than it was in the early years of the cold war. In this introductory chapter I shall try to make sense of the diverse findings reported in the pages that follow by showing the way in which the international system places certain constraints on the foreign policy making of the United States government—even at a time when a government of separated powers became a government divided along partisan lines as well.

A HARD TEST OF THE THEORY

The United States is, in some respects, the last place one would look for international constraints on the making of foreign policy. According to a number of theorists, the international system is expected to have a greater effect on the foreign policy making of small nations as compared to large ones, on the choices of weak nations as compared to strong ones, and on economically dependent nations as compared to economically self-sufficient ones (Katzenstein 1983; O'Donnell 1973). Theorists also expect policy making to be centralized in the hands of the executive when external threats are immediate rather than distant.[1]

If these are correct estimates of the occasions when international constraints are greatest, then the postwar United States is a hard case, a case where external constraints are least likely to be controlling. As a large nation well endowed with natural resources enjoying the world's largest and most self-sufficient economy and containing the world's most powerful military arsenal, the United States was, of all nations, the one best able to compel others to act in accord with its wishes and the one least likely to be subject to constraints imposed by the external environment. If any nation-state can ignore external pressures, it is the richest and most powerful one. Thus, if one discovers that processes within the United States are constrained by external forces, then it is very likely that these constraints are quite general.[2]

Admittedly, the United States was not free of external threats during the cold war.[3] Soviet expansion had to be contained, the possibility of sudden nuclear warfare was frightening, and revolutionary movements supported by the Soviet Union and motivated by communist ideology seemed threatening. As dominant militarily and economically as the United States had become, it hardly felt secure. But the precariousness of the international environment during the cold war was little different from the instabilities of earlier epochs. Thucydides, Machiavelli, and Bodin took a threatening international environment for granted. Wars and rumors of wars marked most of the twentieth century—though the United States sometimes pretended that it could ignore them. Indeed, the bipolar conflict of the cold war seems to have been more predictable and more manageable than the multipolar conflicts that preceded it (Waltz 1979, chap. 9). Hardly before the cold war had come to an end, serious students of international relations became nostalgic about the regularities of bipolarity (Mearscheimer 1990). There is no reason to think that U.S. policy will be less constrained by the international environment in the next half century than it was in the last.[4]

Not only have the external constraints on the foreign policy choices of the United States been less than those facing other nations, but, as Gordon Silverstein shows in the following chapter, the constitutional framework within which the U.S. government operates makes it particularly difficult for U.S. foreign policy to be centrally led by a strong executive free of special interest pressures.[5] By separating the government into three branches, the Constitution insured that a wide variety of groups and interests would participate in decision-making processes. And by assigning most of the governing authority to a Congress divided between a Senate and a House, the Constitution further facilitated the intrusion of parochial considerations into the making of foreign policy.

The weakness of the presidency on issues of foreign policy within the U.S. constitutional framework is not always appreciated. The Constitution makes— and the courts have delineated—no clear distinction between foreign and domestic issues. The only powers given exclusively to the president are the powers to receive foreign ambassadors, grant pardons, and "execute" the laws of Congress. Admittedly, the president is also assigned the responsibility of "commander-in-chief," but no specific powers are granted along with this responsibility, and the Constitution quite specifically grants to Congress the authority to declare war, raise an army, and prepare for the common defense. The presidential powers to appoint ambassadors and make treaties are shared with the Senate. The president can veto congressional legislation, but this negative power can be overridden by a two-thirds vote in both houses. Finally, and ultimately, Congress can remove a president from office, but the reverse is not true. Thus, there is little in the U.S. constitutional framework that encourages executive dominance of the foreign policy– making system.

Over the past twenty-five years the power of the presidency in foreign affairs has been especially weakened by two events that undermined executive branch credibility. The president and his advisers, who had in the decades since World War II enjoyed the enormous prestige that comes from winning a world war, were humiliated in Vietnam by their inability to resolve to their country's satisfaction a conflict with an underdeveloped nation. Simultaneously, a set of illegal and unconstitutional political practices by the executive were exposed as part of the Watergate scandal. For the first time in American history, a president was impeached and forced to resign from office. Under the circumstances, Congress could no longer be expected to defer to professional expertise, the news media could be expected to hunt for presidential peccadilloes, and the public could be expected to become distrustful of the country's political leadership.

Divided partisan control of the legislative and executive branches of government further undermined the basis for a consensual, executive-led foreign policy–making system. The Democratic party controlled the House of Representatives for all but four years during the postwar period and the Senate for all but ten of these years. Meanwhile, until the election of Bill Clinton, the Republican party had won the presidency in every election since 1968, save for the very close election of Jimmy Carter immediately after the Watergate crisis. The ethnic heterogeneity and decentralized internal structure of the Democratic party made it a very effective organization for winning congressional elections, while the more homogeneous, centrally directed Republican party was more suited for electing presidents. The Democratic party had the advantage of holding the more popular position on economic and social issues that tended to influence the outcome of congressional elections, while the Republican party had the political advantage on foreign policy and cultural issues that often played an important role in presidential politics (Jacobson 1990, chap. 6). The leaders of each party — presidential in the Republican case, congressional in the Democratic — had a vested interest in perpetuating the institutional structure and issue orientation that helped it remain in power within its institutional domain. And each party was able to use the political resources of the branch it controlled to facilitate the reelection chances of incumbents.

Consequently, both political parties have developed a set of partisan interests in the institutional power of a particular branch of government. The Democrats, after once having been the party of strong presidents (Jackson, Wilson, Roosevelt, and Johnson), became the defenders of congressional prerogatives. And Republicans, once the congressionally based party (Whiggism, radical Republicans, Henry Lodge, interwar isolationists, anti-New Dealers, and Robert Taft), championed the prerogatives of the executive.

PARTISAN POLITICS AND FOREIGN POLICY

Given these political realities, it is not surprising that foreign policy making became ever more partisan. Party differences existed long before the early 1970s, of course. Harry Truman was accused by Republicans of having lost China and harboring Communists within the State Department. Dwight

Eisenhower scored heavily in the 1952 election when he announced that he would "go to Korea." John Kennedy "discovered" a missile gap as he was launching his presidential campaign in 1960. Republicans attacked Kennedy for the disaster in the Bay of Pigs, and, in the months leading up the Cuban missile crisis, New York Republican senator Kenneth Keating attacked President Kennedy for his inability to identify missiles ninety miles from the Florida coast. These incidents were not exceptional. Robert Pastor tells us in chapter 9 that debates over Central and South America have divided the two parties at least since the Kennedy administration. Similarly, Jay Greene and I show that partisanship was a stable feature of executive-legislative relationships throughout the cold war (chap. 4).

But if parties are endemic to American politics, their role was certainly enhanced after Vietnam. Many, if not most, Democrats on Capitol Hill opposed the bombing of Cambodia in 1970, resisted the Reagan defense buildup of the 1980s, welcomed the nuclear freeze movement or at least called for greater efforts at reaching a nuclear arms reduction agreement, disagreed with President Reagan on the interpretation of the antiballistic missile treaty, opposed Reagan's initial Strategic Defense Initiative, withheld support for the contras in Nicaragua, and condemned the Iranian "arms for hostages" agreement. Nor was partisan opposition simply a matter of Democratic legislators opposing Republican presidents. During the few years that Jimmy Carter was in office, he encountered strong Republican resistance to the Panama Canal and the SALT II treaties.

The growing intensity of partisan conflict is evident in many of the following chapters. Ralph Carter's analysis of defense spending in chapter 7 reveals deeper congressional cuts in presidential defense requests after the Tet Offensive than before. David Rohde shows that partisanship on foreign and defense votes cast in the House of Representatives increased in the seventies and eighties (chap. 5). He also discerns increasing unity within the Democratic party, as northern and southern Democrats became less distinguishable than was once the case. Steven Smith shows that party leaders became increasingly active on foreign policy questions (chap. 6). And within the foreign policy committees assertive questioning became an increasingly partisan affair (chap. 4).

The apotheosis of partisanship may have occurred in the mid-eighties over the Strategic Defense Initiative and the strains it placed on the interpretation of the Antiballistic Missile Treaty, negotiated by Richard Nixon and Leonid Brezhnev. As Alton Frye describes in fascinating detail in chapter 8, the Republican administration headed by Ronald Reagan interpreted the treaty without reference to the debates taking place in Congress at the time of ratification, while a Democratic Congress refused to allow the Strategic Defense Initiative to proceed beyond its understanding of the correct interpretation of that treaty.

This increase in partisan conflict might be thought to have grave implications for the capacity of the executive to conduct foreign policy. For one thing, partisan opposition is effective opposition. While nonpartisan factions and special interests come and go, parties have an identity and a continuity that make their involvement of more long-lasting significance.[6] Members of Congress are usually loyal members of their party, and, if possible, they will support their partisan colleagues in institutional or policy struggles. Also, members of the interest group community and the policy elite often have partisan ties and connections, however much they may wish to appear separate and apart from partisan fracases. Partisan conflict, moreover, is portable. It can move from the legislative arena to the electoral arena quickly and decisively. Presidents cannot simply ignore with impunity the demands and complaints of their partisan opponents.

Less Partisanship in Committees

But though the increase in partisanship conflict was significant, it was not equally evident in all contexts. On the contrary, it was least in evidence in exactly those contexts where it might have been most harmful to the nation's well-being. For one thing, partisan conflict was less pervasive in key congressional committees than on the chamber floor. I. M. Destler tells us that the finance committees helped protect the free trade commitments of the executive against potential threats mounted on the Senate and House floors (chap. 10). Loch Johnson discovered that within the intelligence committees conflict levels failed to increase, even during an increasingly partisan era (chap. 3).[7] Rohde's data on amendments taken up on the House floor are especially instructive in this regard (chap. 5). They indicate that the president's strongest foreign policy supporters in the House are within the armed services and foreign affairs committees. Finally, Smith shows in chapter 6 that party leaders, who mediate relationships between the committees and the floor of Congress, are playing an increasingly active foreign policy role.

Why has conflict between Congress and the executive increased more on the floors of Congress than in its committees? As Rohde points out, legislators with specialized knowledge of foreign policy and defense issues work more closely with the executive than do those more distant from the subject matter. The members of the intelligence, armed services, and foreign policy committees acquired greater expertise and were better able to evaluate international threats to the United States. Among these better informed and more knowledgeable participants, it was easier to fashion a policy consensus. Significantly, it was the members of Congress more distant from day-to-day involvement in foreign policy issues who were more likely to criticize presidential policies. In short, the changes occurring in the post-Vietnam era were particularly evident in settings further removed from the core of the policy-making system.

Differences between Trade and Defense Issues

Not only was partisanship less intense in committees, but it had less of an impact when presidential policies were the most carefully crafted. On trade issues, Destler tells us in chapter 10, the balance of institutional power did not change to any significant extent. The executive branch continued to play the dominant role in determining U.S. trade policy, and, though there were exceptions, the U.S. commitment to free trade continued even at a time when the country's balance of trade deteriorated badly. Although Congress criticized the executive severely and many members strove to impose tighter restrictions on U.S. policy, presidential vetoes, support for free trade within key committees, and artful management of the issue by the party leaders on the chamber floors kept protectionist sentiments at bay.

Military appropriations had a quite different fate during the 1980s. The partisan conflict over defense expenditures seems to have so intensified that it repeatedly led to direct confrontations between Congress and the executive. As Carter points out, defense appropriations were cut sharply in the post-Tet era. Rohde also identifies a much greater increase in institutional conflict over defense than over other foreign policy issues.

The reasons for the distinction are worthy of further consideration. Part of the explanation lies in the nature of the rules of the game in Washington. Defense expenditure happens to be one area in which Congress has the institutional advantage. On most foreign policy questions, the president sets the stage on which actions must be taken. He can commit troops to combat without initially consulting Congress; he can sign executive agreements with other nations that have the full force of law without consulting Congress; he can sign treaties with foreign countries that the Senate then must either ratify or refuse; and he can bring diplomatic pressure to bear, approve covert actions, and threaten and employ economic sanctions. But he cannot spend monies that are not appropriated by Congress. While the president can veto excessive spending, he can, at best, only plead, cajole, or entice a Congress into giving him funds for activities to which a majority on Capitol Hill are not favorably disposed. Containing defense expenditures is one arena in which Congress, if it wishes, can quite easily make its influence felt.

This rule has always given Congress a significant role in matters of defense. But Carter's data indicate that it was not until the post-Vietnam era—and especially in the 1980s—that the issue became a matter of institutional confrontation. Part of the explanation is the increasing interconnection between defense and domestic issues. The struggle to contain a growing fiscal deficit required explicit trade-offs between military and social expenditures. Congressional Democrats could not protect domestic programs of interest to them unless they cut military appropriations (Peterson and Rom 1988). To counter congressional pressures, presidents may have recommended larger defense expenditures than the executive branch itself thought necessary (Stockman 1986). The end result was more intense conflict between the two branches—and more congressional influence—over defense issues than over any other foreign policy question.

In addition, Congress had the better of the argument on many of the defense-related issues. As Alton Frye argues in chapter 8, Congress is likely to become increasingly involved in foreign policy when the choices made by the executive are particularly dubious. Congress refused to appropriate development funds the president requested for the Strategic Defense Initiative because such expenditures violated the Antiballistic Missile Treaty. Similarly, Congress cut defense expenditure in the mid-1980s because the executive's assessment of the international danger seemed unusually extreme. The failure of the Soviet offensive in Afghanistan, the deterioration of the Soviet economy, and the growing pressures for democratization within the Soviet Union all indicated a weakening, not an intensification, of the international threat to the United States.

The comparison with trade is instructive. As Destler points out in chapter 10, most economists have concluded that the United States had little to gain from a protectionist trade policy, no matter how popular such a policy might be with certain industries and constituents in some congressional districts. By adhering to free trade policies, and using the threat of protection mainly to open up foreign markets, the executive branch was choosing a course of action that most disinterested observers regard as in the long-term interest of the country. In this context, protectionist sentiments on Capitol Hill, though loudly expressed, had only a modest policy impact. When the executive was steering a mainstream course considered by policy elites to be in the best interest of the country, congressional pressures were more of a nuisance than a policy determinant.

Executive Direction of U.S. Foreign Policy

Although partisanship has intensified in recent decades, there is no convincing evidence that the executive branch lost control of foreign policy when its assessment of the country's place in the international system was reasonably accurate. Instead, the fundamental responsibility for conducting the nation's foreign policy remained in the hands of the president and his executive-branch advisers. The major decisions were executive decision. It was Jimmy Carter who negotiated the SALT II agreement, which took effect in practice despite the Senate's refusal to ratify it. It was Jimmy Carter who reversed a policy of détente with the Soviet Union, once the Soviet invasion of Afghanistan had taken place. He canceled participation in the Olympic Games, imposed a grain embargo, and instituted a major increase in defense expenditures. It was the Carter administration that facilitated the Camp David agreement between Israel and Egypt. And it was the Carter administration that failed to anticipate the consequences of the Iranian revolution for

U.S. interests, undertook a misbegotten rescue attempt, and finally negotiated the release of U.S. hostages. Next it was the Reagan administration that continued the defense buildup, initiated the Strategic Defense Initiative, and successfully concluded the START and INF arms negotiations. Finally, it was the Bush administration that invaded Panama, defined the U.S. response to the democratization of Eastern Europe and the collapse of the Soviet empire, and committed troops to Saudi Arabia, forcing congressional acquiescence to the Gulf War.

If one turns to international economic policy, the story is much the same. The crucial decision to leave the gold standard and float the dollar was made by the Nixon administration. Congress played only a marginal role in decisions concerning U.S. participation in the International Monetary Fund and the World Bank. The U.S. commitment to free trade was articulated and defended by the executive, with Congress left to complaining and carping from the sidelines. Key issues affecting GATT agreements as well as the Canadian and Mexican trade agreements were resolved mainly within the executive branch.

One can find only a few examples in which, arguably, Congress participated in resolving issues of comparable import. When the Ford administration chose not to recommit U.S. forces to Vietnam even after the North failed to abide by the terms of the 1973 peace agreement, it may have been due to the congressional ban on expenditures for such purposes (though Ford very likely took into account public as well as congressional opposition to renewed conflict in Southeast Asia).[8] Similarly, when the Bush administration negotiated an agreement with the Nicaraguan government, its decision was, in all probability, influenced by the strong congressional opposition to continued aid to the contras. Strong congressional support for Israel has complicated State Department efforts to encourage a resolution of the Palestinian question. Arguably, in most, if not all, cases of clear congressional influence, Congress seems in retrospect to have assessed the national interest more correctly than the executive did. If Congress was exercising somewhat more influence than in the past, its increased role hardly seems to have been dangerous. Instead, the relative openness of the American political system seems to have facilitated an adjustment of policy when executive leadership was misjudging the national interest.

These instances of congressional involvement were not so frequent as to indicate a major shift in power from the White House to Capitol Hill. Quite aside from the resolution of specific controversies, the authority of the executive to conduct foreign policy remained largely intact. The president could still reach executive agreements with foreign countries on almost any and all issues, thereby avoiding the necessity of winning consent of two-thirds of the Senate. Also, as Gordon Silverstein points out in chapter 2, the courts are more assiduously upholding executive discretion today than ever before. Unless a congressional delegation of power is very detailed, limited, and explicit, it finds it very difficult to challenge an executive interpretation of that delegation in the courts. Congressional delegations of authority, moreover, can no longer be hedged by a legislative veto.[9]

Nor is it simply the courts that have protected executive prerogatives. In the concluding chapter, Destler shows that Congress has been no less willing to delegate responsibility for trade policy to the executive in the 1980s than it was in previous decades. Loch Johnson's analysis of the questioning of witnesses by the members of the intelligence committees shows no tendency toward increasing legislative assertiveness (chap. 3), and Jay Greene and I reach a similar conclusion with respect to the foreign policy committees (chap. 4).

In sum, the findings reported in the ensuing chapters do not lead directly to the conclusion that the president has lost his foreign policy prerogatives. As partisan and institutional conflicts increasingly overlapped in the wake of the Vietnam War, foreign policy issues became embedded in the divisive partisan currents that shaped Washington politics during these decades. Yet these partisan conflicts need to be placed in context. For all the congressional conflict that has occurred in the past quarter of a century, the responsibility for governance has been mainly in executive hands. When Congress has decisively intervened, moreover, it has often had a substantive warrant for doing so.

But if conflict over foreign policy has been contained even in the most partisan moments of the post-Vietnam era, it is worth considering theoretically the conditions that make this likely. To understand the relations between the branches, we must appreciate the extent to which day-to-day politics are constrained by the workings of the international system. In this way, we shall identify at the most general level the forces that continue to keep foreign and domestic policies distinct arenas of policy making.

THE TWO PRESIDENCIES

The distinction between foreign and domestic issues has long been noticed. Two decades ago, in a classic essay written under the fetching title "The Two Presidencies," the political scientist Aaron Wildavsky ([1966] 1991) argued that modern presidencies were fraternal—but hardly identical—twins. The one—the domestic policy president—was subject to the debate, pressure politics, and congressional infighting that is a concomitant of the ordinary workings of democratic processes. The other—the foreign policy president—enjoyed an independence, respect, and prestige that enabled him to manage the external relations of the country quite autonomously. Wildavsky identified several factors that differentiated domestic from foreign policy:

1. Since foreign policy questions often require "fast action," they are more appropriate for executive than legislative decision making.

2.   Presidents have vast "formal powers to commit resources in foreign affairs," and they have "far greater ability than anyone else to obtain information on developments abroad."

3.   Since voters know little about foreign policy issues, they "expect the president to act in foreign affairs and reward him with their confidence."

4.   On foreign policy questions, "the interest group structure is weak, unstable, and thin."

5.   Members of Congress follow a "self-denying ordinance. They do not think it is their job to determine the nation's defense policies."

Wildavsky's analysis was not so much an original statement as a summary of a more generally held scholarly perception. Robert Dahl had put forth much the same argument more than a decade earlier: "In foreign policy the President proposes, the Congress disposes," Dahl wrote, adding that "in a very large number of highly important decisions about foreign policy, the Congress does not even have the opportunity to dispose" (1964, 58). Samuel Huntington similarly concluded that "strategic programs are determined in the executive rather than the Congress." "Just as power to legislate strategic programs was at one time, at least in theory, shared by President and Congress, so it is now, very much in practice, shared by the President and a variety of agencies within the executive branch" (1961, 146, 127–28). Richard Fenno's views were little different: "Foreign Affairs members . . . help make policy in an environment strongly dominated by the President. . . . [They] have been hard put to develop any strategic posture other than one calling for responsiveness to executive branch expectations" (1973, 212–13).

As mainstream a statement as the "two-presidency theory" originally was, it has become the subject of steady criticism in subsequent decades. Wildavsky's own empirical test of his generalizations — a comparison of a limited number of roll calls — was woefully inadequate. Subsequent efforts to replicate his results on a wider set of data produced inconsistent and uncertain results.[10] Some of these studies suggested that the "two-presidency theory," though accurate enough for the Eisenhower era, did not explain the politics of foreign policy making in the years following the Vietnam War (Edwards 1991; Sigelman 1991; Peppers 1991). Writing with Duane Oldfield, Wildavsky himself concluded that "as ideological and partisan divisions have come to reinforce each other . . . foreign policy has become more like domestic policy — a realm marked by serious partisan divisions in which the president cannot count on a free ride" (Oldfield and Wildavsky 1991, 188). Finally, two-presidency theory was not much of a theory at all. It was only a set of observations about certain tendencies in American politics at a particular point in time. The structural underpinnings that might produce such a tendency were given little attention in either Wildavsky's essay or subsequent critiques.

But if the two-presidency theory is in disrepair, nothing very substantial has arisen to take its place. Instead, analysts of American politics are drawing few, if any, distinctions between foreign and domestic affairs. It is claimed that both arenas are equally likely to be the subject of partisan debate, voter interest, group activity, and legislative involvement. The president has as much—or as little—control over the one as the other. Within both arenas, the nature of the times, the skill of the participants, and the contingencies of the moment determine outcomes.

When generalizations are made about the making of foreign policy, they mainly chronicle changes that have occurred in the last quarter of a century. Congress is more involved in foreign policy decisions, the process is more partisan than it used to be, the public is more attentive to and polarized by foreign policy questions, and interest groups with foreign policy concerns use the congressional channel more efficaciously than they once did (Franck and Weisband 1979; Sundquist 1981; Blechman 1990; Mann 1990b). It is the new Wildavsky, writing with Oldfield, who once again best expresses the now-revised scholarly mainstream:

> If members of Congress disagree with the basic objectives of a presi-
> dent's foreign policy, deference is much less likely. . . . The press has
> [also] grown less deferential. . . . Ideologically oriented interest groups
> have come to play a greater role. . . . There are also more domestic
> groups with foreign policy agendas. . . . All of these changes have
> added to the difficulty of keeping foreign policy isolated from public
> scrutiny and pressure (1991, 188).

Significantly, the foreign versus domestic policy distinction has not been subsumed under another set of analytical categories. The well-known distinction among distributive, regulative, and redistributive policies promulgated by Theodore Lowi (1964) is not easily applied outside the domestic arena. The contrast between development and redistributive policies that I have used to interpret state and local politics has little direct application to foreign policy making (Peterson 1981). James Q. Wilson's (1980, chap. 10) distinction between policies that have concentrated as distinct from diffuse benefits or costs may be more promising—many foreign policies have both diffuse benefits and costs—but such an approach has yet to be carried out. Indeed, most American politics specialists have tended to ignore the foreign arena altogether, choosing instead to study budgets, deficits, special interest politics, race relations, and other domestic issues.

INTERNATIONAL RELATIONS THEORY AND
DOMESTIC POLITICS

Nor has the vacuum in theorizing about American foreign policy been filled by students of international relations. Theories of international politics typically treat individual nation-states as unitary systems whose internal politics can be safely ignored. "A systems theory of international politics deals with the forces that are in play at the international, and not at the national level," writes Kenneth Waltz. "An international-political theory does not imply or require a theory of foreign policy any more than a market theory implies or requires a theory of the firm," he continues (1979, 71, 72). Instead, each nation-state can be assumed to be governed by a single leader who considers the country's interests within the international system.

In traditional political theory, this point is cast in normative categories. Though Aristotle preferred a mixed constitution, one of the kings for which he recognized a need was "the general with powers delegated for war." Less restrained in his recognition of the necessity of strong leadership, Machiavelli praised "the Roman practice of creating a dictator in emergencies." Not only was the "dictator very useful . . . when the Roman republic was threatened from without but also . . . 'in the increase of the empire' " (qtd. in Mansfield 1989, 135).

In contemporary international relations theory, the stance is analytical but the theme hardly changes. To explain foreign policy decisions, says Hans J. Morgenthau, "we put ourselves in the position of a statesman who must meet a certain problem of foreign policy, . . . and we ask ourselves what the rational alternatives are from which a statesman may choose . . . and which of these rational alternatives this particular statesman . . . is likely to choose. It is the testing of this rational hypothesis . . . that . . . makes a theory of politics possible" ([1946] 1966, 5; as qtd. in Keohane 1984, 66). That Morgenthau uses the appellation "statesman" rather than "politician" indicates that it is the international, not the domestic, political arena that provides the context in which choices are made.

Although Kenneth Waltz's analysis is internally more consistent than Morgenthau's, its point of departure is quite similar. Waltz defines the essential characteristic of the international system as anarchic, a Hobbesian state of nature in which each nation needs to guard its autonomy and security from external threat. This threat is so great—"war may at any time break out"—that individual countries must "worry about their survival, and the worry conditions their behavior" (1979, 102, 105). The external constraints are so great that it is not necessary to understand the way in which responses to these constraints are chosen. On the contrary, trying to explain relations among countries by studying the making of foreign policy within them makes as much sense as trying to understand the fall of the Niagara River by examining the shape of a drop in its spray.

The mutual deterrence theory that guided the United States and the Soviet Union through the cold war relied almost exclusively on the assumption that the nation-state was guided by a single, rational leadership. But it is not only cold warriors and other members of the realist school, represented here by Morgenthau and Waltz, who gave short shrift to internal foreign policy–making processes. The assumption that nation-states are unitary actors acting rationally on behalf of the national interest has been no less important to the increasingly influential political economy school of thought. These scholars suggest that the nation-state may be concerned not so much about maximizing its security as about increasing its wealth. Since the international system has become more stable, nations can—indeed, must—concentrate on maximizing their economic development. Those that fail endanger not just their external security but even their political coherence, as the collapse of the Soviet Union reveals.

Even as these political analysts attend more to economic productivity, finance, and trade than to alliances, armaments, and war, they are more optimistic about the possibilities for international cooperation. These theorists expect that countries will respect international principles and rules designed for their common, long-term good—and not cheat when it seems to be in their immediate interest to do so. Realists agree that some principles are generally respected: most countries do not invade embassies or imprison diplomats. But political economists go beyond realists in identifying an increasingly broad class of activities that are said to be shaped by international rules and principles. The leading industrialized countries of the world respect one another's borders, coordinate their fiscal and monetary policies, have eliminated many tariff and other trade barriers, consult one another when altering the value of their currencies, and draw upon a common pool of funds to assist nations in temporary financial difficulty.

It is too soon to tell whether such coordination can continue over the long run, especially now that the threat of international communism has disappeared. Many analysts believe that current, fragmentary arrangements are only a precursor to a more stable world order in the future. Yet even the enthusiastic proponents of a "new world order" do not ground their expectations in the workings of the foreign policy system of key countries. Instead, they try to show that cooperation is possible among the "rational statesmen" of whom Morgenthau spoke. In Robert Keohane's words, "Rational-egoist models [that assume rational, unitary decision making] do not necessarily predict that discord will prevail in relations among independent actors in a situation of anarchy. On the contrary, . . . if the egoists monitor each other's behavior and if enough of them are willing to cooperate on condition that others cooperate as well, they may be able to adjust their behavior to reduce discord" (1984, 83–84). Similarly, Stephen Krasner (1978) argues that the purposes of U.S. raw materials policy have been determined mainly by the country's national interests, as shaped by threats emanating from the international system.[11]

In short, there is considerable agreement among the various strains of international relations theory that states can be treated as unitary actors. I identify this common assumption underlying otherwise disparate approaches not to bury the theory but to praise it. Still, international relations theorists have—for the most part—yet to work out their theoretical argument to its logical conclusion. If the international system constrains the policies of nations, so also must it influence the way in which nation-states deliberate upon and decide these policies. On this topic, research has barely begun.

Waltz even imposes upon himself a self-denying ordinance, making the peculiar, unwarranted claim that international theory is no more relevant to a theory of foreign policy making than a theory of markets is relevant to an understanding of the behavior of a firm. But, certainly, economists regularly use market theory to analyze—and prescribe—firm behavior. If a firm gave no attention to the bottom line, it would not survive for long. Since it necessarily follows that most firms pay attention to the bottom line, it then becomes a question of understanding the ways in which firms attend to this objective. It may be that information costs, costs of negotiation, and costs of changing practices all limit the success with which the firm can maximize profits. But that hardly makes market theory irrelevant; it only requires a sophisticated elaboration when applying the theory to specific firms.[12]

What Waltz declares inadmissible, Goerevitch (1978) attempts. In a lengthy review of a wide literature, he shows that the international system has often influenced the internal politics of a country. Admittedly, some of his points are well-known truisms: foreign occupation changes domestic politics; defeat at the hands of the enemy can bring about the collapse of the ancien régime (France in 1870, Russia in 1917, Germany in 1918). But Goerevitch also discusses more-subtle ways in which the place of a country in the international system can affect its internal organization—Britain's insular position necessitated a navy but made a standing army pointless; Prussia's permeable border in the middle of the European continent had the opposite consequence. And since the effects an army has on internal politics are different from that of navies, a parliament independent of the monarch was more easily established in Britain than in Germany (1978, 896). But Goerevitch, more interested in the differences than in the common features of nation-states, pays little attention to the way in which the international system structures foreign policy institutions along similar lines. Although he recalls the insights of Machiavelli and Bodin—"Defense of the realm was that quintessential function which required a single sovereign; it required speed, authoritativeness, secrecy, comprehensiveness"—he does not follow up with illustrations and examples (1978, 899). Surprisingly, he does not even mention the tendency of nations to borrow from their competitors those institutional arrangements necessary to defend their autonomy and security. But just as nations steal or copy the military technology of their more advanced opponents, so they adopt and adapt those political structures that seem to work for competitors. For example, Britain, France, and, later, Japan created public bureaucracies that were capable of large-scale, organized activity, once the Prussians had demonstrated the success of this institutional arrangement. Nor does Goerevitch consider the way in which the American presidency grew in power and authority as the United States acquired international responsibilities (Sundquist 1981, chap. 6). Today Americans seem as willing to copy the Japanese as to "bash" them (even while the Russians are frantically trying to copy the United States).

But even if international relations theorists have not written extensively about the way in which the international system structures the making of foreign policy,[13] it may be possible to infer from the theory the obvious hypothesis that the executive is more apt to be dominant on foreign than domestic issues, the point made in the "two-presidencies" literature. What international relations theory makes clear is that the role played by the executive in foreign affairs is not due to transient factors such as the vagaries of public opinion or interest group strategies. Instead, it is rooted in the requirements imposed on the nation-state by the potentially anarchic quality of the international system. Wildavsky hinted at these international sources of executive power in his original essay: "Compared with domestic affairs," he wrote, "presidents engaged in world politics are immensely more concerned with meeting problems on their own terms. Who supports and opposes a policy [at home] . . . does not assume the crucial importance that it does in domestic affairs. The best policy presidents can find is also the best politics" ([1966] 1991, 24). Policy takes precedence over politics because the international system both severely limits the sensible choices a country can make and shapes the processes by which these decisions are reached. International relations theory thus explains not only the policy choices of nations but also the existence of "two presidencies."

Apart from encouraging the rise of a strong executive, what exactly are the requirements that the international system imposes on the domestic policy-making processes of a nation-state? Peter Katzenstein (1983) provides a useful point of departure for answering this question in his study of the small nations of Europe—Austria, Belgium, Denmark, the Netherlands, Norway, Sweden, and Switzerland. Katzenstein points out that small countries are particularly vulnerable to changes in the international environment. Because international trade constitutes a higher percentage of their gross national product, policies must be designed carefully so that they do not adversely affect the country's place in the international system. As a result, he says, "domestic quarrels are a luxury not tolerated in such adverse circumstances." Pointing out that "political metaphors [used by politicians in these countries] often emphasiz[e] . . . that all members of society sit in the same small boat, that the waves are high, and that all must pull on the same oar," he finds that "groups are held together by the pragmatic bargains struck by a handful of political leaders at the summit. Political compromise across the main social cleavages assures political quiescence and . . . reinforces political control within each camp. The greater the degree of segmentation dividing these societies, the more pronounced are . . . arrangements which defuse conflict" (1983, 118, 118–19). In short, Katzenstein finds that in those countries where the international system places the greatest constraints on policy choice, there are strong pressures for elite consensus and centralized decision making.

In summary, if the international system constrains the choices of the United States government, there are likely to be "two presidencies." On foreign policy questions, the executive is dominant, Congress follows a "self-denying ordinance," interest group influence is weak and episodic, and voters look to the president for guidance and action.

INTERNATIONAL CONSTRAINTS ON THE MAKING OF FOREIGN POLICY

The external constraints that differentiate foreign from domestic policy making are evident in many of the findings reported in the chapters that follow. Although several chapters identify genuine partisanship and intensifying conflict between Congress and the president, others indicate that the preponderance of power and authority remain within the executive branch and show that the degree of conflict between the branches has been contained within reasonable boundaries. Silverstein shows that the courts have protected executive foreign policy prerogatives; if anything, the executive is constitutionally better placed to defend its interests than ever before. And in the concluding chapter Destler shows clearly the way in which international requirements limit the congressional role over the making of trade policy.

The finding that congressional committees tend to protect the executive from pressures emanating from the chamber floor further indicates that the policy-making system is constrained by its international environment. Those who are engaged in the making of foreign policy on a sustained basis over the long run are those who are most likely to be aware of the ways in which the international system is constraining choice. Domestic pressures are less likely to influence their deliberations and decisions than those of members who engage in foreign policy issues on a more episodic basis.

Even the notable instances when Congress substituted its judgment for that of the executive do not necessarily demonstrate that external constraints are irrelevant to the foreign policy–making process. In many of these cases, the president's policy proposals constituted a dubious assessment of the country's long-term interest within the international system. Should the United States unilaterally reinterpret an international treaty in a way inconsistent with statements that were made at the time of its signing and ratification? Congress decisively argued against the position taken by the president, and in retrospect it seems to have been warranted in doing so. Congress also moderated the defense buildup in the 1980s; once again, its decisions hardly seem to have done much harm. On the contrary, when

Congress intervened into areas in which the executive branch traditionally exercised its prerogative, the actions seemed as appropriate as they were unusual.

It may even be argued that the need for the executive to defend its foreign policy positions before Congress helps to insure that foreign policy decisions are carefully reasoned. The sharing of information between key congressional committees and key executive branch agencies, and the close cooperation between these institutions, may strengthen the influence of those who are best able to articulate the long-range interests of the country within the framework imposed by the international system. If a country is going to be led by statesmen who take into account the long-term interest of the nation, then policy must be rooted in accurate assessments of the international situation, not based on myths or ideologies. To the extent that one branch or another indulges in fanciful myths or ideological thinking, the other branch should—and often does—become a more influential participant. Congress becomes more influential on defense and arms control policies when executive branch proposals seem unreal and fanciful (see chaps. 8 and 9). But when Congress ignores the interdependence of the U.S. and international economies, as it tends to do in the case of trade policy, the executive assumes a dominant role (see chap. 10). As Morgenthau observed, to explain policy choice "we put ourselves in the position of a statesman who must meet a certain problem of foreign policy, . . . and we ask ourselves what the rational alternatives are from which a statesman may choose. . . . It is the testing of this rational hypothesis . . . that . . . makes a theory of politics possible" (Keohane 1984, 66). And, it might be added, if a statesman is not to be found in the executive branch of government, one will emerge in the legislative.

Chapter Two

★ ★ ★

JUDICIAL ENHANCEMENT OF
EXECUTIVE POWER

★ ★ ★

Gordon Silverstein

Congress responded to the Vietnam War and Watergate with a series of efforts to regain control of foreign policy through legislation, including the War Powers Resolution, the restructuring of the intelligence oversight process, and a series of trade bills and aid appropriations, as well as arms control and emergency powers bills.[1] In the normal course of events, these efforts should have shifted foreign policy power away from the president and toward Congress. Some, indeed, would argue that it has (Rostow 1989; Univ. Miami Law Review 1988; Ripley and Lindsey 1993). But in most of these efforts, Congress not only failed to achieve its stated objective but may have made the imbalance of powers worse, shifting more power to the executive branch.[2]

Whether or not these attempts were wise is not the subject of this study; rather the question here is, why did the legislation fail to achieve its stated objectives? Though the answer is a complex one, part of that answer lies in constitutional interpretation. Since the judicial branch takes a leading role in constitutional interpretation, an understanding of the limits and parameters set by the courts helps explain the difficulty Congress has had in reasserting its authority. An understanding of the judicial doctrine in foreign policy also generates clear signals of what Congress needs to do if it wants to achieve its stated objectives.

Part of the explanation lies in the realities of international affairs. Congress tends to delegate broad discretion to the executive in times of war or perceived international crisis, and international constraints have shaped the making of American foreign policy. But because the American system is governed by a written constitution that is interpreted and applied by all three branches of the government in domestic and foreign policy alike, the distribution of power in foreign affairs influences constitutional interpretation, and foreign policy choices made in time of war or perceived crisis have had implications far beyond their immediate application.

In the years following World War II, presidents have increasingly claimed ever broader discretionary power in foreign policy up to and including claims that foreign affairs authority is part of a broad prerogative power.[3] Many in Congress came to accept some of these claims as legitimate: in a complicated world of nuclear deterrence and permanent cold war, they argued, the president had to be given greater discretion in foreign affairs. As former senator William Fulbright recently put it:

> In a Congress where parochialism still reigned, it was not difficult to be persuaded that modern realities required greater latitude for the President and that proponents of congressional prerogative were agents of unenlightened reaction. Indeed, I concluded that American diplomacy in general, and particularly our need to achieve a measure of regularity in relations with the Soviet Union, would be better served if Congress generally deferred to the President. (in Glennon 1990, xi)

In 1964 Congress capped a series of delegations of broad executive discretionary power in foreign affairs with the passage of the Tonkin Gulf Resolution, in effect following Senator Fulbright's advice that Congress should "give the Executive a measure of power in the conduct of our foreign affairs that we have hitherto jealously withheld" (Fulbright 1961, 1).[4]

Vietnam and Watergate led to an infusion of new legislators in Washington and a renewed commitment by many veteran legislators to the notion that Congress must assert its authority in foreign affairs. A series of new laws were written explicitly designed to reign in the president's broad powers — but these bills still incorporated a commitment to the idea that the modern era required broad latitude for presidential action. One of the most blatant examples of a bill designed to limit the president but which may have unintentionally resulted in a broader delegation of power was the War Powers Resolution of 1973. One of that resolution's original architects, Senator Thomas Eagleton of Missouri, repudiated the bill in its final form and urged its rejection, since, in his eyes, the resolution had become "a 60- to 90-day open-ended blank check" giving the president the legal sanction to "fight the war for whatever reason, wherever" he chose to do so (Eagleton 1974, 212). Another example came in 1977 when Congress attempted to reduce the president's broad powers to exercise emergency powers under the Trading with the Enemy Act of 1917 (TWEA) by replacing that act—which "operated as a one-way ratchet to enhance greatly the President's discretionary authority over foreign policy"[5]—with the International Emergency Economic Powers Act (IEEPA). While the IEEPA was meant to curtail excessive executive discretion, it was also designed to preserve "flexible executive response to emergencies." But "to the degree that IEEPA was intended to restrict the peacetime emergency powers that had been granted the President by TWEA, it failed. IEEPA did not add any significant procedural or substantive restraints to those imposed by TWEA; the powers delegated to the President are still vast and amorphous" (Harvard Law Review 1983, 1120). Similarly, the Intelligence Authorization Act of 1981 can be read as a broad delegation to "permit the executive to conduct covert operations without congressional approval" (Lobel 1986, 1035).

While the congressional failure to recover the power it sought can be explained in part by congressional acceptance of a need for broad executive discretion, it is also partially explained by an inadvertent error: legislators who believed the executive needed broad authority and yet wanted to check undue discretion latched onto the idea of delegating broad powers and checking them with legislative vetoes. This device allowed the broad delegation, and yet made it possible to check the president without having to secure a veto-proof majority in both houses of Congress. This device, however, was ruled unconstitutional by the Supreme Court in 1983 (*Immigration and Naturalization Service v. Chadha*, 1983). While that might have sent Congress back to the drawing board, Congress had taken the curious precaution of making the legislative veto provision severable from the delegation of authority in the War Powers Resolution and in other bills, and the Supreme Court ruled that the broad delegations of power could stand even where the legislative check was invalid.[6] Thus, even where Congress tried to give power with one hand while restraining it with the other, the result was broader power for the president without any additional legislative constraints.

While one would be tempted to blame the Court for this development,[7] it is not the Court that decided Congress had to delegate broad powers to the president; nor has the Court in any way made it impossible for Congress to use its most prominent and accessible tools—the power of the purse and the powers of oversight and investigation—to reassert its authority. A close examination of judicial doctrine in foreign policy cases over the past two hundred years reveals a remarkably consistent doctrine that sends a clear signal to Congress and the president that there are limits in foreign policy, and that there are congressional prerogatives—but that Congress must exercise and police its own prerogatives rather than expect the Court to do so for it. Although the judiciary has very recently begun to accept a broader discretionary role for the executive in foreign affairs, that shift is far less dramatic than might appear to be the case. The truly dramatic changes occurred in the White House and on Capitol Hill, and the courts certified and legitimated those changes.

By examining the evolution of the Court's doctrine in foreign policy, it is easier to see the dimensions of the problem Congress faces in asserting legislative authority in foreign affairs, and perhaps to understand why Congress has in fact lost power despite clear efforts to assert it. Finally, a clear understanding of where the Court stands and what it requires before it will, in fact, rise to the support of congressional assertions of power in foreign policy is necessary should Congress choose to make another effort to assert its authority in foreign policy.

The judicial doctrine in foreign policy cases holds that in foreign affairs the *national government* (the executive and legislative branches) *acting together* is limited in foreign policy only by explicit constitutional prohibitions against infringing individual rights of American citizens without due process. Such invasions of liberty, the Court has consistently held, can be sanctioned only on the showing of explicit pragmatic justification. But this broad power applies only when the national government acts as a unified whole. When the president acts alone, the Court will look to Congress: where Congress is silent or ambiguous, the president is generally upheld; where Congress is formally and clearly opposed, the Court will support Congress and protect what it perceives to be legislative prerogatives in foreign policy. What has changed in recent years is that the Court now insists on ever more precise and determinative opposition from Congress.

The Constitution contains a number of specific, enumerated powers that have been delegated to the national government. In addition, the states have been forbidden to exercise a number of powers, primarily those having to do with foreign affairs and interstate commerce. But the Constitution leaves vague a number of concerns, and few are more vague than the delegation of foreign policy powers. While the Constitution designates the president as commander-in-chief of the armed forces, it gives Congress alone the power to "raise and support Armies," to "provide and maintain a Navy," and to "declare War." Similarly, while the president has the power to make treaties, they must be approved by two-thirds of the Senate. Beyond these specifics, Congress is authorized to "make all laws which shall be necessary and proper for carrying into Execution" the enumerated powers, while the loosely defined "executive power" is vested in the president.[8]

THE DISTINCTION BETWEEN FOREIGN AND DOMESTIC POLICY

From its earliest cases, the Court has argued that the Constitution cannot detail the scope and limits of every possible exercise of power.[9] Thus the Court must decide what is "necessary and proper" for executing the powers that are delegated to the government.[10] As Chief Justice John Marshall acknowledged in *McCulloch v. Maryland*, 1819, all of the powers of the government are limited, and those limits "are not to be transcended" (420). But when it came to national powers, "the government of the Union, though limited in its powers, is supreme within its sphere of action" (405). Marshall picked up on Alexander Hamilton's arguments in the *Federalist* that the Constitution contained delegated, enumerated powers and certain implied powers necessary to execute those enumerated powers. "A government, intrusted with such ample powers . . . must also be intrusted with ample means for their execution," Marshall wrote (407).

Foreign policy needs provided a powerful argument for national supremacy, particularly since the Constitution made no distinction between governmental powers in foreign and domestic affairs. Long before the Court concerned itself with the question of which branch of the federal government had authority in foreign affairs, it first had to resolve the vertical separation of powers between the states and the national government acting as a unified whole. Chief Justice John Marshall saw no constitutional distinction between foreign and domestic policy: if Congress had the power to enact laws that were necessary and proper to carry out its enumerated powers, then it had that power whether or not the subject was foreign policy.[11]

If Marshall was right, however, there was no reason to believe that the Court would be any less intrusive in foreign affairs cases than in cases involving domestic policy: if the Constitution was to be read the same at home and in foreign affairs, then an expansive foreign affairs power might well jeopardize individual state autonomy and provide a way to expand the constitutionally limited role of the national government at home. Alarmed by this interprtation, a number of justices struggled to develop a doctrine that the Constitution was to be read differently in foreign and domestic policy. In the period between the Civil War and the Spanish-American War, Justice Stephen Field and others tried to balance the expanding need for central power in foreign affairs against the inherent threat such an expansion of power posed to the American system of limited and decentralized government at home. Field and his brethren argued that national sovereignty, which conferred no domestic authority on the national government, did indeed confer certain inherent powers on the national government in its dealings with foreign subjects.[12] After the Civil War, such distinctions appeared viable, but as the United States and its international role grew, the artificial constitutional distinction between foreign and domestic affairs inevitably became murkier. The Court confronted this evolution when the justices tried to craft a doctrine that would accommodate the constitutionally unchartered waters of colonial possessions and protectorates following the Spanish-American War. These territories were neither domestic nor foreign, and to develop a doctrine that would allow the national government broad authority to rule these lands without providing a precedent for broad domestic power was a difficult assignment. The solution, a set of confusing and highly technical rulings, produced a doctrine that had little coherence or precedential value.[13]

SUTHERLAND AND CURTISS-WRIGHT: REMOVING THE COURTS FROM FOREIGN POLICY — AND BRINGING THEM BACK IN

As the Court moved away from the expansionist attitudes that were prevalent during the Spanish-American War and closer to the isolationist views that marked the years preceding World War I, it began to read the Constitution far more strictly and literally. For strict readers of the Constitution, the notion that it might apply differently in different circumstances was increasingly hard to maintain. A strict reading would leave the national government with little power at home *and* abroad; or a government with great power at home *and* abroad. Rather than accept that bleak choice, the Court entertained another way of distinguishing foreign and domestic policy: by finding foreign policy to be beyond the scope of the judicial function, the Supreme Court hit on a way to maintain a strict reading of the Constitution at home without hampering foreign policy. Foreign policy, it would be argued, was inherently a political question, and as Marshall had noted in *Marbury v. Madison*, 1803, "Questions, in their nature political, or which are, by the Constitution and laws, submitted to the executive, can never be made in this court" (170).

In a 1917 ruling, the Court offered a standing invitation to future jurists to leave any and all foreign policy questions to the political branches. Writing for the majority, Justice Clarke held, "The conduct of the foreign relations of our government is committed by the Constitution to the Executive and Legislative — 'the political' — Departments of the Government, and the propriety of what may be done in the exercise of this political power is not subject to judicial inquiry or decision" (*Oetjen v. Central Leather Co.*, 1917, 302).

The attempt to remove the courts from foreign policy was short-lived. While many writers argue that it was Justice George Sutherland's famous dicta and opinion in the 1936 case of *United States v. Curtiss-Wright Export Corp.* that removed the courts from foreign policy, the truth is quite the opposite. The Court had steadily moved away from intervention in foreign policy cases until Sutherland reversed that trend with *Curtiss-Wright*. Writing for the Court, Sutherland rejected the earlier invitation to leave foreign affairs to the political branches. He wanted to use the courts to make sure the national government would be empowered to pursue an active foreign policy as unfettered by the states and individuals as possible. Removing the courts from foreign policy altogether would not achieve Sutherland's goal, nor would it have been consistent with his political and legal convictions.

Reflecting on the lessons of America's belated entry into World War I, Sutherland argued that America could and should retain the promise of its written Constitution without sacrificing its ability to perform necessary international duties. In a book published in 1919, before he joined the Court, Sutherland had argued that the United States had to choose one of three options: (1) abandon the Constitution as out of date and inadequate to deal with modern dilemmas, (2) stick with the Constitution strictly interpreted and abandon a world role, or (3) argue, as he did, that the Constitution could be seen differently when applied to domestic as opposed to foreign policy.

Sutherland did not invent his solution out of thin air—quite the contrary. He well understood that the Supreme Court had from the beginning struggled with the dilemma of a constitutional federation of states confronting a world of various types of government. In his book and in his *Curtiss-Wright* opinion, Sutherland reviewed the case history and argued that there was a clear line separating the way in which the Constitution was to be read in domestic and foreign policy. He argued that sovereign power in foreign affairs had to be possessed by every nation, and that the United States was no exception. But unlike domestic authority, foreign affairs authority never passed to the individual states. Rather, foreign affairs powers passed directly from the British Crown to the national government of the United States. Naturally, if powers in foreign and domestic affairs stemmed from different sources, they could and should be treated differently by the courts, or by anyone trying to interpret the Constitution. The national government, Sutherland argued, had broad discretion in foreign affairs, though it was limited by the explicit prohibitions of the Constitution: the national government, acting as a whole, could exercise authority in foreign affairs "unless the powers are prohibited by the Constitution, or unless [they are] contrary to the fundamental principles upon which it was established" (1919, 46).[14]

Curtiss-Wright has come to be perceived as a foundation for executive power in foreign affairs, and though Sutherland did argue that the executive was the key player in foreign policy, the case itself concerned the power of Congress and the executive acting together. The question before the Court was, could Congress delegate to the president broad powers to suspend arms trading with belligerents in fighting between Paraguay and Bolivia? This was not an assertion of executive foreign affairs prerogative, but a question of whether or not Congress had unconstitutionally delegated its authority to the executive. Sutherland embraced the opportunity provided by *Curtiss-Wright* not only to endorse this particular delegation of power but also to announce that the Court did indeed have a role to play in foreign affairs cases. He was unwilling to leave critical questions of constitutional interpretation to the political branches, as a ruling based on the political question doctrine might have done. Instead, he found in *Curtiss-Wright* an opportunity to try to resolve "the key problem facing conservatives who were also ardent nationalists and who somehow wanted strong national powers in foreign affairs but protection for certain states' rights in domestic affairs" (LaFeber 1987, 51). Sutherland's opinion attempted to create a constitutional justification for a strong, centralized government in foreign affairs without sacrificing individual rights or limited government at home. If *Curtiss* definitively resolved anything, it was that the national government, acting in a unified manner, faced few constitutional constraints in foreign policy. What remained an open question was what the courts would do when the branches of government clashed—when the president took action that contradicted the will of

Congress, or when the president acted in an area of uncharted waters, where Congress had not made its will clear.

DEFINING THE "NATIONAL" GOVERNMENT

Although the "national government" has extremely broad discretion in enacting and executing foreign policy,[15] it is critical to understand what the Court means by the national government. The early cases discussed above generally focused on the vertical separation of powers between the states and the national government as a whole, or on questions of substantive constitutional limits on what the national government acting together might or might not do. Modern cases, however, tend to focus more on the horizontal separation of powers among the three branches of the national government, specifically on what the president can do, what Congress can do, and what either one can do in the face of objections from the other. In *Curtiss-Wright*, Justice Sutherland failed to define adequately just what constituted the national government, except to say that the states were not a part of it. To say that the federal government is supreme in foreign policy is one thing, but it is quite another to say that the president acting alone has that power or that the president acting against Congress has that power. And that Sutherland did not say, which is not surprising when one investigates the legal precedents. While various justices have flirted with the idea of executive prerogative in foreign affairs, they have almost always backed away from it.

It is true that Chief Justice John Marshall suggested in *Marbury v. Madison* that those acting under presidential instructions would not be held liable for illegal actions, hinting at some sort of executive prerogative;[16] but by 1804 he had decisively changed his mind, and said so explicitly. Reversing himself from his position in *Marbury*, Marshall rejected the notion that a ship's captain, acting under orders from the chief executive, might be excused for otherwise illegal behavior at sea. Marshall wrote that his brethren on the Court had persuaded him that even in his capacity as commander-in-chief, the president could not authorize a military officer to perform illegal acts: only Congress can make laws, Marshall argued, and regardless of the fact that the president may have ordered his subordinate officer to perform an illegal act, that act was still illegal, and the officer performing that act was responsible for his behavior. Not even a military officer, Marshall wrote, could use the "instruction of the executive" as an excuse for performing an illegal act (*Little v. Barreme*, 1804).

Marshall took note of the difference congressional silence might make, observing that in those areas where Congress had failed to act "it is by no means clear that the President [might] have empowered the officers" to act as he instructed them to do. But in this case "the legislature seem to have prescribed . . . the manner in which this law shall be carried into execution" and did not authorize the executive order.[17] Thus, though the president's action may well have been reasonable and even prudent and, as Marshall noted, far more likely to achieve the ends Congress desired, it was illegal — and any officer who acted under illegal instructions was responsible for his actions.[18]

MODERN REALITY AND THE MODERN COURT DOCTRINE

Despite the paucity of precedent for claims of executive prerogative before *Curtiss-Wright*,[19] after Sutherland's opinion was handed down events overtook the Court: the depression and World War II led Congress to greatly expand the powers it had delegated to the executive in foreign affairs. These events also resulted in a firmly entrenched and greatly expanded role for the United States in world affairs. As the Court came to grapple with foreign policy questions in the modern age, the idea of completely divorcing foreign and domestic policy became less and less realistic. George Sutherland had been a leading proponent of the concept that in America politics could stop at the water's edge, a slogan that "encapsulated the hope that diplomacy could be separated from domestic politics." But as the cold war, Korea, and Vietnam would demonstrate, "Diplomacy could not be separated from domestic politics: An emergency abroad could not be stopped at the water's edge," and the Court could not draw a simple and hard line between the two (LaFeber 1987, 54).

In 1952 domestic and foreign policy collided when the American role in the Korean War became entangled with a domestic labor dispute in the steel industry, and the Court was forced to reexamine its doctrine in foreign policy cases.

An extended strike in the steel mills loomed when the Wage and Price Stabilization Board refused to sanction price hikes in steel that the mill owners insisted were needed to pay for wage increases demanded by the unions. Unwilling to alienate union workers further by invoking the Taft-Hartley Act, Truman ordered the steel mills seized, arguing that the American war effort in Korea, and therefore American national security, would otherwise be imperiled. The Supreme Court overturned Truman's seizure, arguing that the executive had no legislative support for his action, and that in fact there had been a formal and explicit consideration and rejection of his claimed powers (*Youngstown Sheet & Tube Co. v. Sawyer*, 1952).

For every justice in the majority in the Steel case, there was no question but that the national government was constitutionally able to seize the nation's steel mills. But to say that the government could do it was in no way the same as saying that the president could do it: as Justice Frankfurter put it in his concurrence, ". . . the fact that power exists in Government does not vest it in the President. The need for new legislation does not enact it. Nor does it repeal or amend existing law." While it is an open question how the Court might have ruled had Congress never considered what might be done in similar situations, the facts in this case convinced Frankfurter and his brethren in the majority that Congress had considered and explicitly rejected a proposal to give the president the sort of seizure power Truman had used: "In formulating legislation for dealing with industrial conflicts, Congress could not more clearly and emphatically have withheld authority than it did in 1947 [in the Labor Management Relations Act]" (*Youngstown*, 604, 602).

Whether or not Congress had chosen wisely or well, it had acted, and it had authorized the president to deal with industrial conflict without the power to seize property. Absent congressional action, some of the justices, such as Tom Clark, would have been willing to consider the context of the seizure, the gravity of the situation, and the pragmatic arguments of the executive branch. But, Clark (a Truman appointee) argued, "I conclude that where Congress has laid down specific procedures to deal with the type of crisis confronting the President, he must follow those procedures in meeting the crisis; but that in the absence of such action by Congress, the President's independent power to act depends upon the gravity of the situation confronting the nation" (*Youngstown*, 662).

As Justice Jackson outlined it in his concurrence in the Steel Seizure case, separation of powers cases in foreign policy tend to come in one of three varieties: cases where the president acts in concert with the Congress;[20] cases where the president "takes measures incompatible with the expressed or implied will of Congress" (*Youngstown*, 637); and cases that fall in what Jackson termed a "zone of twilight," where the President and Congress may be said to have concurrent powers. Jackson argued that the steel mill seizure was a case where the president acted against the explicit or implied will of Congress, and therefore the president could prevail in court only if the Court were convinced that the "seizure of such strike-bound industries is within [the President's] domain and beyond control by Congress" (*Youngstown*, 640). Congress had not left this field to the president, and seizure clearly was within the congressional domain. Therefore, in Jackson's opinion, Truman could not prevail.[21]

AVOIDING A DECISION: POLITICAL QUESTIONS, FOREIGN POLICY, AND THE MODERN COURT

In cases involving the separation of powers among the branches of the national government, the Court developed a doctrine that held that while the national government, acting as a whole, had broad powers in foreign policy, the president acting without Congress or against Congress was not so free of constraint.

A faithful adherence to the political question doctrine outlined in *Oetjen* would have relieved the Court of the need for this distinction, but despite the occasional flirtation with applying the political question doctrine to all foreign policy cases, it was an invitation the Court consistently refused to accept. While many justices paid lip service to the political question option, it was rarely applied by the Supreme Court. Instead, the justices found other grounds on which to dismiss foreign policy cases they preferred to avoid. Despite what Justice William Brennan labeled the fallacy of "sweeping statements to the effect that all questions touching foreign relations are political questions" (*Baker v. Carr*, 1962), many justices continued to subscribe to the notion that many cases touching foreign policy were, in fact, inherently political questions.

The applicability of the political question doctrine in foreign policy was revived in a 1979 controversy over President Carter's decision to abrogate a defense treaty with the Republic of China (Taiwan). This abrogation was necessary, Carter argued, because it was a condition for normalizing American relations with the People's Republic of China. Arguing that the Senate had a right to a role in treaty termination, Arizona's Republican senator Barry Goldwater challenged the Carter decision in court. The court of appeals held that Goldwater had standing to sue, but that the president had constitutional authority to terminate the treaty without Senate action. Unless there is a specific termination clause calling for a Senate role, the appeals court ruled, the president alone has the power to decide when the treaty has been or should be terminated because of changed circumstances. In this case, the appeals court held, the Senate had made no attempt to reserve a role for itself in the termination of the treaty when it gave its original advice and consent to the pact, and the Senate had made no effort to assert that right since Carter's decision. In essence, the appeals court held that the Senate had the political weapons it needed to fight Carter's decision but had chosen not to use them. Thus the court would not do what the Senate was unwilling to do for itself.

When the decision was appealed to the Supreme Court, the justices were bitterly divided. The Court split and ordered the suit dismissed, but the justices did not agree on why it should be dismissed. *Goldwater v. Carter*, 1979, illustrated the Court's two schools of thought on when it is appropriate to invoke the political question doctrine in foreign policy cases. The *Oetjen* view, expressed by Rehnquist in the *Goldwater* case, held that questions involving "the authority of the President in the conduct of our country's foreign relations" are inherently "political" and "therefore nonjusticiable" (1002). The second school of thought, argued by Justice Brennan, held that the Court had no business reviewing the policy preferences of the political branches, but if "the antecedent question [of] whether a particular branch has been constitutionally designated as the repository of political decision-making power" arises, the questions "must be resolved as a matter of constitutional law, not political discretion; accordingly it falls within the competence of the Courts" (1007). Therefore the Court must, Brennan argued, decide procedural challenges to foreign policy questions. According to Brennan, *Goldwater* was precisely the sort of case the Court was most qualified—and most obliged—to review.

Taking the middle ground, Justice Powell argued that the Court should not do the work of another branch. Powell held that the case was not "ripe" — that since the Senate had not acted, there was no actual case or dispute between the branches. The Senate, he argued, must fight for its own turf before turning to the Court. In a statement attached to the Supreme Court's order to dismiss *Goldwater*, Powell said that the issues raised might well be appropriate for Supreme Court review if there was a standoff between the other branches. At its heart, he wrote, this was a dispute over "the constitutional division of power between the Congress and President" (999).

In hindsight, Powell's position probably was closest to where the Court was headed. The political question doctrine has resurfaced in a number of recent challenges over the War Powers Resolution of 1973. In each of these disputes, members of the House or Senate have sued the president for violating one or another of the provisions of the War Powers Resolution. In 1987 the District Court for the District of Columbia refused to trigger the War Powers Resolution, but not because it was unwilling to involve itself in foreign policy. Rather, as Judge Revercomb put it in his opinion for the court, "A true confrontation between the Executive and a unified Congress, as evidenced by its passage of legislation to enforce the Resolution, would pose a question ripe for judicial review" (*Lowry v. Reagan*, 1987, 339). Should Congress pass a joint resolution stating that hostilities existed in the Persian Gulf, and should the president then refuse to follow the guidelines and requirements of the War Powers Resolution, *then* and *only then* would the court "analyze the constitutional division of powers." For the district court, evaluating "the seriousness of military activities" was beyond its mandate, while weighing and balancing the separation of powers was "within the purview of the judiciary" (341). As Justice Powell had argued in 1979, "A dispute between Congress and the President is not ready for judicial review unless and until each branch has taken action asserting its constitutional authority." As Powell had concluded, "If the Congress chooses not to confront the President, it is not our task to do so" (*Goldwater*, 998, 997).

WHEN THE EXECUTIVE AND LEGISLATIVE BRANCHES DISAGREE

When there is a clear conflict between the branches, the Court has made it clear that such disputes, rare though they are, can have their day in court. As Justice Powell argued in *Goldwater v. Carter*, "if the President and the Congress had reached irreconcilable positions, the specter of the Federal Government brought to a halt because of the mutual intransigence of the President and the Congress would require this Court to provide a resolution pursuant to our duty 'to say what the law is.' "[22]

While the modern Court has generally adopted Jackson's categories, it is increasingly less willing to see those categories as clear and distinct: as

Justice Rehnquist noted in 1980, in foreign affairs most executive action falls "not neatly in one of three pigeonholes, but rather at some point along a spectrum running from explicit congressional authorization to explicit congressional prohibition."[23] The modern Court has moved the threshold for congressional authorization quite a bit, seeming to insist on far more explicit congressional prohibition than it did in the past before it will rule against the executive. Nonetheless, the categories remain, and the Court is still committed to the doctrine that Congress has the right to foreclose certain options to the president at its discretion.

Where Congress is clear, as it was in the Competition in Contracting Act of 1984, the judiciary will support Congress against the president, as it did in *Lear Siegler Inc. v. Lehman*, 1988. When President Reagan signed the Competition in Contracting Act into law in 1984, he did so only after claiming that certain provisions of the act were unconstitutional and instructing the executive branch to ignore those provisions. The law gave the comptroller general a role in managing bidding for military projects designed to steer military contracts to American firms. A military contractor, Lear Siegler, went to court after it lost a Navy contract to a lower bid from a foreign firm even though enforcement of the law as passed by Congress clearly would have resulted in Lear Siegler winning the contract. Lear sued, and the appeals court ruled that the president had no authority to determine which part of the law he would "faithfully execute."[24]

"According to the government," Judge Fletcher wrote for the Ninth Circuit, "these clauses empower the President . . . to declare a law unconstitutional and suspend its operation." That position, the court ruled, was "utterly at odds with the texture and plain language of the Constitution, and with nearly two centuries of judicial precedent" (*Lear Siegler*, 1121). The court ruled that when presented with a piece of legislation passed by both houses of Congress, "the President must either sign or veto a bill presented to him." The Constitution, Judge Fletcher continued, does not empower the president to "excise or sever provisions of a bill with which he disagrees." Such "an incursion into Congress's essential legislative role," the court concluded, "cannot be tolerated" (1124). The court soundly denounced the notion that the president had any broad discretion or prerogative when Congress had spoken so formally, and so clearly.[25]

While Congress *can* and occasionally does win in court, the fact remains that the Court's rising threshold has meant that the president usually wins.[26] Rather than view these cases as conflicts between the president and the legislature, courts have recently been moving these cases into the category of cases Jackson identified as those where the president acts alone—without congressional opposition. While Jackson interpreted this category to be one that encompassed powers not asserted by Congress (i.e., cases where Congress truly was silent), the modern Court has extended the category to those cases where Congress is unclear, and even to those cases where, despite a surface clarity, the congressional intent can be read more broadly than Congress might have planned.

THE COURT AND THE WAR POWERS RESOLUTION OF 1973

Among the most common cases to arise in this category in recent times are challenges brought under the War Powers Resolution of 1973. Although these challenges have often reached sympathetic ears on one court or another, the judiciary has generally held that Congress has not made its own position clear, and the Court is unwilling to intervene in what is not yet a clear dispute.

In 1983 a number of members of Congress sought to stop the executive branch from supplying military aid to El Salvador, claiming that executive branch actions violated the War Powers Resolution. In *Crockett v. Reagan* 1982 (affirmed 1983), the plaintiffs asked that the court trigger the "clock" in the War Powers Resolution; in other words, they asked that the court determine that American forces had been introduced into hostilities or into situations where imminent involvement in hostilities was likely. The district court refused this motion, arguing that determining whether and when American forces were introduced into a hostile situation were questions that were "appropriate for congressional, not judicial, investigation and determination" (*Crockett*, 1982, 898). The court maintained that "Congress must either take action to express its view that the WPR is applicable to the situation and that a report is required, or, if it desires immediate withdrawal of forces, pass a concurrent resolution directing removal of the forces pursuant to . . . the WPR" (1982, 900).

The representatives had laid out an alternative argument in their suit, contending that section 502B of the Foreign Assistance Act precluded security assistance to countries where the government engaged in a pattern of gross violations of human rights. This, they argued, the El Salvador government had done. The plaintiffs sought to have the court declare any further assistance to be illegal, since it violated these standards. But Congress, the court held, "has taken no action to end aid to El Salvador under the Foreign Assistance Act . . . or by other means" (*Crockett*, 1982, 902). And it is Congress that must take that step before looking to the courts for support: "Their dispute is primarily with their fellow legislators. Action by this Court would not serve to mediate between branches of government, but merely aid plaintiffs in circumventing the democratic processes available to them" (1982, 903).

In 1987 this issue was revisited by the district court when 110 members of the House of Representatives sued President Reagan, arguing that the executive had violated the War Powers Resolution by ordering American forces into the Persian Gulf without reporting their introduction into hostilities, and thus without starting the "clock" required by the WPR. Here again the court said this was really a "by-product of political disputes within Congress regarding the applicability of the War Powers Resolution to the Persian Gulf situation" (*Lowry v. Regan*, 338).

Although the courts have made it clear that they will not act to enforce the War Powers Resolution in the absence of formal congressional action, they have made it equally clear that they are willing to hear and decide such a case if Congress takes formal action. As recently as December 1990, a federal district court judge in Washington, D.C., ruled that if a majority in Congress should decide against the use of force in a particular situation, and if the executive refuses to follow that instruction, "the courts would appear to be the only available means to break the deadlock in favor of the constitutional provision" (*Dellums v. Bush*, 1990, 1144n.5). But at the time, there was no such deadlock. "No one knows the position of the Legislative Branch on the issue of war or peace with Iraq," the judge argued, and "it would be both premature and presumptuous for the Court to render a decision on the issue of whether a declaration of war is required . . . when the Congress itself has provided no indication whether it deems such a declaration either necessary, on the one hand, or imprudent, on the other" (*Dellums*, 1149, 1150). In fact, Congress finally did debate the U.S. role in the Persian Gulf, supporting the president's authority to deploy nearly half a million armed troops. But this debate came very late, despite the passage of a special rule that would have allowed the majority leader to recall Congress for a special session while the military decision was still developing. That the debate took place under the circumstances it did says little about the War Powers Resolution, though it says a great deal about Congress and the role it would like to play in war decisions. In the end, despite a great deal of enlightening rhetoric, the president was once again delegated broad discretion in the foreign policy realm, not because the Constitution required it, but because that is how Congress chose to conduct itself. No judge who takes seriously his or her mandate to read and interpret the laws can ignore that reality, though one might argue that, at their most extreme, broad delegations can exceed constitutional limits on delegation.

THE "ZONE OF TWILIGHT"
As Justice Jackson instructed in the Steel Seizure case, there is a "zone of twilight" where the president and Congress may have concurrent authority, or where the distribution of power is uncertain. In such cases "congressional inertia, indifference or quiescence may sometimes, at least as a practical matter, enable, if not invite, measures of independent presidential responsibility" (*Youngstown*, 637). In recent cases this zone has been marked by three types of action: executive initiatives that are derived from enumerated powers where there is no congressional response; long-standing practices that, if not supported by Congress, have at least been acquiesced in; and,

potentially, direct conflict between the branches where each branch has solid constitutional ground for its behavior.

When both branches stand toe to toe, each supported by explicit enumerated powers, the Court has tried to play the role of gentle mediator, refusing to come to either side's aid, urging both to reach a compromise.[27] But such cases are rare: the zone of twilight is far more often filled with cases where the executive has taken an initiative derived from some enumerated power and there is no clear objection from Congress, or where there is a long-standing executive tradition or practice that Congress has acquiesced in, or at least has ignored. In such cases, the modern Court can increasingly be relied upon to support the executive.

In *Goldwater v. Carter* Justice Powell had argued that if Congress were to assert its authority and formally seek a role in treaty termination, it would indeed be a judicial question. But Congress had not done so. What the Senate had done was to provide a termination clause in the treaty itself which did not specify a role for the Senate in termination but merely required one year's notice by either party (the United States or Taiwan) wishing to terminate the treaty. As the court of appeals ruled,

> No specific role is spelled out in either the Constitution or this treaty for the Senate or the Congress as a whole. That power consequently devolves upon the President, and there is no basis for a court to imply a restriction on the President's power to terminate not contained in the Constitution, in this treaty, or in any other authoritative source. (708)

In *Goldwater*, the Senate had consented to a treaty that contained an explicit termination clause. Thus, though there is no textual reference to treaty termination in the Constitution, the Court was able to find Senate acquiescence. But even where there is ambiguous constitutional text, the modern Court has increasingly favored the executive. In 1978 the appeals court was confronted with a suit by Congressman Mickey Edwards of Oklahoma, who challenged the Panama Canal Treaty, arguing that the president could not dispose of U.S. property without the approval of both houses of Congress. Senate treaty approval, he argued, was not sufficient. Unlike the situation in *Goldwater*, the Constitution does mention the disposal of U.S. property, but the court ruled that the text was ambiguous; that the power was not *exclusively* congressional; and that since the disposal of property was part of a broader foreign policy supported by the Panama Canal Treaty, it was valid in this case. While the dissent convincingly argued that the text was far from ambiguous, once again there was no clear effort from the House as a whole to assert its claim, and the Constitution could be strained to bear the reading given it by the majority.

Even without ambiguous textual support, the Court has sided with the executive in the zone of twilight where there is evidence of a long-standing practice acquiesced in by Congress, or at least evidence of congressional tolerance. When the Carter administration negotiated the release of American hostages in Teheran in 1981, part of the executive agreement (it was not submitted to the Senate for advice and consent) set up a process for the disposition of private claims against Iran. Arguing that this process constituted an unconstitutional taking of its property without just compensation, and arguing that the action was beyond the scope of the president's constitutional authority, a firm called American International Group filed suit seeking an injunction against the transfer of frozen Iranian assets. While the president had clear authority to freeze foreign assets under the IEEPA, the court ruled that the President had no express or implied grant of power from Congress in the IEEPA to suspend the claims of American nationals against Iran. Nevertheless, the court found that "there is a long-standing practice of settling private American claims against foreign governments through executive agreements." Here the court found support for an executive initiative in foreign policy not in the Constitution itself, nor in a particular act of Congress, but in the lack of action by Congress and the precedent of a pattern of similar previous behavior.[28] The court was quick to note that it "would be confronted with a very different case if Congress had enacted legislation, or even passed a resolution, indicating its displeasure with the Iranian agreements." Here, the court ruled, Congress had made no effort to foreclose the option chosen by the president; there was a pattern of previous behavior; and allowing this agreement to stand, the court stated, should *not* be read as "foreclosing or eroding any powers to block or amend claims settlements that *the Congress may one day choose to assert*" (*American International v. Iran*, 445, emphasis added).

Recent cases indicate that in the zone of twilight the courts are increasingly insisting on more than a simple assertion of congressional will, looking instead for very specific and explicit legislation before they will rule against the president. In cases in 1981, 1983, and 1985, the courts began to read legislation broadly, and increasingly ruled that where executive action was not specifically foreclosed, the courts would make every effort to authorize broad executive discretion—though the courts were equally clear that executive discretion was not to be equated with executive prerogative.

In 1981 the Supreme Court was asked to rule on the executive agreements reached with Iran over the hostage release. Writing for the court in *Dames & Moore v. Regan*, 1981, Chief Justice Rehnquist argued that the president's actions had been constitutional: even though they were not explicitly authorized by an act of Congress, the IEEPA and the Hostage Act both were clear indications of congressional acceptance of broad executive discretion in circumstances similar to those presented by this case. Rehnquist argued that the courts cannot expect Congress to "anticipate and legislate with regard to every possible action the President may find it necessary to take or every possible situation in which he might act" (678). Taken together with the evidence of other related delegations of power, the Court concluded that "Congress has implicitly approved the practice of claim settlement by executive agreement" (680). But while Rehnquist was willing to find broad executive discretion, he was explicitly unwilling to find executive prerogative: "We do not decide," he wrote, "that the President possesses plenary power to settle claims, even as against foreign governmental entities" (688).[29]

Dames & Moore built court approval on congressional silence combined with an extrapolation of legislation written to delegate authority in similar circumstances. But the courts have stretched even further to authorize constitutionally questionable executive initiatives. In 1983 the Court confronted a situation where Congress explicitly rewrote legislation it perceived to be too broad a delegation of authority to the president, and yet despite this clear intent to limit executive discretion, the Court held that the language of the new bill was sufficiently vague and malleable that the president could extend an existing embargo on Cuba and ban any travel-related spending on U.S. currency there. This, the petitioner argued, was a violation of the IEEPA, which had been passed explicitly to limit the broad delegations of authority under its predecessor, the TWEA.

Writing for the majority, Justice Rehnquist argued that the legislative history was unclear; that the language in the IEEPA was broad, and that the president's action was a logical construction of that language. In a blistering dissent, Justice Blackmun (with whom Justices Brennan, Marshall, and Powell joined) argued that the whole intent of IEEPA was to restrict the burgeoning discretion being exercised by the chief executive. In a separate statement, Justice Powell added that "the judgment of the Court may well be in the best interest of the United States" but that the Court's proper role should be limited to "ascertaining and sustaining the intent of Congress" (*Regan v. Wald*, 262). For Powell as for Blackmun, Brennan, and Marshall, the legislative intent was clear: Congress wanted to limit executive discretion. But the majority found some ambiguity in the legislative record and chose to read the words of the IEEPA rather literally; by so doing, the majority was able to argue that the legislative history was ambiguous, and that since Congress had not clearly foreclosed this particular option, it was within the president's discretionary authority.

While Justice Rehnquist was willing to bend the IEEPA language and legislative intent to legitimate executive discretion in the Cuban and Iranian situations, he changed course two years later, when the president directly contradicted congressional instructions on the imposition of sanctions against countries that violated the International Whaling Commission rules on whale hunting. For years the president had exercised discretion in the imposition of sanctions against countries that violated the whale-hunting rules. Unsatisfied with this behavior, Congress passed an amendment saying that once a country had been certified as a violator, mandatory sanctions had to be imposed. When, in 1984, Japan violated the rules, the administration refused to certify the Japanese as violators and instead concluded an executive agreement trading lack of certification for a pledge on future whaling concessions. When the American Cetacean Society sued, the majority on the Court argued that the legislative history left this sort of discretion available. But Justice Marshall's dissent, in which Brennan, Blackmun, and Rehnquist all joined, argued that the Court was misreading the law and the legislative intent. "This Court," they wrote, "now renders illusory the mandatory language of the statutory scheme, and finds permissible exactly the result that Congress sought to prevent" (*Japan Whaling Association v. American Cetacean Society*, 1986, 243–44).

The majority opinion never contended that the President had the right, in the words of the dissent, to "rewrite the law" (*Japan Whaling*, 246). Instead, the majority argued that the "construction of the statutes neither contradicted the language of either Amendment, nor frustrated congressional intent." Justice White argued that Congress's primary goal was "to protect and conserve whales" and that the executive branch's actions were designed to accomplish those goals (241, 242). Thus, for the majority, the president's choice of means was within his discretion so long as his means served congressional ends. Again, Congress was the key, but the Court made it clear that in the zone of twilight, even what appears to be clear language may no longer be clear enough. Nevertheless, these cases all support the idea that the Court will not entertain arguments of executive prerogative and that should Congress care to write explicit legislation, the Court will continue to support Congress over the president.

WHEN CONGRESS DELEGATES POWER TO THE PRESIDENT

While the courts will strain to find congressional authorization even in legislation that appears to foreclose certain options to the executive branch, the courts are even more prepared to support executive discretion when there is a clear congressional delegation of power. In this category, the Court has made it quite clear that delegation is the key—whether or not that delegation is logical, efficient, or wise. The message to Congress is clear: consider the ramifications of any delegation and do not assume that the Court will support the checks that are built into those delegations. If you don't want to give the executive broad discretion, don't delegate power and authority to the executive branch in foreign policy.

In 1975 a Japanese manufacturer sued the United States, claiming that President Nixon's 1971 unilateral imposition of a tax surcharge on all items subject to import duties was beyond the president's delegated constitutional powers. The appeals court held that the TWEA provided sufficient authority, and that the delegation was within the confines of what the Constitution permitted the Congress to delegate to the executive. While the court agreed that this particular delegation was extremely broad, it noted that it is the judiciary's job to judge presidential actions "in the light of what the President actually *did*, not in the light of what he could have done." And, the court emphasized, "to this we would add 'and not in the light of what he *might* do.'" The court concluded that "though such a broad delegation might be considered unwise, or even dangerous . . . the wisdom of a congressional delegation is not for us to decide" (*United States v. Yoshida International Inc.*, 577, 583–84).

Here, despite fairly clear legislative intent, the Court interpreted the president's action as a logical means to congressionally mandated ends—as indeed it may have been.

THE DILEMMAS OF DELEGATION

It is easy to argue that Congress should simply forgo the delegation of broad authority in foreign affairs, but there are reasons why Congress made these broad delegations, ranging from a desire to avoid electoral responsibility for foreign policy gone awry; to a lack of electoral incentives to do otherwise; to a sincere belief that "the need to act quickly, to understand the technology involved, and to maintain important secrets" were needs only the executive was capable of meeting (Warburg 1989, 35). Despite Vietnam and Watergate, Congress was convinced that the executive had to have broad discretion in foreign policy, but Congress wanted to delegate that authority and yet retain some measure of control. One answer Congress increasingly came to rely upon was the legislative veto. Starting with the New Deal's attempts to confront the Great Depression, Congress became enamored with the legislative veto as a way of delegating authority to the executive that would allow speed, discretion, and broad latitude without surrendering congressional oversight.

In foreign affairs, this apparently congenial solution was disrupted in 1983 when the Supreme Court ruled that the legislative veto was unconstitutional, since it violated the Constitution's presentment clause (*Immigration v. Chadha*, 919).[30] To complicate matters further, the Court has since ruled in a number of cases that the legislative veto provisions can be severed from the rest of the legislation—in effect, that the broad delegations of power and discretion to the executive can stand, but the tool designed to make those delegations "safe" is unconstitutional.

In 1987 the appeals court made it clear that in foreign policy the ability to sever a legislative veto from a broad delegation of power to the president would in fact be used by the courts to find authorization for broad executive discretion. In *Beacon Products Corp. v. Reagan* an emergency embargo ordered by the president under authority granted by the National Emergencies Act

(NEA) and the IEEPA prevented a Massachusetts manufacturer from trading with Nicaragua. Since the NEA had a legislative veto provision, the plaintiff argued that it was unconstitutional, and the president therefore lacked the authority to impose the embargo. The court ruled that the veto was severable from the legislation, and the president therefore had adequate authority. In effect, the control is invalid, but the delegation of power still stands.

CAN CONGRESS ASSERT ITSELF IN FOREIGN AFFAIRS?

If any delegation is interpreted by the courts to be a broad delegation, if the Court won't allow Congress to improvise a solution to the problem by accepting the legislative veto as legitimate, and if Congress insists on delegating authority to the president in foreign affairs,[31] is it possible for Congress to regain control of foreign policy? The answer is mixed: If Congress wants to maintain control of the process and the expenditures, it certainly has the tools to do so. If it wants to continue to delegate broad authority in foreign affairs to the president and yet still retain control, it faces a far more difficult task.

How did Congress get into this predicament? In large measure it was a response to a world that seemed very different from the one that shaped the thoughts and concerns of the founders. The development of nuclear weapons at the end of World War II, and the prolonged cold war in which the United States led an international coalition of countries in a bipolar struggle, combined to convince many in Congress to give the executive even greater authority, for two reasons: nuclear weapons meant that there might be no time for deliberation, and that ultimate responsibility for these weapons had to rest on one person; and the cold war allowed the executive to accrue extraordinary power by arguing that the United States was engaged in a national emergency, though that emergency—and the legislation that supported it—lasted for more than forty years.[32]

While presidents starting with Harry Truman began to develop a new interpretation of the constitutional authority vested in the president, it was Congress and congressional leaders who paved the way to this new interpretation. As Wisconsin's senator Wiley argued in 1946, "in this atomic age" the president needs to have broad powers that will "make it possible for government to take appropriate action in any emergency." Wiley admitted that he was uncomfortable with this broad delegation, but argued that it was unavoidable: "There are those who would fear such legislation. A decade ago I would not have been in favor of it, because I could see no reason for it at that time. But in this tremendously challenging period . . . I would have available and ready for any eventuality every instrument which, with foresight, I could bring into being" (*Cong. Rec.*, 29 May 1946, 5899).

When, in 1950, Truman sent U.S. troops to Korea on his sole authority as commander-in-chief and in accord with a United Nations' resolution, many echoed the views expressed by Senator Lucas, a Democratic leader, who argued that the times mandated extraordinary powers for the president: "With communism creeping into every nook and corner where it can possibly go," Senator Lucas argued, if the president believes "that the safety, the security, and the honor of this country are involved as a result of what is going on in the Orient, he had a right to move as he did with the powers he had under the Constitution as Commander in Chief of the military forces" (*Cong. Rec.*, 28 June 1950, 9328).

For their part, members of the executive branch began to articulate a new reading of the Constitution, particularly in reference to foreign affairs. This executive prerogative argument held that in foreign affairs the president alone had final authority, and when the national security was imperiled (a judgment left to the executive), the president was legitimately entitled to override constitutional constraints to preserve and protect that security. While this doctrine emerged slowly through the Truman, Kennedy, and Nixon administrations, it has been fully and articulately expounded by recent administrations. While Congress has been delegating power, the president has increasingly insisted that the executive power in foreign affairs is plenary and that there is, in fact, a prerogative power. As two senior legal advisers to the Bush administration wrote recently, the executive power "includes a foreign affairs power . . . and a discretionary power, sometimes termed the 'prerogative,' which includes both a broad authority to meet national exigencies by acting for the public good and a residual power that encompasses all authority not expressly delegated to the other branches of government" (Block and Rivkin 1990, 50).[33] While Congress is far from endorsing this extreme version of prerogative power, it is true that in the years since the end of World War II Congress itself increasingly came to accept the need for ever greater executive discretion in foreign policy. Thus when, in the 1970s, Congress sought to reassert its authority, it did so on top of a host of legislative precedents ceding power to the executive. Rather than repeal these, Congress passed legislation that either tried to give power with one hand while checking it with the other or merely installed an overlay of control on top of a foundation of delegated authority.

WHY THE COURTS WON'T RESCUE CONGRESS

A review of the Court's doctrine in foreign policy illustrates the challenge Congress faces. The problem with broad delegation is multilayered: by delegating broad authority, Congress implicitly supports executive claims to discretion in foreign policy bordering on prerogative; Congress also hurts its case in court, since the judiciary has made it clear that in foreign policy cases judges will give great weight to any sort of delegation as an indication of broad congressional support for executive initiatives.[34] The courts have also made it clear that long-standing practices acquiesced in by Congress, or at least not actively opposed, also constitute a signal of congressional support for executive discretion. The courts interpret the law, and laws are written by Congress. Even if the courts were hostile to the prerogative arguments of recent administrations, the fact that this interpretation has been implicitly woven into the very legislation designed to reassert congressional authority would naturally lead the Court to add its weight and legitimacy to this new interpretation. The Court can only rule on what it is given, and if it is given legislation that legitimates executive prerogative in foreign policy, then we should hardly be surprised that it will not rescue congressional prerogatives. In fact, far from being hostile to the new interpretation, the lower courts have become increasingly receptive to this new reading, and the changing composition of the Supreme Court also indicates that it too is getting closer to this view of the Constitution in foreign policy.

Only Congress can decide whether or not broad delegation of power in foreign affairs is wise: presidents will continue to assert such claims and act on them, as George Bush did in the Iraq conflict, and the executive as well as the judicial branch will look to Congress for the next move. With the cold war apparently over and with foreign affairs increasingly being seen as having a direct effect on local constituents, perhaps the incentive structure will change. But with or without a clear shift in the incentives, legislative options are both limited and clear: legislators can concede foreign policy power to the president formally or informally; they can try to replace the legislative veto with a constitutionally more acceptable device that will allow them to delegate broad power without surrendering control; they can pass a constitutional amendment to legitimate the legislative veto; or they can roll back the broad delegations of power from the years since World War II and assert the power they never lost—the power of the purse and the power of oversight and investigation.

Congress can assert itself. In foreign policy, though the record is largely one of failed attempts at control, there are some success stories, particularly in the military budget, in arms control, and in weapons sales.[35] In each of these areas the sort of electoral incentives with which we are familiar are strong.[36] If Congress has the will, the Constitution provides the way, and the judicial branch has clearly indicated that it will support such action. The current distribution of power in international affairs suggests that Congress may have a unique opportunity to reassert itself. But Congress must be decisive and unambiguous.[37] That is the message one reads clearly from a close look at the evolution of judicial doctrine in foreign policy cases, and it is a message those who would like to see a more assertive Congress would do well to heed.

Part II

PRESIDENTIAL ADVISERS AND CONGRESSIONAL COMMITTEES

Chapter Three

★ ★ ★

PLAYING HARDBALL
WITH THE CIA

★ ★ ★

Loch K. Johnson

INTRODUCTION

The studies presented in this volume examine the question of executive and legislative involvement in the making of U.S. foreign policy, and the extent to which the levels of this involvement have undergone change in the postwar period. The central hypothesis posits that a dangerous, anarchic international environment sharply constrains foreign policy decision making within a nation, and that, mindful of these external dangers, Congress has usually deferred to the executive branch for foreign policy guidance, relying on its attribute of secrecy, its vast store-house of information on international events, and its ability to act with dispatch. This chapter explores the extent to which this hypothesis has been valid for strategic intelligence—America's secret foreign policy.

More specifically, the research offered here probes the efforts by Congress to supervise and instruct one of the most controversial and hidden entities within the executive branch: the Central Intelligence Agency (CIA), America's premier intelligence service. In light of the shroud of secrecy that envelops the CIA (known simply as "the Agency" among insiders), its supervision represents a difficult challenge for Congress—arguably the most severe test faced by legislators in their role as overseers and would-be makers of foreign policy. For Congress must carry out its monitoring of intelligence operations largely without the assistance derived from the extensive media coverage, interest-group articulation, and unfettered debate that informs legislators about the activities of most government agencies—virtually all of which are markedly more porous and open to public scrutiny than the CIA.

In reaction to newspaper allegations in 1974 of illegal spying at home by the CIA, congressional leaders announced their intention to watch the government's secret agencies with greater care (Johnson 1988). How well have legislators carried out this objective? To what extent has Congress been a serious player in the guiding of America's secret power abroad? One answer can be found in an analysis of public hearings held by the intelligence oversight committees in the House and the Senate, and by ad hoc committees established by legislators on two occasions to investigate intelligence controversies.[1]

THE RESEARCH STRATEGY

Formal Legislative Supervision

The supervision of executive activities by Congress assumes many forms, both formal and informal (Aberbach 1990; Johnson 1980; Kaiser 1977; Ogul 1976; Ogul and Rockman 1990). On the formal side are, at the extreme, full-blown investigations costing millions of dollars and lasting several months, with elaborate public hearings conducted before the klieg lights of television cameras and a standing-room-only crowd of spectators—genuine media events with a nationwide audience. Within the category of formal oversight, one also finds hearings that are less celebrated than showcase inquiries into scandals but that nonetheless subject executive branch officials to close—sometimes heated—interrogation. On the formal side as well are debates and colloquies in the chambers of Congress, explicit agency reporting requirements, inspections of an agency's facilities at home and abroad, and, among other activities, the publication of committee reports bearing on an agency's programs.

In this study, even hearings on new legislative proposals affecting CIA programs are treated as a supervisory activity, since here again legislators are attempting to control the agency's policies and practices. For some, this perspective may seem too inclusive, blurring the traditional distinction between legislative activity (lawmaking), on the one hand, and the supervision of existing programs, on the other hand. Yet, legislators spend much of their time looking at federal agencies in order to understand not only how well existing statutes are working but what changes in the law (and executive regulations) may be desirable. These two concerns are part of a seamless web of legislative oversight. Where supervision ends and legislating begins (or vice versa) is often difficult to say, and the distinction is artificial anyway; both represent efforts to place—or sometimes remove—controls on an executive agency.

Informal Oversight

On the informal side of legislative supervision stands another long list of activities, far less visible (and therefore knowable) to the researcher but often of consequence in the daily affairs of government. Here are the winks and nods across the green baize tables in committee rooms; the private dinners where tacit policy understandings are reached between agency directors and legislators; and the tennis matches, golf at the Congressional Country Club, and bourbon-soothed "socials" in the hideaway offices of the Capitol, where executive-legislative relations can deepen into bonds of trust and friendship. Obviously, much of this side of legislative supervision lies beyond the purview of most researchers—though some have witnessed and reported on these events as former officials and aides themselves, and others have journeyed into the inner sanctums of government by developing a rapport with members of Congress and observing their behavior (Fenno 1990).

Formal Hearings as a Research Focus

From the wide range of supervisory activities engaged in by Congress, formal and informal, this analysis focuses on one of the most significant: participation in formal public hearings on the CIA, both investigative and routine. The thick volumes of open testimony gathered over the years by the congressional intelligence committees (and their ad hoc investigative surrogates) provide a rich chronicle for studying the role of Congress in foreign policy making. These documents disclose the attendance records of members at hearings and, of still more value, the thoroughness of their questions and remarks (Q & Rs).

Which members were in attendance is easily determined by reading the transcripts of the hearings. Simple, too, is the task of gathering frequency statistics on the number of Q & Rs offered by each legislator—another index of a member's degree of involvement in this forum of agency supervision. More qualitative, and thus more difficult to measure, is the *seriousness* with which members participate. To what extent do overseers delve deeply into the inner workings of an agency and its programs? For this aspect of oversight, one must turn to the methodology of content analysis.[2]

To examine the quality of legislative participation in CIA hearings, this study sorts the utterances of overseers into four categories: deferential, factual, probing, and adversarial. This sequence reflects a rising intensity in the critique offered by legislators of the CIA's activities.

The Legislator as Pal. As the term implies, the first category (deference) is the repository for questions and remarks of a warm and supportive nature—in some cases, an obsequiousness toward CIA officials and their programs. At times, the purpose of the deferential Q & R will be to build rapport with the witness. Occasionally, the deferential approach seems to have little intent beyond exhibiting unalloyed support for the Agency. In a farrago of sychophancy, the CIA witness is offered assurances that his (there have been no female CIA witnesses) organization is functioning without flaw; in fact, if fault is to be found, it is with the Congress itself.

The chief complaint of one leading deferential member of the House committee, for example, had nothing to do with any shortcomings of the CIA but, instead, with (unsubstantiated) "egregious leaks of information" from Capitol Hill; another House committee member opined that legislative guidelines had usually served only to "inhibit good intelligence."[3] From these vantage points, the less oversight the better—especially to prevent the unauthorized disclosure of information by the Congress. "This place [Congress] has more leaks than the men's room at Anheuser-Busch," commiserated a deferential senator during a hearing with CIA witnesses.[4]

In contrast, overseers of a more skeptical bent are inclined to raise troubling questions about the legal aspects of CIA activities as well as the quality of its intelligence: Is the Agency obeying the law? Is it reporting reliable, unvarnished information to high decision councils—speaking truth to power? The skeptics also worry about civil liberties and the rights of the American people.

Like other agencies, much of what the CIA does is laudable and warrants praise from overseers. So a degree of deferential Q & R is expected. Few would deny that Congress ought to acknowledge the good work of bureaucrats, not just criticize work that is shoddy. Still, a legislator who offered only deference could hardly be viewed as a hard-nosed overseer, diligently upholding the checks and balances meant to safeguard the American system of governance from the abuse of power. Surely, quality oversight involves the asking of some demanding questions about an agency's performance—even, from time to time, sharp criticism about its failures. What this research seeks to examine is the mix of deference and skepticism present in Congress's public examination of CIA programs and personnel.

The Legislator as Fact Finder.   With the second category (factual questioning), the attention of the overseer turns toward the marshaling of basic information about an agency's activities. At this level of inquiry, the legislator is content to ask routine, factual questions about the CIA or the witness's role in its operations, such as: "How long have you served as chief of the Covert Action Staff?" "Which component of the Agency is responsible for approving the use of covert propaganda aboard?"

The Legislator as Interrogator.   At the next level of questioning (probing), the overseer shifts from basic fact-finding toward a more prickly line of inquiry into past performance, anticipated operations, and even charges of malfeasance. The questioning can extend from well-researched and thoughtful explorations about how an agency functions (beyond the mere recitation of organization tables) to a courtlike cross-examination of alleged policy failures, misuse of funds, or violations of the public trust.

At this level the legislator stops short, though, of rendering a value judgment against the Agency. An illustration: "If [the CIA] puts out a story [overseas] which is totally false propaganda, how do you protect [Americans] against the domestic feedback of the planted story?" So probed a member of the House intelligence committee into the problem of propaganda "blowback" during a hearing with a former Agency director. Or: "What is your understanding of the legality of the covert mail operation?" asked a Senate overseer while questioning the CIA's chief of counterintelligence during an investigation into charges of unlawful opening of mail.[5]

The Legislator as Adversary. The final category of Q & Rs exhibits a more explicit skepticism, sometimes even hostility, toward the Agency's programs or witnesses. At this level, the legislator is no longer content to be impartial; he or she (only one woman has served on an intelligence committee) becomes an adversary. The CIA is chided for inefficiency, lambasted for error, ridiculed for stupidity, excoriated for abusing power, or shamed for transgressions against the law, the Constitution, American traditions, or commonly accepted norms of propriety. As distinct from the roles of booster, fact finder, or prober, the legislator is now a jurer. Here is the use of hearings-as-oversight in its harshest form.

Some examples: "You do not want to inform [the President] in the first place, because he might say no. That is the truth of it," said a senator to a senior CIA official, concluding with disgust and heavy sarcasm: "And when [the President] did say no [to an illegal mail-opening program], you disregarded it—and then you call him the Commander in Chief." Similarly, a member of the House sharply rebuked a CIA counsel for trying to control what information Congress could release: "The executive branch is not going to have this thing both ways with the legislative branch. . . . You come in here and bug our rooms, you throw us out for forty-five minutes and yet you feel free to go out and tell anybody and everybody you want whatever you choose. . . . I resent it."[6]

Softball versus Hardball

In a democracy, some verbal sparring between executive and legislative officials is arguably healthy as a means for informing the public about policy disagreements, failures, and violations; however, overheated confrontation between the branches—Edward Corwin's "invitation to struggle" run amok— would result in a tense and ultimately unworkable government. Still, the opposite extreme of legislative fawning (overlook instead of oversight) represents a breakdown of auxiliary precautions, exposing the nation to concentrated, untended, and, in this case, secret executive power—the very dangers that animated the drafting of this nation's Constitution.

The first two roles of the overseer—deference and fact-finding—are, from an agency's point of view, relatively benign: at worst (in the case of fact-finding), a mildly intrusive intervention into its business. Probing and adversarial roles, however, represent significant interventions, threatening at their worst (accusations of wrongdoing) an agency's reputation and funding—perhaps even its raison d'être.

Some legislators are satisfied to emphasize the first two roles—known colloquially in Washington as "playing softball." The questioning consists of easy pitches and long home runs—an agency's favorite sport. Others reject this approach (particularly deference) as a manifestation of co-optation. They prefer hardball: tough pitches, with many strikes. This study, then, is about softball and hardball on Capitol Hill, as played by legislators and "spooks" (CIA slang for spies).

THE FINDINGS

The Frequency of Hearings

From 1975 to 1990, the intelligence committees averaged only 1.6 hearings in public per year. In some years—1976, 1985, and 1990—neither House nor Senate overseers met openly with CIA officials. The peak periods of open oversight, as measured by the frequency of public hearings, took place in the House intelligence committee. In 1979 and 1980 its subcommittees on oversight and on legislation (led by Les Aspin, D-Wis., and Morgan Murphy, D-Ill., respectively) produced in a burst of energy a series of thirteen public hearings with CIA officials—54 percent of the committee's total from 1975 to 1990. As veterans of the Pike committee investigation in 1975, Aspin and Murphy knew more about the CIA than most legislators; moreover, both men were ambitious, bright, skeptical—and the chairmen of subcommittees with authority to conduct their own hearings.

By 1979 Aspin and Murphy had reached full stride in their interest in and knowledge of intelligence issues; and, in step, their self-confidence as subcommittee chairmen came to full bloom. With their departures from the committee in 1981, much of this panel's energy and dedication to CIA supervision went with them, emphasizing the importance of individual personalities in the conduct of oversight responsibilities (Johnson 1989a, 230–31).

Thus, the frequency of public hearings with CIA officials during the era of "New Oversight" (1975–90) was low. Yet the public hearings that were held demonstrated the feasibility of carrying out a meaningful discussion of intelligence issues in an open forum. Among the several good examples are the inquiry of the House oversight subcommittee into the relationship between the CIA and the media in 1977 and 1978; the Senate committee's review of a wide range of CIA activities at home and abroad in 1980; and the House committee's exploration of oversight procedures for covert action in 1983.[7]

Attendance Patterns

A rudimentary indicator of a legislator's commitment to an involvement in foreign policy is his or her attendance at hearings on this subject. Each of the intelligence committees held (coincidentally) twenty-four open hearings during this period at which current or former CIA officials testified. By far the highest participation rates for legislators occurred during times of formal investigation into alleged CIA abuses: a 100 percent attendance rate during the inquiries of the Church and Pike committees in 1975; and, again, 100 percent on the Senate side (75 percent for the House) during investigative hearings into the Iran-contra affair in 1987, held by the joint Inouye-Hamilton committees.

Only in about one-third of the instances (35 percent) did the intelligence committees muster a majority for public hearings. The Senate committee surpassed this threshold considerably more often than the House committee (65 percent), despite a senator's greater number of committee assignments and supposedly more frenetic schedule. The Senate committee members also proved more regular in their attendance, averaging 51 percent turnout per session compared to 39 percent for the House committee. These last two statistics are inflated by the high participation of legislators during investigative hearings; if one looks only at routine hearings, attendance rates drop to 47 percent for senators and 35 percent for representatives.

The extent of member participation in routine hearings varied according to the sponsoring unit—either committee or subcommittee. When the full committees convened, the turnout rates averaged 55 percent attendance in the House (though the House intelligence committee met only five times in this fashion) and 48 percent in the Senate (twenty-two meetings).

In the House, the high-water mark for full committee participation in a routine hearing was a 69 percent turnout (the Boland committee in 1978, shortly after the creation of the House panel); and the low-water mark, 39 percent in 1982 (again the Boland committee). On the Senate side, the Boren committee reached a high mark of 93 percent in both 1986 and 1987 during confirmation proceedings for the director of Central Intelligence (DCI) and his deputy director, held in a Washington atmosphere charged with rumors of the Iran-contra machinations. (The formal Iran-contra investigation would soon erupt.) The Goldwater committee—whose leader, while a member of the Church committee investigation, had opposed the creation of the very panel he now ironically had come to chair—tallied the low mark, at 7 percent in 1983 (and averaged only 38 percent turnout for its six public hearings).

When open hearings were held at the subcommittee level (typically the case in the House), attendance rates fell significantly: to 32 percent in the Senate and 31 percent in the House. Usually only the members of the subcommittee attended these hearings, with one or two additional legislators from the full committee dropping in for a brief question or two.

For the intelligence committees in their public forums, then, two scandal-driven bursts of high activity (1975 and 1987) bracketed a profile of fluctuating—but much lower—participation rates during the intervening years of routine hearings. After the Iran-contra investigation of 1987, participation again fell off sharply. It took extraordinary circumstances — major scandals — to bring the members out in full force, drawn in part no doubt by the phototropic effect of television lights. More-routine oversight, the unglamorous job of weeding out abuse before it seeds, was a burden taken up by far fewer hands — almost always a minority of the members on the two intelligence committees. Woodrow Wilson once observed that "Congress in its committee-rooms is Congress at work" ([1885] 1956, 69). Applying this celebrated adage to CIA public hearings, one can only draw the conclusion that a good many legislators failed to show up for work.

The Frequency of Individual Q & Rs

For those committee members who did show up, what did they do? The frequency of questions and remarks proffered by legislators provides one useful measure.

Total Q & Rs. During these fifteen years of the New Oversight, the CIA found itself on the receiving end of 10,196 Q & Rs advanced by overseers on the two intelligence committees in public hearings. On the House side, members generated 4,677 questions. Only thirteen legislators (out of fifty-nine committee members during these years) posed more than 100 questions. The mean rate of questioning was 79 questions per overseer, with sixteen committee members remaining utterly mute. Perhaps accustomed to their more lenient rules of speech, senators spoke more often than House members: an additional 842 Q & Rs, for a total of 5,519 — though no senator came close to Congressman Aspin's herculean individual effort of 997. Walter "Dee" Huddleston (D-Ky.), a veteran of the Church committee investigation, set the record on the Senate committee at 623. Only nineteen senators, out of fifty-five, asked more than 100 questions. The mean rate of questioning for senators was 100 questions per overseer (21 higher per member than on the House committee), with five who chose complete silence.

Between the two committees, then, twenty-one overseers (18.4 percent of the combined membership) never asked a single question. Even among those who did, the Q & R rates were often extraordinarily low. Representative Clement J. Zablocki (D-Wis.), for instance, put in seven years of service on the House intelligence committee, averaging but one question per year.

Per Year Q & Rs. The CIA faced 22 questions annually in public from each of its House committee overseers, on average; and 24 from each of its Senate committee overseers — not exactly a withering barrage. The most intensive per-year questioning came, as one might expect, from the members of investigative committees, especially the Pike and Church committees. The chairmen of these two panels pitched the largest number of Q & Rs at

CIA witnesses, averaging 154 and 110, respectively. So, each year the CIA faced relatively few inquiries in public from the vast majority of its overseers—though a few legislators came well armed.

Softball and Hardball at the Committee Level

The next question involves the more qualitative aspects of CIA public hearings, namely, the mix of lenient (softball) and challenging (hardball) questions directed toward CIA witnesses. The tendency in both chambers has been to throw mostly softball questions. Yet despite the emphasis on fact-finding seasoned with a leavening of deference, both oversight panels have fielded a fair number of hardballers. Well over a third of the questions advanced by members of the Senate and the House committees have been in the hardball category (39 percent and 36 percent, respectively), with about 10 percent for both panels posed in a rather heated, highly skeptical (adversarial) manner.

This year-by-year degree of hardball questioning is shown in figure 1. The highest levels of rigorous interrogation occurred in the Senate: 57 percent in 1975 (the Church committee), 59 percent in 1987 (the Inouye committee II investigation into Iran-contra, along with three related hearings), and 57 percent in 1989 (the Boren committee, still provoked by the Iran-contra affair). These are the only instances in which the Senate committee recorded a majority of hardball questions.

The most robust interrogations on the House side (though each time with a lower hardball quotient than the Senate) were 51 percent in 1975 (the Pike committee) and 54 percent in 1983, when Representative Wyche Fowler (D-Ga.) led the Boland committee through a sustained interrogation of Agency witnesses regarding their responsiveness to oversight procedures. These are the only two instances in which the House committee fired a majority of hardball questions. Thus, the oversight committees played hardball with the CIA chiefly during times of scandal (1975 and 1987), as one might anticipate, and when an individual member (Fowler in the House) chose to pursue a lengthy, critical inquiry into a particular foreign policy topic.

Form Follows Function

The level of intensity in oversight questioning has varied according to the topic of the hearing: investigations into alleged abuses; examinations of procedures (such as CIA censorship of works written by current and former officials, or its use of the polygraph); proposed legislation; foreign intelligence (the CIA's operations abroad, a topic avoided altogether in Senate public hearings); and, in the Senate (by constitutional prerogative), leadership confirmation. The Church (1975), Pike (1975), Inouye II (1987), Hamilton II (1987), and Boren (1987–90) committees all recorded a majority of hardball questions; and each was either involved in a formal investigation

Fig. 1. The Percentage of Hardball Questions and Remarks Directed toward CIA Witnesses in Public Hearings, U.S. House and Senate Intelligence Committees, 1975–1990.

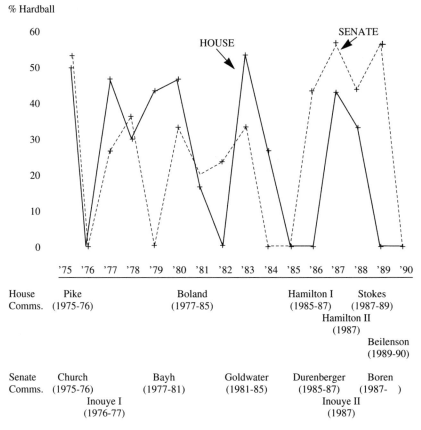

The Senate intelligence committee held no public hearings with CIA witnesses in 1976, 1979, 1984, 1985, and 1990; and the same with the House intelligence committee, in 1976, 1985, 1986, 1989, and 1990. In 1982 the House committee held a hearing with Agency witnesses but asked no hardball questions.

or, in the case of the Boren committee, operating in the atmosphere of the Iran-contra scandal, which settled over Washington from 1986 to 1988. Clearly, as one would predict, oversight committees engaged in scandal-driven investigations behaved more aggressively toward witnesses than those conducting routine hearings (in Smist's dichotomy, "investigative" versus "institutional" oversight [1990, 19–23]).

While investigative hearings elicited the most acrimonious questioning, confirmation hearings in the Senate stood a close second as an occasion for playing hardball (table 1). The Senate committee rejected two presidential appointees for DCI: Theodore C. Sorenson in 1977 and Robert M. Gates in 1987.[8]

Next in order for hardball questioning were House hearings on CIA procedures, which often touched on civil liberties issues dear to liberal legislators (though procedures proved the most lenient topic for Senate questioning), on proposed legislation, and, lastly, on foreign intelligence — often an exercise in Soviet bashing by conservative legislators during the cold war, but now and then leading to a critical examination of the CIA's overseas operations. Hearings on legislation have sometimes ignited debates over the proper scope of congressional oversight; more frequently, though, they have served as forums for factual questioning about the likely effects of a proposed statute.

Individual Styles of Intelligence Oversight

Most members of the intelligence committees offered a blend of questions, spanning the range from deferential to adversarial. A few, though, specialized in specific styles of interaction with CIA witnesses. Senators Church and Arlen Specter (R-Pa.), among others, were clearly inclined toward hardball, while at the other extreme, GOP senators Goldwater and Lyman Chafee (R-R.I.) much preferred softball — the latter the record holder for easy pitches. And recall that twenty-one overseers chose a style of total quiescence.

This study turns next to a multivariate analysis of the softball-hardball differences among members of the intelligence committees. How have ideology, party, seniority, and other influences on congressional behavior shaped the style of supervision chosen by intelligence overseers?

WHO PLAYS HARDBALL AND WHY

A model of intelligence oversight questioning in the Congress should take into account several possible influences on a member's behavior in public hearings. The association between the dependent variable (hardball questioning) and a series of key independent variables is presented in table 2.

Involvement

The results indicate that those overseers who were deeply involved in the hearings, as indicated by high attendance records and lengthy questioning,

Table 1
Rigor of CIA Oversight by Type of Hearing, House and Senate Intelligence
Committees, 1975–1990

| Hearing Type | Softball | | Hardball | | Total |
	Deference	Fact-finding	Probing	Adversary	
House					
Investigative	305 (16.6)	609 (33.2)	723 (39.5)	195 (10.6)	1,832 (100)
	914 (49.9)		918 (50.1)		
Procedures	259 (20.8)	419 (33.7)	482 (38.7)	84 (06.8)	1,244 (100)
	678 (54.5)		566 (45.5)		
Legislation	329 (28.4)	339 (29.3)	310 (26.8)	179 (15.5)	1,157 (100)
	668 (57.7)		489 (42.3)		
Foreign intelligence	29 (06.5)	265 (59.7)	106 (23.9)	44 (09.9)	444 (100)
	294 (66.2)		150 (33.8)		
Senate					
Investigative	144 (09.5)	508 (33.6)	655 (43.3)	206 (13.6)	1,513 (100)
	652 (43.1)		861 (56.9)		
Procedures	52 (20.8)	136 (54.4)	52 (20.8)	10 (04.0)	250 (100)
	188 (75.2)		62 (24.8)		
Legislation	423 (31.5)	445 (33.2)	385 (28.7)	89 (06.6)	1,342 (100)
	868 (64.7)		474 (35.3)		
Foreign intelligence	—	—	—	—	—
Confirmation	367 (15.2)	862 (35.7)	962 (39.9)	223 (09.2)	2,414 (100)
	1,229 (50.9)		1,185 (49.1)		

Note: Figures in parentheses are percentages.

Table 2
Multiple Regression of Hardball Questioning of CIA Witnesses in
House and Senate Intelligence Committees, by Selected Influences on
Legislative Behavior, 1975–1990

Independent Variables	Hardball Regression Coefficients (β)			
	House Intelligence Committee		Senate Intelligence Committee	
	Total	By Year	Total	By Year
Involvement				
Attendance	.46**	.21	.37**	−.10
Volume of Q & Rs	.96**	.66**	.93**	.59**
Ideology				
ADA	.86**	.87**	.43**	.40**
NSI[a]	.41*	.56*	.18	.15
Party	.79**	.77**	.51**	.52**
Seniority				
Chamber	−.16*	−.14*	−.11*	−.11*
Committee	−.11	−.35**	−.14**	−.35**
Divided government	.17*	.02	−.29**	−.25**
Periodical coverage	.56**	.68**	.43**	.41**
Superpower cooperation	.20**	.19**	.02	−.15**
Constant	−110.22	−42.72	1.18	−5.27
R² (Adjusted)	.35	.42	.35	.29
No. of observations	4,677		5,519	

*p ≤ .10 **p ≤ .05

[a]National Security Index, with a 100 score indicating a legislator unerringly in support of increased defense funding (see Lindsay, 1990).

were more apt to engage in hardball during their tenure on an intelligence committee. Generally, the more time spent on the playing field, the more intense the play.

The relationship between involvement and hardball stands out more starkly still when a member's volume of questioning is examined. The more an overseer participates in questioning, the more likely he or she is to be a hardballer. For both committees, the total volume of questioning reveals the strongest correlation with hardball.

The Importance of Ideology

Ideology has proved to be a powerful correlate of voting behavior in the Congress (Lindsay 1990; Bernstein and Anthony 1974; Fleisher 1985), and it it also a significant variable in this study. The policy preferences of committee members reveal a definite correspondence with their readiness to ask difficult questions in public hearings. The index of ideology tabulated by the Americans for Democratic Action (ADA) is an especially significant predictor of hardball for House committee members. Those on the conservative side of the political spectrum were more inclined to express trust and support for the CIA; conversely, liberals expressed more skepticism. What most concerned the softball legislators (to quote from various hearings) was the need for "better secrecy," "fewer restrictions," less "micromanagement," "stopping leaks," and "improving CIA cover." In contrast, key buzz words for the hardballers included concern for "the rights of the American people," "a free society," "civil liberties," "access to information," and "prior notification" to Congress of important CIA operations.

Partisanship

Republicans in Congress tend to be more conservative on interest-group ratings than Democrats (the inclusion of conservative Southern Democrats notwithstanding); therefore, one would expect from the ideological results in table 2 to find more hardballers among the Democratic overseers on the intelligence committees. The findings confirm this expectation. In both chambers, Democrats on the intelligence committees have been more inclined to engage in hardball questioning than Republicans. Party has been a more powerful predictor of hardball questioning in the House than in the Senate, though party in the Senate, unlike the House, demonstrates somewhat greater predictive strength than ideology.

Seniority

Time in service proves a weak indicators of hardball questioning. "Youngsters" and "oldsters" are nearly alike in their willingness to ask searching questions, with a slight tendency toward hardball among younger members. In one category, however, the relationship reveals strength: in both the House and the Senate, members with low seniority—newcomers—are inclined toward hardball on a by-year basis, though the relationship diminishes as they accrue longevity. Whether the questioning of inexperienced hardballers mellows with the added insight and appreciation for the CIA's programs they may gain over the years, or whether the overseers are won over (co-opted) through skillful Agency lobbying, cannot be answered with these data. My observations of the committees since 1975 indicate the presence of both phenomena.

Divided Government

Throughout the era of the New Oversight for strategic intelligence, America's government has almost always been divided. The exceptions were when a Democratic president (Jimmy Carter) served with a Democratic Congress from 1977 to 1980, and when a Republican president (Ronald Reagan) enjoyed a partial respite with a GOP majority in the Senate from 1981 to 1986.

The relationship between divided government and hardball, summarized in table 2, is explored in finer detail in table 3. The proposition that Congresses controlled by Democratic legislators are consistently tougher on GOP presidents than they are on Democratic presidents fails to hold up with respect to intelligence policy. It is true that the most rigorous series of questions were directed toward the CIA during the Reagan administration from 1981 to 1986 by Democratic overseers on the House committee, when they posed 94.9% of the total number of hardball Q & Rs (table 3). Nevertheless, congressional Democrats as a whole were much harder on the CIA during the Carter presidency (84.9% hardball, averaging both chambers) than they were during the combined Reagan-Bush presidencies (70.0%).

Table 3
Hardball on House and Senate Intelligence Committees, by Party and
Administration, 1975–1990

	% of Hardball Questioning					
Party	Ford (1975–76) WH = R H = D S = D	Carter (1977–80) WH = D H = D S = D	Reagan I (1981–86) WH = R H = D S = R	Reagan II (1987–88) WH = R H = D S = D	Bush (1989–90) WH = R H = D S = D	Average
House						
Dem.	83.8 (640)	83.5 (740)	94.9 (168)	80.6 (154)	–	85.7 (426)
GOP	16.2 (124)	16.5 (146)	5.1 (9)	19.4 (37)	–	14.3 (79)
Senate						
Dem.	66.9 (462)	86.3 (493)	75.6 (118)	49.1 (472)	50.0 (34)	65.6 (316)
GOP	33.1 (229)	13.7 (78)	24.4 (38)	50.9 (489)	50.0 (34)	34.4 (174)

Notes: WH = White House, H = House, S = Senate, D = Democrat, and R = Republican. So, in 1975–76, e.g., the Republican party controlled the White House, and the Democratic party controlled the House and the Senate.

The percentages in the table represent the portion of hardball questions and remarks posed by each party as a fraction of the total number of hardball Q & Rs for the period. (The House held no public hearings with CIA witnesses in 1989–90).

Figures in parentheses are *N*s.

Democratic overseers were also tougher on the Carter CIA than were GOP overseers, by a wide margin; and the mildest Democratic questioning on both intelligence committees occurred during the latter years of the Reagan administration (1987–88). The Democrats on the Senate intelligence committee, for example, proved to be far more lenient in their questioning of the CIA during the Iran-contra travails than were selected Republican overseers.[9]

While it is true that the Senate committee, when controlled by the GOP (1981–86), asked only a low percentage of the total number of hardball questions directed toward the Reagan CIA (24.4%), Republican overseers advanced an even lower percentage of hardball Q & Rs against the Carter CIA (11.6%). In every instance but one (the Senate in 1987–88), the Democrats on the intelligence committees were far more rigorous in their questioning of *each* administration than were GOP legislators.

Lights, Camera, Questions

During the years examined here, the years 1975 and 1987 were among the most intense times of hardball questioning on Capitol Hill—and the bleakest moments in the CIA's history since the Bay of Pigs fiasco, brought on by Operation CHAOS (domestic spying) and the Iran-contra affair, respectively. During these two years, the CIA also endured its most widespread periodical coverage (as reflected in *Reader's Guide* index entries).

Whether the hearings spurred the coverage or vice versa is a complicated matter that cannot be resolved here. Most likely, the media allegations of CIA abuse (reported in the *New York Times* in 1974 and a Middle East magazine in 1986) stirred Congress into investigative hearings, which in turn brought media reporting on the hearings and further encouraged legislators to participate in questioning—at least until the media executives calculated a declining public interest and pulled the plug on the television lights.[10] This much is speculation, though grounded in observation and interviews with legislators, staff, and CIA officers. What the coefficients in table 2 do indicate is a reasonably close correspondence between broad periodical coverage of the CIA and legislative hardball. Presumably both are driven— in a complex, interactive manner—by allegations of wrongdoing in this subterranean tier of government.

Détente

Ransom (1987) has argued that legislators are more likely to engage in serious oversight when superpower tensions are relaxed, for when these relations are taut, overseers may be reluctant to criticize the CIA as it faces a sharply hostile adversary. The results of table 2 indicate some support for this hypothesis during the House committee's public hearings; but on the Senate side, by-year hardball questioning actually showed some increase (though weak) during periods of détente. The measurements of U.S.-Soviet cooperation used here are crude, however, and these findings must be viewed as quite tentative.[11]

DISCUSSION

The supervision of strategic intelligence by Congress since 1975 has undergone a dramatic increase over earlier years, when legislators were by and large content to rely on the president to guide America's secret power. From among the wide range of new oversight activities, hearings—public and in executive session—have been the most important. When asked which forms of supervision he considered the most valuable, the staff director of the Senate intelligence committee motioned toward the committee's hearing room and replied emphatically: "Down there, with the members."[12]

The Importance of Public Hearings

Between the two types of hearings, public and private, clearly most often the intelligence committees have chosen to meet behind closed doors. This allows members the freedom to explore any aspect of intelligence without fear of inadvertently revealing classified information. Nevertheless, public hearings provide a significant window into the content and quality of oversight by the committees. Those legislators who participate effectively in public tend to repeat this behavior in private; members do not suddenly change their personalities, styles, and interests depending upon the openness of the forum wherein they find themselves. Indeed, in some respects, open hearings provide a better measure of oversight at its high-water mark: the attendance of members at public hearings tends to be much higher (especially when the media is present), and legislators are likely to prepare themselves more thoroughly when on public view.

The hardball questioning by intelligence committee members in open hearings corresponds well with the most significant instances of CIA transgressions and subsequent major efforts by Congress at intelligence reform. Among the most conspicuous periods of hardball questioning in this study are 1975, 1977–78, 1980, and 1987—the years when the following important oversight efforts took place: investigations into Operation CHAOS and controversial covert actions (1975); the years of successful wiretap legislation (the Foreign Intelligence Surveillance Act of 1978) and an attempt, which failed, to enact sweeping "grand charter" legislation for the intelligence community (1977–78); another, far more modest, and this time successful try at passing "mini-charter" legislation (the Intelligence Oversight Act of 1980); and the investigation into the Iran-contra scandal (1987).

Oversight and the Eye of the Beholder

Accepting that public hearings do offer useful insights into the monitoring of the CIA, what does the evidence in this analysis suggest about the quality of the New Oversight? How has the congressional role been changing? Are legislators now playing a major role in the formation of foreign policy? Is this leading to greater conflict with the executive? What are the policy consequences?

Judgments made on these vital questions depend to some extent on one's point of view. If the historical benchmark is the state of oversight before 1975, it can be concluded with confidence that the present level of congressional participation in this aspect of foreign policy is remarkably more robust and effective—if, that is, one believes that the activities of the CIA ought to be subjected to legislative guidance in the first place. A prominent school of thought, which includes some members of the intelligence committees, maintains that, on the contrary, the best oversight is to strengthen the CIA as much as possible and let it proceed in its struggle against America's enemies in the back alleys of the world. For this school, congressional involvement merely impedes America's self-defense and its pursuit of global objectives.

The Iran-contra Affair

Even for those who believe in close congressional supervision and guidance for the CIA and find the comparison with the pre-1975 era heartening, the Iran-contra affair might well lead one to conclude that the New Oversight has failed. In rebuttal, many observers argue that Iran-contra is more accurately viewed as an aberration—a distressing glitch in the intelligence partnership between Congress and the executive branch that, since 1975, officials have been hammering out on the anvil of experience. The failure of oversight during the Iran-contra affair is blamed on officials in the executive branch who lied to Congress and evaded the law in order to achieve their policy objectives in the Middle East and Central America. Under such circumstances, maintain defenders of the New Oversight, no system of accountability would have worked this side of heaven.

"Were it not for a fortuitous leak of the secret Iran arms-sale operation in a Middle East magazine," concedes a senior staffer on the Senate intelligence committee, "the Iran-contra affair would probably not have been discovered through normal oversight activities."[13] Adds a senior staffer on the House Intelligence Committee: "When the nation's national security adviser and other top officials look you in the eye and tell you that the [Iran-contra] rumors are false, the inclination is to believe them."[14] According to interviews with senior staffers on the intelligence committees, the chairman of the House panel, Lee Hamilton, relied on the word of these officials and, like his Senate counterpart, David Boren (D-Okla.), failed to pursue the Iran-contra rumors. Presumably, in the wake of the Iran-contra experience, congressional overseers have learned again (the lesson is ancient) to be more doubting of those in power. Still, the government could scarcely work without some sense of comity and trust between the branches. Therein lies the rub.

Feckless Accountability

Yet the argument that Iran-contra was merely an aberration is too glib for critics of the New Oversight; they see more-fundamental flaws (e.g., Parry and Kornbluh 1988). Certainly, the findings of this study indicate that most members of the intelligence committees have fallen far short of robust attendance at public hearings—and even if present, have failed to ask weighty questions about CIA activities. The conclusion of some researchers (Johnson 1980; Ogul 1976; Ransom 1975, 36) that congressional oversight has generally been uneven and episodic, relying on the dedication of a few legislators, is reinforced by this analysis of how CIA witnesses are questioned.

The testimony of some former DCIs indicates that even the CIA's leadership has found legislative guidance weak and ineffectual. Noting that "Congress is informed to the degree that Congress wants to be informed," William E. Colby, DCI from 1973 to 1976, places many of the inadequacies of congressional supervision squarely on the shoulders of legislators, some of whom have not tried very hard to become informed (U.S. House 1983, 29).

More direct, and more damning, is the testimony of Admiral Stansfield Turner. The DCI during the Carter administration, Turner—who came to the job from outside the ranks of intelligence professionals—can speak to the question of oversight with a certain detachment lacking to those former directors with career-long ties to the CIA. Appalled by the failure of legislative overseers to pursue Iran-contra leads more aggressively, Turner recalled in testimony before the House intelligence committee "being incensed at the time [in 1986, when rumors of scandal flitted around Washington] that nothing was being done in the media or in the Congress to stop this," adding: "I would say with all candor that in my four years when I think we had a very cooperative relationship, I believe the committees of Congress could have been more rigorous with me . . . it would be more helpful if you are probing and rigorous" (U.S. House, 1987, 66).

This view animates the activists among the current crop of CIA overseers on Capitol Hill. Yet a number of legislators still prefer to march under the banner of Justice Sutherland's dicta in *United States v. Curtiss-Wright* (1936), with an added twist: the president should be the sole organ of strategic intelligence.[15]

Bones of Contention

The debate over the proper role of Congress in supervising and providing direction for strategic intelligence will continue, of course; the nation's founders were of many minds themselves on the proper interbranch responsibilities for foreign policy. With respect to the CIA, disagreements have been—and will continue to be—most heated on five main issues:

when the Agency should report on its activities to the intelligence committees: before or after their implementation; and if after, how long after? (the present expectation on Capitol Hill is *before* in most cases, but in extraordinary circumstances, "within a few days");[16]

how covert action differs from secret diplomacy or traditional secret military operations (i.e., definitional disputes);

whether, in their handling of secret intelligence, legislators can be trusted to molt no feather;[17]

whether Congress has created too many stifling regulations that only inhibit the CIA (yes, say the *Curtiss-Wright*ers; no, say the civil libertarians and those wary of unsavory covert actions); and,

whether CIA officials will be sufficiently forthcoming with legislators to allow them a meaningful role as intelligence overseers—the lingering odor of Iran-contra mendacity.

Suppressio veri, suggestio falsi

This issue of misleading Congress gnaws at the minds of foreign policy activists on Capitol Hill. In his subsequent attempt to explain why he deceived legislators during the Iran-contra affair, the CIA's chief of the Central American Task Force (C/CATF) argued that in his sworn testimony he had been "technically correct, [if] specifically evasive." As so often in the past, legislative overseers had been placed in the position of having to ask precisely the right question, narrowly tailored, to have any chance of ascertaining the truth. In response to this limp defense, Senator William Cohen told the C/CATF that "if Congress is satisfied that it is being told the truth and the whole truth, then the distrust of the Agency will evaporate and that is what has to happen" (U.S. Congress 1987, 142, 153).

In the absence of forthright reporting by executive agencies, the opportunities for meaningful congressional involvement in intelligence policy will never be much more than a sandcastle, washed away in the next tide of deceit. Here again is the C/CATF in post-Iran-contra testimony:

C/CATF: . . . I think that the final prerogative to make a decision and the man with his hand on the helm is the President and he [Ronald Reagan] wanted to do it. . . . Congress passed a very awkward law [the Boland amendment], put us in a terrible position. . . . I just couldn't understand it. There was a law. Why give us half a loaf, why give us something that we couldn't implement right? It was just ludicrous and it was partisan politics because the Congress didn't like [DCI William J.] Bill Casey and the Congress didn't want CIA in because of the mining of the [Nicaraguan] harbor[s] and we couldn't get over our internecine warfare and it shouldn't have been that way (158).

In response, Senator George Mitchell (D-Maine, later named majority leader) offered the pertinent lesson in Civics 101:

I think it is simply preposterous to suggest that those who opposed contra aid did so because they didn't like Bill Casey. I would hope you would have a somewhat higher opinion of the motives of those who happen to disagree with you on an issue . . . every executive branch official has an obligation to obey and uphold the law, and not to select which laws will be obeyed or not (158).

CONCLUSION

In response to the central research question in this volume about change in the making of foreign policy, several conclusions may be drawn about the new era of congressional involvement in strategic intelligence. First, the degree of participation by Congress in this policy domain has risen markedly since 1975, although it continues to remain relatively limited compared to the potential, just as the central hypothesis would anticipate. The few public oversight hearings, the limited attendance of members at these sessions, and the often anemic quality of the questioning, all point to a lower level of legislative supervision than the record of errant CIA operations in the past (Bay of Pigs, CHAOS, Iran-contra, et al.) would seem to warrant.

Second, despite its uneven attention to public hearings on the CIA, other evidence indicates that Congress is nevertheless now a actor in the conduct of strategic intelligence policy. Between 1986 and 1990, for example, the oversight committees received a vast amount of information from the CIA through closed hearings and briefings. In 1986 Agency officers briefed the committees on 1,040 different occasions; in 1987, 1,064; in 1988, 1,044; in 1989, 947; and in 1990, 1,012.[18] These sessions have served as occasions for members and staff to explore CIA programs. Moreover, the briefings have armed Congress with considerable ammunition in its struggles with the executive branch over the interpretation of world events and how best to react as a nation.

With its greater responsiveness to congressional requests for information, the CIA has helped to level the playing field between the branches. The intelligence committees now have a definite role in shaping strategic intelligence policy (by demanding greater attention to human intelligence, or HUMINT, among other examples), and, now and then, they have forced the president to abandon some misguided secret operations. The Boland amendments are the most well-known recent examples of congressional involvement in intelligence decisions, but there have been other significant instances.[19]

Third, the rise of Congress as a player in the field of strategic intelligence has sharpened conflict between the branches. This is not saying much, however, since before 1975 the executive branch had its own way altogether. The extent of the new institutional conflict should not be exaggerated. The intelligence committees, the White House, and the CIA have agreed on well over 90 percent of all U.S. intelligence operations. Most of these activities have been sensible efforts to collect information about potential dangers to the United States, and even most of the more aggressive covert actions have been widely accepted in Congress as modest but useful attempts to shape international events in favor of America's best interests. Only occasionally, as with the covert actions in Nicaragua during the 1980s, have strong disagreements erupted; on these occasions, the American public itself has been of two minds on appropriate policy, and this division—not surprisingly—has been reflected in congressional debates and votes.

Further, the vast majority of intelligence professionals are law-abiding citizens sensitive to restrictions placed upon them by Congress and the nation's traditions. The CIA is probably no more a "rogue elephant" than other agencies, and this helps to keep interbranch conflict in check—though, to be sure, the CIA has "gone off the reservation" at times, and when it does, its secretiveness and expertise at manipulation give it a particularly threatening quality, emphasizing the need for close supervision in this dark realm of government.

Fourth, judging the overall policy consequences of the New Oversight is, to some extent, a subjective matter. Those with a *Curtiss-Wright* perspective will long for the abolition of the intelligence committees and a return to the happier days of full executive control over intelligence. No more "micromanagement." Those more sanguine about congressional activism point to the solid contribution legislators have made to strategic intelligence: keeping the CIA on its toes, urging improved analysis, encouraging more-organized counterintelligence, advocating wider HUMINT, and minding the budget. Their bottom line: secret operations benefit from a more collegial policy review, involving the executive branch *and* the Congress—not unilateral decisions made by the White House or the DCI alone, with all the risks that attend concentrated power. (This school also appreciates, though, the need for some degree of secrecy, which must at times confine oversight to the well-guarded inner sanctums of the intelligence committees.) The idea is to make intelligence policy more representative of the goals and ideals of the American people, as reflected in the judgments made by their elected surrogates in the White House and on Capitol Hill.

Bringing Intelligence under the Constitution

The most remarkable aspect of the experiment in stronger congressional involvement in strategic intelligence is simply this: most participants in both branches now acknowledge the value of participation by legislators. In the view of one recent DCI, William H. Webster, "On balance, the oversight process has clearly been useful and helpful"[20] Similarly, William Colby concludes, "I think that supervision is absolutely essential," adding: "We have to run American intelligence under our Constitution and under the law. I think it is the Congress's job to make sure that happens" (U.S. House 1978, 106).

Admiral Turner concurs:

> I am a strong supporter of congressional oversight of intelligence, because unaccountable power is power that can be misused. That is not because the people using it are necessarily malicious, but because any of us, when faced with not being accountable, can be less judicious, less careful in making decisions. Therefore, the role of this [House Intelligence] Committee, and its counterpart in the Senate, is very important in terms of making the intelligence community recognize they will be held accountable for the decisions they make. (U.S. House 1983, 74)

These "modern" views stand out in bold relief from the philosophy and practice of the pre-1975 era. They are by no means uniformly shared. The controversial DCI William J. Casey expressed the view in 1984 that "the business of Congress is to stay out of my business."[21] Through evasiveness, Casey did his best to help Congress adopt his standard. Surely one objective for those who wish to see rigorous oversight succeed ought to be to ensure, during confirmation hearings, that would-be DCIs with Casey's outlook on the role of Congress are barred from this sensitive office.

Many of the most useful means for providing a check on the CIA's potential abuse of power lie beyond the focus of this study. "The most important form of oversight goes unseen," comments a senior staffer on the Senate intelligence committee. "The CIA worries that Congress is looking over its shoulder; therefore, it is less reckless. It makes them [intelligence officers] think twice before they act" — the well-known law of anticipated reactions.[22] The media will also continue to provide an important check, as illustrated by the *New York Times*'s reporting on Operation CHAOS in 1974. "Don't forget the Freedom of Information Act," adds an intelligence committee staffer, pointing to the use of this law by private citizens to unearth the most recent case of improper FBI domestic surveillance (Operation CISPES). "It has been the best of all external overseers."[23]

These and other checks have been important (Johnson 1989b; Johnson 1992–93, 67–69). And, based on this analysis, one can add another: more-frequent public hearings. As DCI Turner stressed in his call for a more open discussion of intelligence policy, "A well-informed public is the greatest strength of our nation"[24]

From 1975 to 1990, the intelligence committees averaged less than two public hearings a year with CIA witnesses. Yet in the House, subcommittee

chairmen Aspin and Murphy (among others), and in the Senate, full committee chairmen Bayh, Boren, and Inouye (among others), have demonstrated
that routine open sessions can be held on intelligence without jeopardizing
security interests—all the better to inform the public and the overseers
themselves about CIA policy; all the better to keep Agency officials steadily
aware of the congressional presence; all the better to deter, or at least
discover, the next Iran-contra transgression before it gathers steam. This,
coupled with increased member attendance and more hardball pitches, is
likely to improve the quality of intelligence supervision on Capitol Hill—and
have James Madison cheering from the high bleachers.

METHODOLOGICAL APPENDIX

The Committees

The official names of the permanent intelligence oversight panels in Congress are the Senate Select Committee on Intelligence and the House
Permanent Select Committee on Intelligence. Established in 1976 and 1977,
respectively, these committees are referred to more simply in this study as
the Senate and House intelligence committees. The ad hoc investigative
panels include the Pike committee (officially, the Select Committee on
Intelligence, serving in 1975–76 and led by Otis Pike, D-N.Y.); the Church
committee (officially, the Senate Select Committee to Study Government
Operations with Respect to Intelligence Activities, serving in 1975–76 and
led by Frank Church, D-Idaho); and the joint Inouye-Hamilton committees
(officially, the Senate Select Committee on Secret Military Assistance to Iran
and the Nicaraguan Opposition and House Select Committee to Investigate
Covert Arms Transactions with Iran, serving in 1987 and led, respectively,
by Senator Daniel K. Inouye, D-Hawaii, and Representative Lee H. Hamilton, D-Ind.).

Senator Inouye chaired two committees involved in intelligence oversight:
the first, designated here as Inouye committee I, was the permanent select
committee on intelligence (1976–77); and the second, designated Inouye
committee II, was the Senate Iran-contra investigative committee (1987).
Representative Hamilton fulfilled a similar dual role, chairing the House
intelligence committee from 1985 to 1987 (Hamilton committee I) and,
jointly with Senator Inouye, the House Iran-contra investigative committee
in 1987 (Hamilton committee II).

In this study, these permanent and investigative committees are treated
together as part of a continuum of intelligence oversight stretching from 1975
to 1990—the era of New Oversight for intelligence policy. (A listing of these
various intelligence oversight committees can be found in figure 1, along
with their dates of service.) The House intelligence committee (including the
Pike and the Hamilton II incarnations) held twenty-seven public hearings

from 1975 to 1990, twenty-four of which included incumbent or former CIA officials as witnesses. The Senate intelligence committee (including the Church and Inouye II incarnations) also, coincidentally, held twenty-seven public hearings from 1975 to 1990, again twenty-four of which included incumbent or former CIA officials as witnesses.

Executive Sessions

For the CIA, the differences between its closed and open supervision by Congress cannot be tested in any satisfying manner at the present time, since the overwhelming majority of executive-session hearings conducted by the intelligence committees remain classified. Despite the obvious importance of executive-session oversight, however, some observations can be made that support the relevance of public hearings as a research focus even for the CIA. As a participant-observer (a senior staff member on the Senate and the House intelligence committees sequentially from 1975 to 1979), I have listened to hundreds of hours of closed-door testimony by CIA officials and questioning by legislators. The behavior of committee members showed little variation from the private to the public forum. Those who attended the public hearings were likely to attend the closed hearings; those who were energetic in public hearings were energetic in closed hearings; those who were deferential in public were deferential in private. Moreover, a close examination of the four closed hearings of the Senate intelligence committee that have subsequently been declassified (not a part of this study) reveals questioning patterns closely similar to those disclosed in this analysis of open hearings.

Some observers have been highly critical of the executive session as a meaningful forum for legislative supervision of the CIA. Representative Pike, chairman of the House intelligence committee in 1975, put it this way — in frustration — after consenting to shut the door to the public during hearings with the CIA: "We went into executive session and the result could only be described as acutely disappointing. . . . we went round and round for a while; and the fact of the matter is that we got absolutely nothing out of our executive session. . . . the public thinks that [the CIA] has indeed been forthcoming in executive session. . . . But the fact of the matter is that we learn more in open session than we do in executive session." In Pike's view, "we gain absolutely nothing by going into executive session, except the newspapers somehow get the appearance that we are learning things which in fact we are not learning" (U.S. House 1975, part 1, 168).

Chapter 4

★ ★ ★

QUESTIONING BY THE FOREIGN POLICY COMMITTEES

★ ★ ★

Paul E. Peterson and Jay P. Greene

Conflict between the executive and legislative branches over foreign policy is generally thought to have dramatically increased in the last two decades. In the words of one analyst, "Because Congress was so willingly deferential for most of the cold war, the actual problem of institutional power sharing was minimized. The 1970s, however, changed all that. . . . Like other areas of policy, foreign policy is no longer held above politics, no longer considered immune to political conflict and contention, no longer kept at the water's edge" (Jentleson 1990, 148–49; see also Blechman 1990; Sundquist 1981; Haass 1979). This view is usually supported by anecdotal evidence that suffers from selective recall. Recollections of the early postwar period typically overlook the debate over who lost China, the aftershock of Sputnik, the inquiry into the bomber and missile gaps, and the accusatory language that followed the failure at the Bay of Pigs. Once these events are remembered, it is more difficult to conclude that interbranch relations were perfectly harmonious before Vietnam.

Some analysts cite measures of increased congressional activity as evidence of growing conflict between the executive and legislature (e.g., Blechman 1990, 12). They note the proliferation of subcommittees monitoring foreign policy, the increase in the size of congressional staffs, the length and detail of budgets, and the growth in congressional requests for reports and testimony. To cite just one frequently mentioned statistic, the size of congressional staffs between 1947 and 1975 more than quadrupled. But while there is certainly more congressional activity on foreign affairs, there is more of virtually everything in Washington. Just as the number of congressional staff has increased, so the number of executive branch personnel whose job it is to respond to congressional requests for information and testimony has also risen. Top-level executive positions increased by more than sevenfold in the first thirty years after the end of World War II (Heclo 1977, 57–59). Although executive officials may complain about the nuisance of congressional oversight, executive resources may well have kept pace with the increase in congressional demands.

The mere fact that Congress is more actively involved in foreign policy making does not necessarily imply that interbranch relations have grown more acrimonious. One might better describe heightened activity as signifying enhanced interbranch collaboration. Many studies of political participation report that participation enhances mutual cooperation and understanding rather than alienation and resistance (Kornhauser 1959; Coleman 1957; Berry, Portney, and Thomson 1992). If these findings can be generalized to the policy-making community in Washington, one would expect increased congressional involvement to reduce rather than increase conflict.

In this study we offer more-systematic evidence about the level and causes of interbranch conflict in foreign affairs throughout the postwar era. Our data suggest that, contrary to the prevailing belief, the degree of conflict between the executive and Congress over foreign affairs has not risen over the four decades since World War II. We do not find any dramatic shift following the war in Vietnam, as might have been expected. Our findings do show, however, that while the level of conflict between the branches has not increased, the direction of congressional criticism has changed. Members of Congress in recent years tend to chastise the executive for excessive diligence in protecting national security, when they previously criticized the administration for not being diligent enough. We have also found that interbranch conflict, even though it is no more severe, has become more partisan in nature. Our study also reveals that conflictual behavior in committee has important electoral consequences. Perhaps our most surprising result is that threats emanating from the international system, and the differential institutional perceptions of their magnitude, are important determinants of conflict between the executive and Congress.

THE AUTHORIZATIONS OF THE USE OF FORCE

Perhaps the best way of illustrating our findings is to remind the reader of the extraordinary differences in the way in which Congress reacted to two of the best known instances of presidential requests for congressional support for a major foreign policy–making initiative—the Gulf of Tonkin Resolution of 1964 and the Persian Gulf Resolution of 1991. While most commentators see in these two cases evidence of the deterioration of executive-legislative relations, we see examples of a number of other changes. If we looked only at these two incidents we might think that interbranch relations on foreign matters have become more conflictual, but our systematic evidence shows that the changes in the nature and direction of conflict illustrated by the Gulf of Tonkin and Persian Gulf resolutions are the more significant developments.

The Tonkin Gulf Resolution authorizing the president to use all necessary force to respond to a presumed attack on U.S. naval ships was approved by the Senate with only two dissenting votes. The president won overwhelming congressional support despite a number of military and international considerations that made the undertaking a dubious one: The United States was violating the military's pledge after Korea "never again" to become involved in a land war in Asia. It was also reversing the Eisenhower decision to avoid entanglement in the French struggle in Vietnam, attempting to suppress a nationalistic uprising against a corrupt regime, acting without U.N. authorization, and engaging in a war with little support from its European allies. The United States was already committing a high percentage of its national resources to defense purposes; any increase in this commitment would bear heavily on the U.S. taxpayer. In short, the United States was hardly assured of winning an easy military victory. Even though the political dangers of becoming embroiled in a conflict were not unlike those that had doomed the Truman presidency, Congress lent its support to this presidential initiative with hardly a dissent.

Twenty-three years later Congress once again resolved to support a presidential request for the use of all necessary force to turn back aggression, this time in the Persian Gulf. But in contrast to the Tonkin Gulf Resolution, the margin of victory was very narrow. In both Senate and House the president's request was opposed by the congressional majority leadership and some of the most influential foreign policy spokesmen on Capitol Hill. The resolution received less than 60 percent of the votes cast, and the vote, though widely said to be a matter of conscience, divided Congress along party lines. Nearly every Republican voted in favor of the resolution, and 85 percent of the Democrats voted against it.

Congressional reluctance to support the president persisted even though the use of force was not to suppress a nationalistic uprising but to prevent aggression by a regional power against its weaker neighbor; the terrain was a desert instead of a jungle, and few strategists doubted the likelihood of a military victory, should war prove necessary; the United States was acting within the framework of a Security Council resolution; and European and regional allies were fully supportive of U.S. policy. Inasmuch as a good deal of the armament was to be taken from supplies already destined for the garbage dump, the war could be undertaken at little additional cost to the national economy. Most analysts expected the president to achieve a great political as well as military victory.

Six factors seem to account for the different congressional response to these presidential requests. First, time had marched on. When the Tonkin

Gulf Resolution was proposed, the seemingly relevant historical analogue was Munich. When the Persian Gulf Resolution was proposed, the apparent historical analogue was Munich for some, the Tonkin Gulf for others. Second, the apparent international threat differed significantly. Support for the Tonkin Gulf Resolution was requested at a time when an aggressive North Vietnam was openly backed by a seemingly powerful Soviet military force and the Vietnam leadership was spouting an anti-imperialist, anticapitalist ideology that threatened Western-oriented regimes throughout the sub-Asian continent. Although Iraq's aggression threatened Saudi Arabian as well as Kuwaiti oil wells, Saddam Hussein acted without the backing of any of the Great Powers.

Third, President Johnson's most active political opposition came from hawks on the right wing of the Republican party, who felt that he had been doing too little to counter Communist influence. They could hardly oppose the president when he was asking for "all necessary means" to retaliate against the aggressor. President Bush's problems were very different; his most active political opposition came from Democratic doves, who felt that neither Reagan nor Bush had been sufficiently responsive to Soviet disarmament proposals. Fourth, the opposition that Bush faced was much more favorably situated than was Johnson's opposition. At the time of Tonkin Gulf the same party controlled both Congress and the White House, while the Persian Gulf Congress was firmly under the control of the partisan opposition. Fifth, this division of governmental power was reinforced by a partisanship on foreign policy questions that had been less evident in the early postwar era.

Finally, electoral circumstances were different in the two cases. Johnson asked for support immediately before the presidential election of 1964, which he was expected to win by an overwhelming margin. Standing up to the president on the eve of a presidential reelection campaign would have been politically risky. The electoral situation was less menacing for the Democrats in the winter of 1991. While Bush was still an unusually popular president, the midterm elections were safely behind the legislators, and the 1992 presidential race was still two years away—long enough, perhaps, for the public to forgive and forget any decisions made with regard to the Persian Gulf.

SOURCES OF INTERBRANCH CONFLICT

It may be possible to generalize from these cases to the overall pattern of interbranch conflict during the postwar era. Admittedly, no two issues are identical, and any specific conflict may simply be a function of the particular personalities involved. Yet it is reasonable to hypothesize that the following historical, international, institutional, political, and electoral factors influence the patterns of conflict and cooperation between the president and Congress.

Historical Trend

Many observers have suggested that trends over time have significantly affected interbranch conflict on foreign policy issues. In the immediate postwar period Congress was in disarray, while the executive branch benefited from the great prestige it enjoyed at the close of World War II. Congress was receiving the blame for the isolationism that gave rise to the Smoot-Hawley protectionist legislation, said to have caused the recession and aided the rise of Hitler. Congress had also been reluctant to appropriate money for defense, even in the face of increasingly aggressive behavior by Germany in Europe and Japan in Asia. By contrast, the executive could point to its triumphant execution of the war, and the sophistication with which it constructed an interdependent, democratic postwar international community in both Europe and parts of Asia.

Over time, the memory of prewar congressional failures and wartime executive successes waned, and eventually they were replaced by new memories associated with the Vietnam War, blamed largely on Lyndon Johnson and Richard Nixon. Congress blamed itself only for not examining executive policies more closely.

International Context

Apart from the changes that time alone renders, the international context seems to influence domestic conflicts. Its effect is unlikely to be simple and uniform. In crisis situations, the more serious the threat, the more likely the president is to get strong congressional backing. In more protracted situations, a severe threat may provoke interbranch conflict, as political elites blame one another for failing to eliminate or otherwise respond to the threat. Once the threat lessens, domestic tranquillity may increase; however, it may be that political elites will disagree over the speed with which swords can be turned into plowshares.

In other words, while the international threat creates the context for decision making, interbranch conflict may depend not only on the magnitude of the external threat but also on the interaction between that threat and the most likely source of active opposition to the president. The source of congressional opposition is likely to be from hawks when the international threat is great, from doves when the international threat is of lesser magnitude. Stated more generally, it may be hypothesized that congressional opinion responds with greater elasticity to changes in the international situation, perhaps because the executive has the main responsibility for responding to external threats and has the best sources of information on the nature and extent of that threat. But it may also be because its personnel changes slowly, its organizational structure changes hardly at all, and it inevitably responds sluggishly to changes in the external environment. By comparison, Congress may respond more quickly because it has less access to confidential information and is less able to process and interpret information that is available, making it more likely to overreact to international change. And Congress could well be more responsive because its staff is continuously changing and its members have incentives to promote new ideas and introduce novel solutions. For both good and bad reasons, then, Congress may be more likely than the executive to respond with greater elasticity to changes in the external environment. From the perspective of Capitol Hill, Johnson was not doing enough in response to the Gulf of Tonkin, while Bush was doing too much in the Persian Gulf. Differences in institutional perception such as these may generate conflict between the branches.

Partisanship

Quite apart from differential institutional perspectives, partisan factors may affect the degree of interbranch conflict. The comparison of the two cases suggests that when Congress is in the hands of the opposition party, it will control the machinery necessary to generate conflict over foreign policy questions. It is unclear whether this proposition can be generalized, however. Scholarly opinion has reached no consensus with respect to the proposition that divided partisan control affects the functioning of governmental institutions. On the one side, it is argued that only when both the legislative and executive branches are in the hands of the same party can the country move decisively to address major international and domestic problems (Sundquist 1987). Not so, responds a second group of scholars. It makes little difference whether the legislative and executive branch are in the same or different hands, because the need for extraordinarily large majorities to pass legislation dampens narrow partisan inclinations (Mayhew 1992).

Independent of the existence of divided government, one may expect to find greater partisanship by individual members of Congress in more recent years than in the immediate postwar era. The two parties have become increasingly internally homogeneous and distinct from one another on both domestic and foreign policy questions, voting behavior in Congress has increasingly been defined along partisan lines, and congressional procedures have been revised to give the majority party greater control (and bipartisan committee majorities less influence) over legislative outcomes.

Institutions

It may also be hypothesized that the degree of conflict will vary by the institutional setting in which foreign policy is discussed. Specifically, it can be expected that the Senate and the House of Representatives will approach foreign policy issues differently. The Senate has the constitutional responsibility for ratifying treaties and approving presidential nominations for the secretaries of state and defense and the director of the Central Intelligence Agency, as well as for lower level appointees. As a result, it has historically been more directly involved in the formation of policy. Presumably, it has developed a body of procedure, expertise, and information that allows it to work more closely with the executive.

The two chambers also differ in the rules by which they make decisions. The most important difference is the rule in the Senate that permits unlimited debate unless 60 percent of the senators vote for cloture, a requirement that makes it difficult for the majority party to govern without the cooperation of the minority. Bipartisan, coalitional politics have thus become the institutional norm in the Senate—in contrast to the House of Representatives, where majoritarian democracy is more evident. The large size of the House of Representatives, the ease with which its debate can be closed, the long-term dominance by the Democratic party, and the tight control over rules and procedures achieved by the Democratic majority has structured policy making in this chamber tightly along partisan lines (Bach and Smith 1989; Smith 1990; Reichley 1985; Shepsle 1989).

Elections

The effects of elections on interbranch conflict is somewhat uncertain. On the one hand, the case studies suggest that congressional criticism in times of crisis is an electorally risky strategy. Electoral considerations may have mitigated criticism of President Johnson when he asked for a resolution of support in the wake of the Tonkin Bay incident, and the Democratic reluctance to support President Bush on the eve of the Persian Gulf War may yet prove to have been an electorally counterproductive decision. On the other hand, the electoral consequences of legislative criticism in crisis situations may differ from criticism under more routine circumstances. The ordinarily cooperative member may win access to departments that can be turned into special favors and pork for his or her district or state. But the regularly critical member can capture public attention, demonstrate independence of mind, and avoid blame for presidential policies that go awry— characteristics that may be more electorally beneficial, at least in the short run. The importance of partisanship for interbranch conflict suggests that there are, indeed, electoral benefits that come from finding fault with executive branch officials of the opposite party. But these electoral benefits probably come at a cost to the member's reputation inside Washington. Going along is the best way of getting along inside the Beltway. For those who can safely ignore constituency pressures, it probably makes more sense to pull one's punches in one's relations with foreign policy officials within the executive branch.

STUDYING TESTIMONY BEFORE CONGRESS

To evaluate these hypotheses we gathered data on the degree of conflict that occurred when executive branch officials appeared before the hearings of the foreign policy committees of the House and Senate. Committee hearings are the one and only public setting where congressional-executive exchanges regularly take place. These hearings also provide a window into the activities of the committees and subcommittees, where most legislative work is thought to be done.[1] These hearings are available for public examination in libraries throughout the United States, yet apart from use as a source of anecdotes or case-study detail, they have seldom been subjected to systematic analysis.[2]

Using public hearings as a source of information about congressional behavior is not without its limitations.[3] Only publicly recorded exchanges can be studied. It is possible that these are contrived events that have no connection to the real world of interbranch communication. It may be that actual relationships can be ascertained only by either reading insider accounts or attending private meetings of congressional and administrative officials. But to dismiss committee hearings as unconnected to the real world of politics ignores the fact that what happens at committee hearings can itself be politically important. Members can ask politically embarrassing questions, executive branch officials are expected to respond truthfully to questions, the news media waits expectantly for controversy, and interested third parties watch the discussions closely. Executive branch officials avoid testifying only at considerable risk to their political credibility and budgetary authority.

The political significance of hearings is evident from the fact that the choice of topics and witnesses is carefully shaped by the committee chair and by other influential members of the committee (Cohen 1952; Keller 1981; Meier and Van Lohuizen 1978). Testifying at hearings is the tactic most frequently used by interest groups for exercising influence, and it is thought by group leaders to be second in importance only to personal contact with public officials (Schlozman and Tierney 1986). As a means of overseeing executive agencies, congressional staff also regard public hearings as second in importance only to direct personal communication with executive officials (Aberbach 1990, 135).

If committee hearings neither make up the entire executive-legislative battlefield nor provide direct information on the calculations taking place within the tents of the commanding generals, they can at least provide a sustained look at the struggle from a well-placed treetop overlooking the lines of conflict. If one observes the combat from the same viewpoint over a sustained period of time, there is good reason to believe that overall changes in the nature of the conflict will be as apparent from this site as from any other.

Some of the findings reported in table 1 give us confidence in relying on committee hearings as a source of valid information about congressional-executive relationships. Although these findings are not substantively significant, they help validate our methodology. First, the fact that our findings account only for the questioning of administration witnesses and do not similarly explain the interrogation of nonexecutive witnesses suggests that our results are not merely an artifact of some aspect of our methodology. Second, we found that Senator William Fulbright asked more conflictual questions than did other senators, a finding quite consistent with his reputation for being one of the Senate's foremost curmudgeons. Third, we found that when cabinet officials were being examined, the questioning by members was more critical. When high-ranking officials are testifying, the most controversial issues are very likely under discussion, producing greater conflict. And fourth (but not shown in table 1), we found that when public hearings were more lengthy, presumably a sign of their newsworthiness, questioning tended to be more aggressive. Apparently, the hotter the issue, the more conflictual the questioning process. We shall control for these variables as we examine the impact of the substantively more interesting variables to which we now turn.[4]

TESTING THE HYPOTHESES
Three main dependent variables were included in the analysis: (1) the degree to which disagreement emerged between questioner and witness, (2) the extent to which members of Congress explicitly raised domestic considerations in their questions, and (3) the change in the margin of victory experienced by a House member between the previous election and the one after the questioning (for a further explanation of variables, see the Methodological Appendix).

Apart from the personality and issue characteristics mentioned above, five categories of independent variables were included in the analyses: (1) trends over time, (2) perceptions of the international environment, (3) partisanship, (4) institutional arrangements, and (5) electoral considerations.

Historical Trend
Since there is reason to believe that time alone has affected the degree of interbranch conflict, we were interested in ascertaining whether or not there was any historical trend in the degree of disagreement in the questioning of administration witnesses in committee hearings. Also, it was felt that it was best to control for any annual trend when determining the importance of other factors affecting interbranch conflict. Many variables have drifted in a particular direction over the past forty years and one might easily attribute to any specific variable an influence that is more appropriately attributed to a more generalized set of changes occurring over time. If one takes into account any year-by-year trend, the specific contributions of other factors are more easily isolated.

International Context

The perceived threat to the nation's security was measured most directly by calculating the percentage of the annual gross national product expended for defense purposes.[5] Not all money spent in the name of defense is efficiently used to protect the nation from aggression. Nonetheless, this measure seems to be a better indicator of the genuine as distinct from rhetorical commitment of the political leadership to defending the country from well-identified international threats. For one thing, it indicates its willingness to tax the resources of the nation for defense purposes.

A second measure of the perceived international threat—the percentage of change Congress makes in the president's defense budget—captures the differences in the perceptions of those on Capitol Hill from those within the executive branch.[6] This measure of comparative congressional hawkishness takes a higher value if Congress increases the defense budget over and above what the president requests, and it takes its lowest values when Congress cuts the president's budget most severely. The president's request consists of his initial request to Congress for the following fiscal years plus all subsequent requests for supplemental funding. The congressional response is measured by the total congressional appropriations for the fiscal year in question.

Our third measure of the perception of the international situation is the interaction between the overall perceived threat and the differences between congressional and executive perceptions. It was hypothesized that Congress would be particularly critical of the president under two quite different but equally conflictual circumstances: (1) if the threat was high and Congress, in a hawkish mood, felt the executive was not taking adequate measures in response; and (2) if the threat was low and Congress, taking a dovish view of the situation, felt the executive was expending an excessive amount of the nation's limited resources for defense purposes. This varaible reaches its maximum under two quite contrasting circumstances: (1) when Congress increases the defense budget even when the percentage of GNP spent on defense is high, or (2) when Congress cuts a defense budget even at a time when the percentage of GNP spent on national defense is low. Its minimum value is reached when Congress cuts a defense budget when the percentage of GNP spent on national defense is high, or when Congress increases a defense budget when the percentage of GNP spent on national defense is low.

Partisanship

Many studies of interbranch conflict have emphasized both the importance of growing partisan differences over foreign policy questions and the frequency with which Congress and the presidency are controlled by opposite political parties, thereby dividing governmental power between them. To capture the separate effects of each, partisanship is measured in two ways: (1) the "divided government" variable distinguishes circumstances when the chamber holding the hearing is controlled by the party opposite that of the president from instances when the chamber is controlled by the same party, regardless of the individual asking the question of the witness. (2) "Opposition questioner" distinguishes questioning of administration witnesses by a member from the party opposite that of the administration from questioning by a member from the same party as that of the president, regardless of control of the chamber.

Since the case studies implied that partisanship was contributing to higher levels of conflict in the post-Tet era, an interaction term calculating the effects of party in the pre-Tet period was included in the analysis as well.

Institutions

Relationships between the president and Congress may vary by chamber. Not only may the conflict level be generally higher in the House of Representatives than in the Senate, but it may vary more along partisan lines and in response to the international situation. These chamber differences were taken into account by including an interaction term that multiplies divided government and opposite party questioning by the chamber in which the questioning is taking place. A separate measure of overall chamber differences in questioning styles was also included.

Elections

The impact of electoral considerations on interbranch conflict was measured most directly in a separate analysis of conflict between the executive and members of the foreign affairs committee of the House of Representatives (reported in table 2), for whom information on the margin of victory in both the election preceding and following the questioning could be ascertained. In the absence of direct information on the margin of victory of members of the Senate, a proxy variable—whether or not a member came from the South— was used to estimate the safety of the seat the member held. Many southerners run unopposed in elections, and many other southerners win by large margins in a region of the country that remains overwhelmingly Democratic in nonpresidential elections. Although this is an imperfect proxy, it does have a .22 simple correlation with margin of victory in the previous election of House members, and it became a statistically insignificant variable in the House analysis once the more direct measure of seat safety—margin of victory in previous election—was included.

RESEARCH FINDINGS

Table 1 reports the results of our analysis of the determinants of conflictual questioning within the foreign policy committees of the House and Senate between 1949 and 1989. It allows us to evaluate the evidence for each of the five sets of propositions elaborated above.

Table 1
Factors Affecting Degree to Which Foreign Policy Committee Members
Disagree with Witnesses, 1949–1989

Factors Affecting Conflict	Administration Witnesses Only		Nonadministration Witnesses Only	
	Coefficient	(t)	Coefficient	(t)
Historical Trends				
Time only	−0.00	−0.3	−0.01	−2.8***
Time, Controlled for:	−0.004	−0.9	−0.00	−0.0
International Context				
Threat	0.69	3.0***	0.12	0.4
Hawkish Congress	−0.10	−1.1	0.10	1.1
Threat by Hawkish	1.82	4.7***	−0.19	−0.4
Partisanship				
Divided government	0.15	1.5	−0.07	−0.8
Opposition questioner	0.39	3.4***	—	—
Opposition questioner by				
early period	−0.29	−2.6***	—	—
Institutions				
Senate	0.15	1.5	−0.03	−0.3
Threat by Senate	−0.71	−2.9***	0.02	0.1
Threat by Hawk by Senate	−1.56	−3.5***	−0.60	−1.1
Opposition questioner by				
Senate	−0.21	−1.6*	—	—
Divided government by				
Senate	−0.17	−1.4	0.14	1.1
Elections				
Southerner	−0.18	−2.2**	0.09	1.1
Issue and Personality				
Cabinet-level witness	0.21	2.7***	—	—
Fulbright	0.48	3.8***	−0.11	−0.7
Constant	2.75	22.4***	2.86	24.5***
Corrected R^2	0.08		0.07	
No. of observations	1,410		1,075	

*$p < .1$. **$p < .05$. ***$p < .01$.

Historical Trend

There is no evidence in our data that congressional-executive relationships became increasingly conflictual over time. There was no statistically significant relationship between the year in which the foreign policy committee hearing was held and the amount of disagreement between questioners and witnesses. Both in a simple analysis of the relationship between time and

Table 2
Factors Affecting Degree to Which House Foreign Affairs Committee Members
Disagree with Witnesses, 1949–1989

Factors Affecting Conflict	Administration Witnesses Only		Nonadministration Witnesses Only	
	Coefficient	(t)	Coefficient	(t)
Historical Trends				
Time only	−0.00	−0.6	−0.01	−2.5**
Time, controlled for:	0.00	0.0	0.00	0.4
International Context				
Threat	0.72	2.4**	0.28	0.8
Hawkish House	−0.03	−0.2	0.15	1.1
Threat by Hawkish	1.54	3.1***	−0.19	−0.3
Partisanship				
Opposition questioner	0.32	−2.2**	—	—
Opposition questioner by				
early period	−0.17	−0.9	—	—
Divided government	0.17	1.5	−0.04	−0.3
Elections				
Safety of seat	−0.08	−2.0**	−0.02	−0.6
Constant	2.71	14.9***	2.77	16.1***
Corrected R^2	0.11		0.06	
No. of Observations	587		505	

$**p < .05. ***p < .01.$

questioning style and in a multivariate analysis controlling for other factors, one finds no trend over time in the amount of disagreement. The extent to which committee members bring up domestic issues did change over time, however. As can be seen in table 3, both the simple and the multivariate analysis reveal a decline over time in the frequency with which domestic matters are explicitly raised. The trend is in a direction opposite of the one congressional critics might have anticipated. If some may feel that members too frequently let domestic considerations shape their view of foreign policy, such considerations are less apparent now than they once were.

International Context
Conflict between Congress and the executive increases as the threat from the international environment increases (table 1). This relationship between threat and congressional behavior is particularly evident in the House of Representatives (tables 1 and 2). Congress also pays less attention to domestic considerations when the international threat is greater (see table 3).

Table 3
Factors Affecting Likelihood Questions Contain Domestic Concerns, 1949–1989

Independent Variables	Coefficient	(t)
Time only	− 0.004	− 3.8***
Time, Controlled for	− 0.009	− 7.4***
Threat	− 0.47	− 7.6***
Senate	0.07	3.0***
Subcommittee	0.13	5.1***
Constant	− 2.57	− 76.6***
Corrected R^2	.03	
No. of observations	2,869	

***$p < .01$

Whether Congress is relatively hawkish or dovish seems to have little direct effect on the level of disagreement. Whether Congress is passing defense budgets that are larger than presidential requests or cutting presidential requests sharply is not related to the level of conflictual questioning within the foreign policy committees. However, the interaction between the international threat and the congressional mood does have an effect on interbranch disagreement. If the international threat is relatively high and Congress is more concerned about that threat than the executive is, then Congress is clearly more assertive in its questioning. Conversely, if the international threat is relatively low and Congress is less concerned than the executive branch with the threat that remains, then Congress once again becomes quite assertive in its questioning of the administration.

This point can be elaborated by considering the evidence in table 4, which identifies the factors that affect the relative hawkishness on Capitol Hill — that is, the factors that induce Congress to spend more, or at least not much less than, the president requests. Congress overspends when war fever sweeps the country in the early years of an international conflict, but it underspends as the war becomes protracted. Also, Congress spends more when the international threat is greater. Put more precisely, Congress is willing to increase the military budget when the military budget, as a percentage of the gross national product, is already very high; it wants to cut the budget more deeply when expenditures are relatively low.

Some may see this as greater facility on Capitol Hill to develop more rapidly an appropriate policy response to changes in the international environment. Others might see this as the overreaction of policy makers with less access to relevant information and less direct responsibility for the nation's welfare. In any case, the fact that congressional reactions seem to be

Table 4

Factors Influencing Relative Hawkishness of Congress (Willingness to Raise or
Not Significantly Cut President's Budget), 1949–1989

Independent Variables	Percentage Increase or Negative Decrease in President's Budget	
	Coefficient	(t)
Threat	0.45	1.6*
War	−0.38	−2.0**
Early war	0.60	2.4**
Constant	0.05	0.6
R^2	0.10	
No. of observations	41	

$*p < .1. **p < .05.$

more elastic than the reactions of the executive branch identifies an important and enduring source of interbranch conflict. Whatever the change in the international situation, Congress will want to be there "firstest with the mostest" but will be less likely to stay the course, and this is likely to cause institutional discomfort between the branches.

The nature of the international environment and differential congressional and executive reactions to that threat do not account for disagreement between committee questioners and nonadministration witnesses, however (tables 1 and 2). Whereas members of Congress hold the administration accountable for the nation's response to a changing international environment, any disagreements that may exist do not seem to spill over and affect relations with those outside the government. In other words, the changing international situation has a specific effect on the relationships between the legislative and executive branches—not a general effect on the way in which members relate to witnesses appearing before them.

These findings help explain the widespread perception of an increase in congressional-executive conflict in recent years—especially by those concerned about the adequacy of the country's national security arrangements. In the early postwar period, congressional assertiveness took place in an environment in which the threat from the Soviet Union was widely recognized, and Congress was at least as concerned about that threat as was the administraiton. In more recent decades congressional assertiveness has generally occurred in a context of lowered international tensions, and Congress has regarded executive commitment to defense expenditure to be excessive. Most commentators on the congressional role in foreign affairs tend to have hawkish preferences and may find Congress's recent assertiveness more bothersome and therefore more noticeable. Yet it is not the degree of assertiveness that has changed; it is the direction from which that assertiveness comes that is new.

Partisanship

Partisan differences shape interbranch conflict in the House of Representatives in a variety of overlapping and reinforcing ways. If the questioner in the House is from the party opposite that of the administration witness, the witness is subjected to more critical questioning. It also seems that the level of disagreement increases when the party in control of the House chamber differs from the party in control of the executive branch, as can be seen in tables 1 and 2.[7] Together they create a highly partisan context for foreign policy deliberations within the House of Representatives. Table 1 also reveals that the effect of an individual member's partisan affiliations on conflictual questioning in the House increased after the Tet Offensive. In the earlier period there was no significant relationship between party affiliation and questioning behavior. Nor was there any relationship between divided government and the questioning of nonadministration witnesses. (Nor any reason to expect any such relationship.)

Institutions

The partisanship evident in the House of Representatives is not apparent in the Senate. Senators are not significantly more likely to examine critically an opposition witness than a witness from their own party. Nor does it make much difference whether the party in control of the committee is the same as the party in control of the White House. (This can be ascertained in table 1 by adding together the "divided government" and the "divided government by Senate" variables: the sum is not significantly different from zero; a similar procedure is to be followed for the "opposition questioner" and "opposition questioner by Senate" variables). These differences between House and Senate may be due to the greater and increasing importance of partisan affiliations in the organization of the larger chamber.

The Senate also differs from the House in that changes in the international threat and the interaction between that threat and congressional hawkishness do not affect the level of disagreement between the Senate committee and administration witnesses. Apparently, the Senate's greater constitutional obligations—treaty making, confirmation of presidential appointments—help to stabilize its relationships with the executive branch. Acting with less information and less expertise, the behavior of House members seems to fluctuate more in response to changes in the international environment. This may also account for the greater partisanship in the House than the Senate. Lacking the same constitutional responsibility for treaty ratification and for confirming presidential nominations to key foreign policy positions, House members may act with less sense of responsibility, less information, and less-sophisticated advisers. Under these circumstances partisan cues may have a larger effect on committee behavior.

These results should not lead one to the conclusion that interbranch conflict is confined to the House of Representatives. After partisan and other factors are taken into account, the Senate committee may, if anything, be slightly more likely to engage in critical questioning of administration witnesses.[8] It is the sources, not the amount, of conflict that differ by chamber. House members seem to react with greater elasticity to changes in the international threat, and they respond more clearly along partisan lines. In general, they act as one would expect of less informed and more marginal members of the policy-making process.

Elections

Partisan controversy is generally good for a House member's reelection chances (table 5). Committee members who question administration witnesses of the opposite party more critically improve more on their margin of victory in the next election than do members who defer to such witnesses. While all members have been improving on their margin of victory over time, the gains have been larger for those committee members who ask tough questions of an administration of the opposite party. As might also be expected, critical questioning of administration witnesses from one's own party does not improve one's election chances.

Members of the House seem to recognize this electoral reality. If members enjoyed a larger margin of victory in the preceding election, they were less likely than their more endangered colleagues to question administration witnesses critically (table 2). This table also shows that electoral considerations did not affect the treatment of nonadministration witnesses.

Table 5
Factors Affecting Changes in Margin of Victory of House Members, 1946–1989

Independent Variables	Administration Witnesses		Nonadministration Witnesses	
	Coefficient	(t)	Coefficient	(t)
Conflictual questioning	2.35	0.6	−4.18	−0.9
Conflictual questioning of opposition party	7.21	2.5**		
Time	1.16	3.1***	−0.13	−0.3
Constant	−32.17	−2.4**	21.36	1.2
R^2	.03		.002	
No. of observations	604		524	

**$p < .05$. ***$p < .01$.

We do not know whether similar electoral considerations affect behavior in the Senate as well. We expect that they do, since southerners were less likely to be critical of administration witnesses than members of Congress from other parts of the country. We suspect that this is due to the safer electoral margins of southern members, but further research is necessary before any firm conclusions can be reached.

INTERPRETATION

Conflict between Congress and the president over foreign policy questions has not increased over time, but it has changed in character and direction. The changes are best understood as a by-product of the steadily declining military and ideological threat to the United States posed by the Soviet Union. In the immediate postwar period the United States faced a strong challenge from a militarily strong, aggressive world power whose ideological doctrine justified claims for world domination. Soviet troops marched into Eastern Europe, China was absorbed into the Communist empire, Germany and Korea remained divided, and Communist-inspired, Soviet-assisted nationalist movements appeared throughout the third world. In the United States, there were sharp divisions within both parties over the appropriate response to Soviet aggressiveness, and various persons (e.g., Alger Hiss) and institutions (e.g., the State Department) were held responsible for Communist successes. Gradually, the intensity of the international threat subsided, as a policy of containment was agreed upon, international institutions were created to carry out the policy, and Soviet objectives adjusted downward to a level more consistent with the country's internal resources. The share of the U.S. economy allocated for defense purposes declined steadily. The Vietnam War interrupted but did not reverse these long-term trends, whose logical culmination has only recently become apparent.

This change in the international system influenced opinion among those politicians and professionals who think about, discuss, and shape U.S. foreign policy. Over the decades, opinion among these professionals has moved steadily in a dovish direction. At one time, most doubted the veracity of Soviet leaders, and the vast majority of credible experts thought that only the constant vigilance of the United States could keep the Soviet threat contained. But the Soviet Union's economy could not keep pace, its control over its Warsaw Pact allies waned, its threat to Europe became negligible, its support of third world allies paid few dividends, and its once-vaunted technological capacity fell behind. Gradually, policy makers in the United States began considering the possibility of reaching arms limitation agreements with the Soviet Union, engaging in trade and cultural exchanges, and cooperating with the Soviet Union on an increasingly broad range of international issues.

This change in elite opinion in the United States was uneven. Although the overall trend was in the dovish direction, the groups, think tanks, and professionals associated with the Democratic party provided its leading edge, while Republican-oriented ones remained relatively hawkish, if not quite so hawkish as they once had been. In the aftermath of the Vietnam War, opinion among Democrats shifted so rapidly that some foreign policy experts closely identified with what became known as the Jackson wing of the party began to feel more comfortable in Republican circles. In short, even while elite opinion was generally becoming more dovish, partisan differences over foreign policy questions were enlarging.

A parallel development was creating divisions of opinion between the two major governing institutions. In the immediate postwar era the executive branch was not quite as hawkish as the most vociferous opinion on Capitol Hill. Although most members of the policy-making elite were concerned about the threat posed by the Soviet Union, the executive was much more reluctant to use force to reverse any changes that had already occurred. From both sides of the aisle, some in Congress were demanding first the liberation of Eastern Europe, then involvement in the internal conflicts on the Chinese mainland, next the bombardment and invasion of Manchuria, and finally the defense of French interests in Indochina. The executive was reluctant to embrace these demands, in part because the executive had too much responsibility for the well-being of the nation to use rhetoric or pursue policies that could risk nuclear annihilation, and in part because the political cost to the president of failure would be overwhelming. Containment was a less exciting but, ultimately, both a more responsible and a politically more savvy doctrine than one that committed the United States to freeing the world from totalitarianism.

But just as the executive was originally less hawkish, so it moved less dramatically in a dovish direction than did the less responsible and therefore less constrained legislative branch, especially within the House of Representatives. In the aftermath of Vietnam the tide of dominant congressional opinion turned decisively against the use of force in third world countries. On Capitol Hill communism was no longer thought to be a monolithic political force directed by the Kremlin but a slogan used by many groups and leaders for diverse and competing purposes. Many thought there was no longer much need for U.S. intervention against groups claiming to be allied with the Soviet Union. Opinion within the executive branch was less certain that Soviet intentions had changed and less convinced that its capacities were increasingly limited. Even when Democratic Jimmy Carter became president, policy makers treated the Soviet Union with caution. And after the betrayal that Afghanistan seemed to represent, the Carter administration became much more determined to forestall further aggression: it cut off grain sales to the Soviets, boycotted the Olympic Games, withdrew its request that the Senate ratify the SALT II agreement, and called for a major arms buildup.

CONCLUSIONS

The interpretation set forth in this paper is exploratory, not definitive. Our analysis relies on a new methodology, the systematic examination of congressional hearings. While this approach offers a fresh look at interbranch relations, it may be further refined with greater use. We nonetheless expect that subsequent research will corroborate the major findings in this paper, namely:

1. Conflict between the two branches over national security policy has not increased over time.

2. The nature of the conflict has changed in two important ways: (a) Congressional (and especially House) opinion fluctuates more widely in response to changes in the international environment. In times of high threat, Congress is more hawkish than the executive; in times of low threat, Congress is more dovish. This greater fluctuation in congressional than in executive opinion contributes to interbranch conflict. (b) Conflict has taken a more partisan coloration, especially in the House of Representatives.

3. Partisan conflict is electorally beneficial, inducing members from more-marginal districts to contribute to interbranch conflict.

Some of this description of interbranch relations in foreign policy is at odds with the conventional wisdom in the field. Most observers believe that Congress was deferential to the executive in the early postwar years but became increasingly conflictual after Vietnam. It is also implicit in most analyses that congressional influence on the executive usually comes from one direction: Congress restrains the executive from pursuing more-active foreign policies.

A number of factors may explain the divergence between our findings and this conventional wisdom. First, we employ a systematic method that may avoid the biases of selective case studies and insider recollections. Relatively few analysts have witnessed first hand forty years of foreign policy making, and those who have may not fully recall the intensity of old conflicts. Second, as we have noted, conflict between the executive and Congress has become more partisan in recent years. Partisan conflict may be more visible and disconcerting, especially in a political culture that expects partisanship to end at "the water's edge."

Third, the direction of congressional criticism of administration foreign policy has changed from rebuking the executive for failing to be sufficiently vigilant in defense of the national interest to challenging the executive for excessive diligence. Observers may perceive the latter as more conflictual, either because it threatens policies they prefer or because they believe that it is wiser to be too cautious than not cautious enough. Yet congressional pressure on the executive to respond more vigorously to external threats during the early postwar period may have influenced policy in ways as undesirable as later, more dovish, congressional pressure. The controversy over who lost China may have directed more attention than was warranted to developments on the Asian mainland. Congressional urgings to close an apparently fictitious bomber and missile gap may have produced unnecessary expenditures and accelerated an arms race. And congressional criticism after the Bay of Pigs may have significantly influenced Kennedy's response to the Cuban missile crisis. Thus, commentators may overlook these earlier examples of interbranch conflict even though they are no less important than controversies following the war in Vietnam.

Our central claims, that congressional response to events in the international system is more elastic than the executive's and that the House displays this characteristic more than the Senate, are actually consistent with a long tradition of thought on the design of the U.S. government. In fact, the differing conduct of the branches and of each chamber of Congress that we observe seems remarkably close to the behavior anticipated by James Madison when he wrote in *The Federalist Papers*, "The necessity of a senate is not less indicated by the propensity of all single and numerous assemblies to yield to the impulse of sudden and violent passions" (Hamilton, Madison, and Jay 1961, 379, No. 62).[9] While it is reasonable to be concerned about excessive interbranch conflict, we find no evidence to support the concern of some that executive-legislative relations in foreign affairs have seriously deteriorated and must be corrected by constitutional or institutional reforms.

METHODOLOGICAL APPENDIX

Procedures

A random sample of questions or what have been termed "lines of inquiry" was drawn for each year between 1946 and 1989. Each line of inquiry was identified by selecting a question drawn at random from each year's public collection of hearings. Hearings and page numbers were chosen at random; when a page with a question was identified, the first question on the page was selected for coding. Coders read up to one page of testimony subsequent to the chosen question, unless the questioner or witness changed. If so, the coder examined in addition the testimony before the chosen question up to a total of one page. If a full page of testimony did not take place without a change in questioner or witness, then the coder relied upon the less than one page of testimony that was recorded. Courtesy questions (e.g., would you please sit down? would you speak into the microphone?) and statements by members of Congress unaccompanied by a question were excluded.

A line of inquiry was coded for the degree of conflict that occurred in the course of the discussion (measured by the apparent assertiveness of the questioner); for the degree of information the questioner displayed; and for the extent to which the questioner mentioned domestic issues or considerations. For the conflict variable a six-point scale was developed by using a two-step coding procedure. Coders first ascertained whether they thought there was agreement or disagreement between questioner and witness by answering the following question: During the course of the line of inquiry, is there any sign of disagreement between the questioner and the witness? If the answer was yes, the coder then coded for the intensity of the disagreement; if no, the coder indicated whether agreement included explicit praise of the witness or the witness's testimony; if the coder was uncertain, the coder indicated whether it seemed as if there was agreement or disagreement. The domestic considerations variable was a simple three-category variable: yes, no, or unclear.

A variety of other information about the questioner (title, party, seniority, house of Congress, district or state), witness (member of executive branch, lobbyist, or policy expert), month, year, time and length of hearing, and the topic of the hearing was recorded. The topic of each hearing was classified under the following headings: foreign aid; military; arms control; international organizations; human rights; trade; nominations and appointments; organization of the State Department; and terrorism, international crime, and drugs.

Initially, one hundred lines of inquiry were coded for every year; since preliminary analysis revealed a stable pattern of results, it was decided that the number of observations could be limited to thirty per year. Data could then be gathered for every year over the postwar period without exceeding resource constraints.

Questions were randomly selected by first selecting hearings at random, then selecting pages from hearings at random, and finally selecting the first question on the selected page. One question was selected for every one hundred pages of a hearing's length—up to thirty questions per year. (When a hundred observations per year were being made, one question was selected for every fifty pages.)

The sampling approach employed in this study may have undersampled longer hearings. We do not think this is a major problem, because our findings did not change when we controlled for the length of the hearings. Since limited resources preclude identification of the total number of questions asked in a given year, the number of pages in a hearing serves as a proxy.

To keep the coding process from being contaminated by contextual knowledge of partisan relations or the reputation of particular individuals, students who were not particularly well informed about the history of congressional-executive relations coded the data. The hypotheses of the study were not discussed with coders during the coding process.

The two coders differed systematically in their assessment of the degree of conflict. Apparently, conflict, like beauty, is to some extent in the eye of the beholder. By using coder as a dummy variable in all conflict equations, the systematic difference in coder judgments was controlled. In addition, once it became clear that judgments differed, coders were assigned years randomly in order to make sure that any coder bias would not be systematically related to trends occurring over time. Estimates of other relationships do not change significantly, depending on whether the coder correciton is included or excluded from the analysis. Presumably, random errors in the coding process reduce the significance of statistical relationships.

The total number of observations was 2,906. The sample was drawn separately for each year; thus the data set is not a random sample of all questions asked over the forty-four years. Hearings held in executive session that were subsequently published were excluded.

The results presented here are based on the ordinary least squares (OLS) technique. We use OLS because the coefficients are more easily interpreted and because many readers are more familiar with OLS. A logit analysis of the data produced results that were substantively very similar.

Definition of Variables

Conflict—Ranges from 1 to 6, with 6 representing the highest level of disagreement.

Time—Ranges from 1 to 44, with the year 1946 taking the value 1 and 1989 taking the value 44.

Threat—Percentage of GNP expended for defense. This variable was centered at its mean so that it is positive when the threat was above average and negative when it was below average. A change of 1 in the measure of this variable is equal to a change of 10 percent of the portion of GNP used for defense. It ranges from $-.35006$ to $.63994$.

Hawkish Congress—The percentage change of the president's defense budget requests, including supplementary requests. This variable was also centered at its mean so that it is positive when Congress authorizes more than the president requests or when they cut his request by a small amount. A change of 1 in this measure of the variable is equal to a change of 10 percent in the president's defense budget request. It ranges from $-.8484$ to 1.1996.

Threat by Hawkish—Threat multiplied by Hawkish.

Divided Government—A dummy variable that takes the value 1 when chamber is controlled by the party not in control of the presidency. Takes the value 0 when both are controlled by same party.

Opposition Questioner—A dummy variable that equals 1 when an administration witness is not of the same party as the questioner.

Opposition Questioner by Early Period—Opposition Questioner multiplied by a dummy variable that equals 1 when a question is asked before 1968.

Senate — A dummy variable that takes the value 1 when a question is asked in the Senate. It equals 0 otherwise.

Threat by Senate — Senate multiplied by Threat.

Threat by Hawk by Senate — Senate multiplied by Hawkish Congress multiplied by Threat.

Opposition Questioner by Senate — Senate multiplied by Opposition Questioner.

Divided Government by Senate — Senate multiplied by Divided Government.

Southerner — A dummy variable that equals 1 when questioner is from a state that was once part of the Confederacy.

Cabinet-level Witness — A dummy variable that equals 1 when the witness is a member of the cabinet.

Fulbright — A dummy variable that equals 1 when a question was asked by William Fulbright.

Safety of Seat — The difference between a representative's percentage of the two-party popular vote and 50 percent. This variable was rescaled so that when a representative won 99 percent of the vote (the safest members), the variable takes the value 4.9. When a representative wins with barely 50 percent (the least safe members), the variable takes the value 0.

Domestic Concerns — Ranges from 1 to 3, with 3 representing greater domestic content.

Subcommittee — A dummy variable that equals 1 when a question is asked in subcommittee.

War — A dummy variable that equals 1 for any year in which the United States was engaged in hostilities for more than half of that year.

Early War — A dummy that equals 1 for any year during the initial years of hostilities. It equals 1 for 1950, 1951, 1965, 1966, and 1967.

Change in Margin of Victory — The difference between a representative's percentage of the two-party vote and that member's percentage in the previous election.

Part III

PRESIDENTIAL INFLUENCE ON THE CHAMBER FLOOR

Chapter Five

★ ★ ★

PRESIDENTIAL SUPPORT IN THE
HOUSE OF REPRESENTATIVES

★ ★ ★

David W. Rohde

On 12 January 1991 the House of
Representatives adopted a resolution authorizing President George Bush to
use military force to compel Iraq's withdrawal from Kuwait, setting the stage
for Operation "Desert Storm." The vote was 250–183, and the president's
position in favor of the resolution received the votes of virtually all Republicans and about one-third of the Democrats. Yet only three months later, on 17
April, with the president's approval ratings at extraordinarily high levels in
the wake of Desert Storm's success, the House resoundingly rejected his
proposals for the fiscal 1992 federal budget. The amendment incorporating
Bush's views received only 89 votes (all from Republicans), while 335
members were opposed.[1]

The contrasting outcomes on these important votes illustrate a phenomenon that has interested political scientists for a quarter of a century, since
Aaron Wildavsky (1966) propounded what he termed the "two-presidencies"
hypothesis. Wildavsky argued that there were two different presidencies,
one related to domestic policy and the other to foreign and defense policy,
and that the president was much more successful in the foreign arena than in
the domestic. As we will see, most subsequent analyses of Wildavsky's
hypothesis have agreed that there had been a presidential advantage on
foreign versus domestic issues, and that this advantage declined over time.
There has been disagreement, however, about the timing and reasons for the
decline. In this analysis I will try to offer new perspectives on these matters
by focusing on some issues that have not been extensively addressed in the
literature.

My central thesis is that changing presidential success in the House on
foreign and domestic issues has been due primarily to two factors. First,
patterns of agreement and disagreement between the president and represen-

tatives have shifted on various issues, primarily as a consequence of changes in the preferences of their respective electoral coalitions. Second, the relationship between House committees and the membership on the floor has also changed, owing mainly to the House reforms of the early 1970s. In my view, the president's advantages in foreign and defense policy rested on strong agreement with the president's views among the members of the relevant House committees, and on the ability of those committees to dominate floor decisions on their bills. As both agreement and committee dominance declined, so did presidential success.

With regard to policy preferences, the Eisenhower-Kennedy-Johnson administrations were all characterized by an anticommunist foreign policy and by a commitment to substantial defense spending. These views were generally supported by members of both parties in the House, in committee and on the floor. As a result of political conflict over the Vietnam War, however, the partisan consensus on foreign and defense issues ended, and northern Democrats came more and more to favor a less bipolar foreign policy and reductions in defense spending. On the organizational side, House committees were able to dominate policy making within their jurisdictions until the mid-1970s. Thus even though Presidents Nixon and Ford faced greater disagreement on foreign and defense policy from the Democratic majority, they were still frequently able to have legislation reflect their views if they had the support of committee members. Then the reforms of the 1970s undermined committee autonomy and made it easier to change committee bills on the floor. As a consequence, during the Reagan administration defense and foreign policy legislation came to reflect more and more closely the increasingly consensual views of House Democrats, which were usually opposed to those of the president.

THE SEARCH FOR "TWO PRESIDENCIES"

Wildavsky contended that the greater presidential advantage in foreign policy matters stemmed from, among other things, the immediacy of the cold war, greater formal powers, the need for secrecy in foreign policy and the resulting information advantage for the president, and greater personal attention by the president. His brief article devoted only a little space to the presentation of evidence. Data on congressional actions on presidential proposals between 1948 and 1964 (compiled by Congressional Quarterly Inc., and generally known as the presidential "box score") demonstrated a higher rate of passage for foreign and defense policy proposals than for domestic ones. Taking the importance of the issue into account, Wildavsky asserted that in "the realm of foreign policy there has not been a single major issue on which Presidents, where they were serious and determined, have failed" (1975, 449).

Subsequent analyses sought to assess whether Wildavsky had been correct about the existence of the two presidencies, and whether conditions had changed since his original study.[2] Two of the most extensive examinations of Wildavsky's hypothesis are also among the most recent, and both are part of more general analyses of presidential success in Congress. George Edwards (1989) studied levels of support for presidential positions on roll calls in the House and Senate from the Eisenhower years through the latter part of the Reagan presidency (1953–86). By including all presidential-position roll calls, rather than just "key votes," Edwards's study encompassed a much larger set of votes than earlier studies. His analysis showed that Eisenhower had received substantially more support from Democrats on foreign policy than on domestic policy, although there was no such advantage among Republicans. Under subsequent presidents, however, the higher levels of foreign policy support from the opposition party were reduced, and eventually became almost nonexistent.

Given the change in support and its timing, Edwards argued that conventional explanations of bipartisanship and congressional deference to the president on foreign policy were not persuasive explanations for the existence of the two presidencies. Moreover, the impact of the war in Vietnam or Watergate was not a persuasive explanation for its decline. Instead, he said, the explanation involved the changing appeal of presidents' foreign policies to the opposition party.

The other major recent effort to examine the two-presidencies hypothesis is contained in the work of Jon Bond and Richard Fleisher (1990). They also employed the presidential-position roll-call votes used by Edwards, but instead of looking only at levels of support among individual congressmen, they focused particularly on the frequency of presidential victory or defeat. Examining the data from this vantage point, they also concluded that there was some evidence of greater presidential success in the foreign policy area, but that the increase occurred only under Republican presidents. The source of this greater success was primarily increased support among liberal Democrats in both houses and among conservative Democrats in the House. For Democratic presidents, the only substantial increase in support was among liberal Republicans. Since this has been such a small faction, it didn't do those presidents a great deal of good.

In one partial contrast to Edwards, Bond and Fleisher did not show as much decline in the advantage of Republican presidents in terms of success and support over time. Their analysis further indicated that when attention was limited to relatively "important" votes, "the two presidencies phenomenon for Republican presidents disappears in the House and diminishes considerably in the Senate" (1990, 168).[3] They concluded that their findings tended to dispute Wildavsky's original theory, which they maintained was intended to apply particularly to more-important issues. They argued that the explanation for the advantage of Republican presidents was that these situations involved divided government, in which case the president and the opposition majority share responsibility for maintaining the operations of government. This may constrain the majority to be more cooperative with the president on foreign and defense policy preferences than they would be based only on their own preferences.

VARYING AGENDAS: SOME THEORETICAL AND EMPIRICAL CONSIDERATIONS

Vote Types and Issues

As I have indicated, except for the earliest studies of the two-presidencies hypothesis, most analysts have employed presidential-position roll calls to test it. In accordance with their primary focus, they controlled for whether a foreign or domestic issue was involved, but otherwise they treated roll calls as equivalent across time. However, there has been significant variation in the types of roll calls in the House, and this variation may affect the patterns of presidential success and support.[4] For example, after the Johnson years there was a substantial increase in the proportion of presidential-position votes that were taken on amendments. From 1961 to 1968, only 7.2 percent of the votes were on amendments, while from 1981 to 1988, amendments accounted for 44.8 percent of the presidential-position roll calls.

This shift was a direct consequence of changes in House rules in the Legislative Reorganization Act of 1970. Before this time, roll-call votes on amendments were rare. In the House, most amendment activity on the floor takes place in the Committee of the Whole (which is merely the full House operating under a more relaxed set of rules), and until the 1970 Reorganization Act record votes were not permitted on amendments in that forum. As a consequence, a roll call could only be had on an amendment if it had previously *passed* in the Committee of the Whole (on a voice or other nonrecord vote). From 1971 on, however, a record vote could be taken on a proposed amendment if as few as twenty members requested it. This permitted amendments to become a significant part of the record-vote agenda on the House floor.[5] In turn, the shares of the agenda accounted for by votes on final action (passage of bills, conference reports, suspension of the rules, etc.) and by procedural votes declined.[6]

This type of variation in the agenda is relevant in two ways for the analysis of presidential-congressional interaction. First, if we were to expect that presidential success or support would be systematically different across different types of votes, failure to control for these variations could lead to incorrect conclusions from the patterns we see in the data. That is, some relationships might turn out to be spurious when the types of votes are controlled for, while new, previously unseen relationships may appear. To assess this potential problem we need to consider theoretical expectations about presidential success or support on various types of votes.

Second, considering types of votes separately will permit us to address new aspects of the questions of interest here. We will be able to draw inferences about elements of the legislative process that the aggregated data do not permit us to deal with. For example, considering amendments separately will allow us to assess, in a general way, the responses of rank-and-file members and the president to committee recommendations.

Another kind of variation in the roll-call agenda relates to the kind of issue involved. In drawing contrasts with domestic issues, most analysts have grouped foreign policy and defense issues together. However, as table 1 shows, there have been important variations in the distribution of votes between these categories over time.[7] If we anticipate that congressional responses to presidential positions should be similar in both areas, there will be no difficulty. If, however, we have reason to expect different patterns of conflict and support between these issues, then we must consider them separately. With these characteristics of the agenda in mind, we can now return to theoretical issues.

Committee Actions, Presidential Positions, and Responses on the Floor

Congressional Reform and the Policy Agenda. Presidential-congressional interactions over policy, and their variation over time, will be shaped by many factors. Among the most important are changes in congressional organization and the ways that organization shapes the policy agenda members face. Probably the most salient feature of congressional organization has been the division of labor through the committee system. Between the 1950s and the 1980s, the House's committee organization and related institutional arrangements underwent radical changes, which can only be briefly outlined here.[8]

Table 1
Distribution of Foreign and Defense Policy Presidential-Position Roll Calls,
by Administration, 1953–1988

Administration	Foreign Policy Votes (%)	Defense Policy Votes (%)	Total (%)
Eisenhower (1953–60)	69.5	30.5	100.0 (82)
Kennedy-Johnson (1961–68)	76.7	23.3	100.0 (133)
Nixon-Ford (1969–76)	39.0	61.0	100.0 (136)
Carter (1977–80)	72.8	27.2	100.0 (151)
Reagan (1981–88)	29.9	70.1	100.0 (254)

Note: Figures in parentheses are *N*s.

Before the reform era, the House was characterized by strong and largely autonomous committees, powerful committee leaders, and relatively weak party leaders.[9] Committee chairman mostly ran their committees as they saw fit, with little constraint provided by party leaders or rank-and-file members. There was, moreover, a pronounced conservative cast to these arrangements. The Democratic party had ideological divisions along regional lines on domestic policy during the 1950s, and these splits grew much more severe during the 1960s as Democratic presidents pressed for innovations on civil rights and social welfare.[10] The senior ranks on most major committees were dominated by the conservative coalition of southern Democrats and Republicans. They were able to keep much legislation favored by liberal Democrats from reaching the floor, and to shape to their liking most bills they reported out. In addition, the inability to take record votes on amendments limited the practical ability of members to change bills on the floor, even when the sentiment existed to do so.

Liberal Democrats believed that these institutional arrangements were unfairly biased against their policy preferences. They launched the reform effort of the 1970s in large part as an effort to remove that bias. One set of reforms (popularly known as the "Subcommittee Bill of Rights") struck at the autocratic powers of committee chairmen. The makeup and leadership of subcommittees were put outside of their control; subcommittees were given fixed jurisdictions and adequate staffs, and bills within their areas usually had to be referred to them for consideration. Full committees were empowered to hold meetings if their chairmen refused to do so, and bills could not be bottled up in a committee without the assent of a majority of its members.

Furthermore, the House Democratic Caucus adopted rules for automatic secret-ballot votes on committee chairmen at the opening of every Congress. Thus chairmen were no longer provided absolute protection by the seniority system. If a chairman's behavior dissatisfied a majority of Democrats, he or she could be voted out. Nor was this an idle threat; three southern chairmen were removed from their positions in 1975. The reforms also established Democratic party caucuses on each committee, which were empowered to shape the rules for committee operations and could remove subcommittee chairmen who were deemed unacceptable.

Another important set of reforms significantly strengthened Democratic party leaders. The independence of the Rules Committee, which had long been the major hurdle for liberal legislation, was sharply reduced. The Speaker was granted the power to appoint, with the consent of the caucus, both the chairman and the Democratic members of the committee. The Democratic Steering and Policy Committee was created, most of whose members were part of the leadership or were appointed by the Speaker. It was intended to help articulate party policy, and it soon was also given authority to make Democratic committee assignments. This increased leadership influence over the allocation decision most important to members. In another move that further undermined the autonomy of committees, the Speaker was empowered to refer bills to more than one committee and to set deadlines for those committees to report.

The combined effect of these organizational changes was to undermine the independence of committees in shaping policy, to reduce substantially the power of committee chairmen, to increase the influence of the majority leadership, and to make both committees and the Democratic leadership more responsive to the policy preferences of House Democrats when there was substantial consensus among them. Only a fraction of the legislative activity of the House was relevant to the partisan interests of members of the majority, and in the late 1970s and 1980s Democrats were (as we will discuss shortly) still divided on a number of issues. However, on that subset of important issues salient to the parties, and on which the majority was relatively united, committees and their leaders had to respond to the wishes of Democratic members. They could not simply withhold bills that were wanted, and in shaping bills for floor consideration they had to take into account the preferences of their party colleagues outside the committee.

Political Coalitions, Member Preferences, and the Policy Agenda. The reforms discussed above have substantial relevance in determining the nature of the alternatives that make up the agenda for decision making in the House. But members' decisions, and the outcomes that result from them, are the consequence not only of the alternatives that face them but also of their preferences about policy. Those preferences are in turn shaped by constituencies, interest groups, the members' own views about what is desirable, pressures from party leaders and presidents, and so on. The patterns of preferences among members of the House changed in important ways over the course of these four decades, especially in the ways they varied within and between parties.

As noted above, there were divisions on domestic policy issues among Democrats in the 1950s, which became much sharper in the Kennedy-Johnson years. Southern Democrats frequently sided with Republicans against their northern colleagues. However, by the end of the Johnson administration, domestic policy wasn't the only locus of intra- and interparty conflict. There were varying degrees of disagreement about foreign policy and defense issues as well. Before the Vietnam War, there had been widespread consensus in both parties in favor of a strong military establishment and for the containment of Communist expansion, although there were ideological variations in the degree of commitment to these positions. While these views also provided a substantial base for foreign military aid, there was much less consensus for economic aid. Conservatives of both parties were basically opposed to such programs, but the Eisenhower and Kennedy administrations garnered support from conservatives by portraying foreign aid as a device to stave off the advance of communism.[11]

The Vietnam experience changed these preference patterns significantly. Antiwar sentiment in Congress began with a small number of liberals in both parties, but it eventually came to encompass almost the entire northern wing of the Democratic party, as well as enough other members to make a majority. In the process, liberal Democrats came to favor cuts in defense spending and foreign military aid generally, to question particular weapons systems, to support international agreements limiting nuclear weapons, and to attack the wisdom of the policy of Communist containment. On each of these policies there was substantial conflict with the views of conservative Democrats and Republicans. There was, moreover, growing sentiment in Congress to channel foreign economic aid through international agencies. This approach reduced the ability of the U.S. government to attach "strings" to the aid, which undermined the limited support for it among conservatives.

Thus by the early 1970s, there had been important changes in the partisan and ideological pattern of preferences across various issues among members of the House. These patterns were not static from that point on, however. Further changes occurred, as the effects of the organizational reforms began to be felt. We will discuss those developments below, as we examine the implications of these organizational and preference changes for presidential-congressional conflict from the Eisenhower to the Reagan years.

AGENDA AND PREFERENCE CHANGE
AND POLICY CONFLICT

At the beginning of the period under study, during the Eisenhower and Kennedy years, the House experienced little overt policy conflict over foreign and defense policy, and committees dominated the issues within their jurisdiction. The president's attempts to achieve his legislative goals had to focus primarily on the committees that controlled the policy areas of concern to him. His goal was to get committees to shape their bills in accordance with his preferences, because committee bills that came to the floor almost always passed.[12] Furthermore, because of the restrictive amendment rules, the principal features of committee bills were only rarely changed on the floor.

Under Eisenhower there were natural partisan conflicts between presidential and congressional preferences on domestic issues, conflicts that were lessened (although they didn't disappear) under Kennedy. On foreign and defense policy, however, there was comparatively little disagreement during this time, and the committees tended to defer to the president's wishes. For example, Richard Fenno characterized the policy coalitions in the realm of the House foreign affairs committee as "executive-led." Presidential leadership on policy was primary, and both the committee and the House membership were inclined to accede to it on most matters. On the one issue with some significant partisan-ideological conflict—foreign aid—the committee contingents of both parties tended to be dominated by aid supporters (Fenno 1973, esp. 27–30). The picture was similar with regard to the armed services committee and the defense appropriations subcommittee. The latter was of crucial importance because annual authorization of defense did not begin until 1961, and it was not until late in the decade that the authorized portion became substantial. Edward J. Laurance, in a review of the literature on defense policy making, offered the following generalizations for the period through 1967:

The committees which process defense policy are prestigious and consist of senior, conservative members who are pro-military and support a strong defense posture. . . .

The military committees are well integrated and rarely in conflict over defense policy, resulting in little opposition to executive-formulated defense policies. . . .

Decisions made by the military committees are always accepted and approved by the house and senate as a whole. (1976, 219–20)

As Samuel Huntington said in a more general vein: "Although perhaps not obsolete, like the Crown's veto over legislation, the veto power of Congress over military programs certainly was dormant" (1961, 132).

Thus we would expect decreased presidential-committee conflict on domestic issues in the Kennedy-Johnson administrations compared to the Eisenhower years.[13] This would be reflected in increased satisfaction with the bills reported from committee and passed by the House, although there would likely still be significant (and perhaps even greater) conflict over these bills on floor votes. On defense and foreign policy, on the other hand, low levels of disagreement between committees and the president in both periods should have yielded high levels of presidential satisfaction with bills and infrequent floor conflict.[14]

The later years of the Johnson presidency and the Nixon years saw significant changes from the previous period. In the area of domestic policy, the issues of civil rights and the "Great Society" created sharp ideological divisions among Democrats. In the 89th Congress (1965–67), after the Democrats' landslide presidential and congressional victories in 1964, Johnson had enough liberal Democratic votes to overwhelm conservative resistance. However, after the reversals in the 1966 elections, the conservative coalition was able to assert itself again. Southern Democrats voted frequently with the Republicans, and many of the president's domestic initiatives were blocked in committee or couldn't carry the day on the floor. Then when Nixon took office, presidential domestic preferences changed sharply. Conflict with liberal Democrats increased, while conservative Democrats and Republicans became more satisfied. Of course, it was the latter two groups that controlled most of the major committees, and that was the situation that gave rise to the reform movement.

On defense and foreign policy there were also some significant preference changes. Vietnam shattered the Democratic consensus on a commitment to a strong defense. An increasing percentage of liberal Democrats turned against the war, and most also came to support cuts in the defense budget and limits on nuclear and conventional weapons. Here too the Democrats were divided on sectional lines, with most southerners retaining strong pro-defense positions. The defense committees were still dominated by conservatives, so the committees' proposals were still shaped in accordance with the president's views, but the reform rules permitting record votes on amendments expanded the incentives and opportunities for challenging committee positions on the floor.

Foreign policy issues, particularly at this time foreign aid, show the potential contrast between presidential and congressional interests even when partisan and ideological views are shared. Conservative Republicans in the House were still mostly opposed to foreign aid, as were many southern Democrats. One might have expected Nixon to side with them, but the president (and Henry Kissinger) saw aid as a useful foreign policy tool. For example, in the early 1970s, over six times as much money from the "Food for Peace" program went to South Vietnam and Cambodia as went to areas in Africa that were experiencing severe famine.[15] The internationalist majority on the foreign affairs committee also favored these programs, so the president's position had committee support, but on this issue it was recalcitrant conservative Republicans who had the incentive to seek to amend committee bills on the floor. On other matters, however (like war powers and human rights), conflict between the foreign affairs committee and the president increased significantly. The committee received an influx of liberal activist members, and the committee reforms permitted the various subcommittees to challenge the executive on a number of fronts.[16]

When the Democrats regained the White House in 1976, presidential preferences changed notably in some areas and less so in others. Jimmy Carter was a moderate southern Democrat in domestic policy. Thus he was more in favor of traditional Democratic positions than was Nixon, but not as much as many liberal Democrats would have preferred. This, coupled with Carter's style, caused more conflict with congressional Democrats than might have been expected.[17] Intraparty conflict also developed on some aspects of defense policy. Carter largely shared the antipathy of liberal Democrats to nuclear weapons and made great efforts to reach a strategic arms agreement with the Soviet Union. This caused the president some problems with the defense committees, as when he sought to cancel the B-1 strategic bomber. In the conventional arms area, on the other hand, Carter supported spending increases that garnered committee support but were less than enthusiastically received by northern Democrats.

In foreign policy, it was interparty conflict that increased. Carter was strongly committed to international support for human rights and for channeling foreign economic aid to international agencies. These views were generally supported in committee but were strongly opposed by the growing conservative wing of House Republicans, especially after their gains in the 1978 elections.[18] Here, then, Republican incentives to seek changes on the floor in foreign policy bills were substantially increased.

Finally, there was the period of Ronald Reagan's presidency. Reagan was the most conservative of the presidents we have considered, with the most consistently ideological agenda—an agenda for which he believed he had a mandate from the voters.[19] He wanted a major reduction in the size of government in the domestic arena, cutting back social and regulatory programs. On defense, however, he favored substantial increases in spending, and he supported a more aggressively anticommunist foreign policy.

During the Reagan years, significant changes in congressional preferences also became apparent. These were the result of shifts in the electorate, particularly in the South, in response to the changing positions and images of the two parties.[20] Among Republicans, the growth of the right wing continued. Southern Democrats, on the other hand, (especially those first elected after 1980) held policy views more like those of their northern colleagues. Their views were not identical, and southerners remained on average more conservative, but homogeneity within the party increased; and, most important, the majority of southern Democrats held positions on most issues that were closer to those of northern Democrats than to those of Republicans. Meanwhile, the reform mechanisms that were designed to permit removal of committee leaders whose policy views conflicted too often with those of the party majority induced more support for party positions among senior southern Democrats in committee and on the floor. Furthermore, the increased powers of the Democratic leadership helped to encourage further party homogeneity and to shape the policy agenda (through the control of the rules committee, for example) to the party's advantage.

The increased homogeneity among the majority Democrats, matched with the president's conservative preferences, caused substantial conflict, especially after Reagan's first year, when his approval ratings in public opinion polls declined. If the committee reform mechanisms were working as designed, then the bills reported from committee on issues that were important to House Democrats should have reflected party preferences and been relatively unsatisfactory to the president. Thus the House Republicans and the president should have had increased incentives to seek changes on the House floor through the amendment process.

Of course, the statement about committee bills reflecting the views of House Democrats should have been more true on committees whose membership was representative of the House or tilted toward Democratic positions, and less true for committees biased toward the Republicans. This point is important with respect to defense policy and the armed services committee. As we noted earlier, armed services had long been dominated by conservative prodefense representatives. This continued after the majority of congressional Democrats became less supportive of defense spending, and the committee's Democratic membership became significantly different from the caucus generally.[21]

So there was a tension between the preferences of committee members and the pressure to represent the Democratic membership's views. This tension was so acute that at the opening of both the 99th and the 100th Congresses House Democrats voted down two different sitting chairmen of the committee, in large part because of the belief that they didn't effectively represent the positions of the caucus.[22] Thus in the defense area we would expect that House Democrats would have been relatively less satisfied with committee bills than in other areas and would have more reason to seek to amend them, while the president would have been much more satisfied with the committee's product.

BILLS, AMENDMENTS, AND CONFLICT ON THE FLOOR

In accordance with the earlier discussion regarding the different types of votes that make up the roll-call agenda in the House over time, we will focus separately on particular kinds of votes. There is not enough space to consider every category of vote, so we will confine our attention to two types: first-degree amendments and the initial regular passage of bills.[23] First, however, we will examine the frequency with which bills favored by the president received near unanimous support. These data will show that, before Nixon, presidents usually got their way on defense issues without much evident disagreement.

This will be followed by an analysis of floor amendments. Support for amendments indicates dissatisfaction with policies drafted by committees. Using this perspective, the analysis will show that through the Reagan years the president found committee products more satisfactory in the defense area than on other issues, and the position he favored on the amendments in that area was more often successful. However, presidential success did decline over time in all issue areas. This is what the theoretical discussion would lead us to expect: the greater support in committee for presidential views on defense was an asset, but a declining one as committee autonomy and support in the full House waned. Finally, an analysis of votes on bill passage will show that over time, on foreign policy as well as domestic issues, the final product passed by the House was less likely to be in accord with presidential preferences and more likely to reflect the growing consensus within the Democratic majority.

The Frequency of Presidential-Congressional Conflict

As argued above, when one is seeking to analyze presidential support and success, it is potentially misleading to focus only on conflictual roll-call votes. One also needs to know how often the Congress went along with the president without internal disagreement. Since the evidence employed here also involves only roll-call votes, it can shed only a limited amount of light on this issue, but some relevant statistics can be presented.

One question we can address is, what was the frequency of consensual support for the president's position on roll calls on bill passage across issues and over time? If committees produce bills that are satisfactory to the president, and then on the floor members overwhelmingly endorse the bills, we would have to conclude that the president was successful and his support was high on that issue. Figure 1 shows the proportion of presidential-position roll calls on which the president favored passage and 90 percent or more of the members voted aye.[24] (I will refer to votes by this margin as "consensual votes.")

On domestic issues the proportion of consensual support is similar over time, except in the Kennedy-Johnson years (when it is higher), and in the Reagan years (when it is very low).[25] Foreign policy bills show even less variation; the proportion of consensual votes for bills the president favored was low in every administration. Clearly, there was usually at least a small minority willing to disagree with the president. On defense bills, however, the existence, and then the shattering, of the defense consensus is clearly illustrated. Consensual support for the president's position declined from 100 percent under Eisenhower to virtually nothing under Carter and Reagan. Thus we can see that, even from this limited perspective, there was a noteworthy difference between defense issues and domestic and foreign policy issues regarding the amount of conflict, and a substantial change on defense over time.

Issues and Conflict in the Amendment Process

As the discussion of reform indicated, there were few record votes on amendments before 1971, and they are not comparable to those that occurred after that date. Thus our analysis of first-degree amendments must be confined to the 92d through the 100th Congresses.[26] First, in figure 2, we see trends regarding presidential support for amendments.

With only three Nixon-Ford Congresses, those years are all grouped together. However, the large numbers of amendments in the Reagan years permit us to separate his two terms. We see that Republican presidents were more likely to support amendments on domestic issues than was Carter,

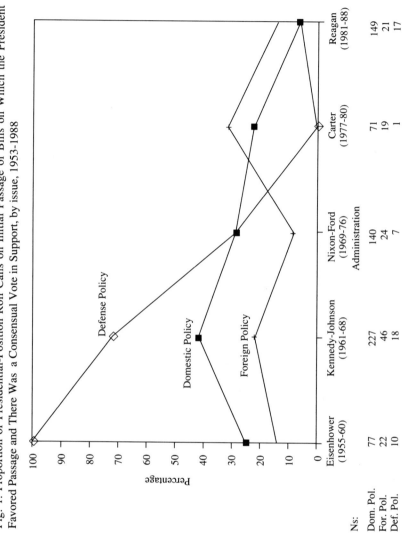

Fig. 1. Proportion of Presidential-Position Roll Calls on Initial Passage of Bills on Which the President Favored Passage and There Was a Consensual Vote in Support, by issue, 1953-1988

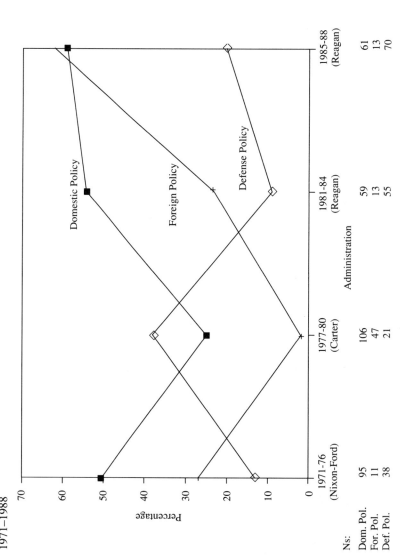

Fig. 2. Proportion of Presidential-Position Amendments on Which the President Favored Passage, by issue, 1971–1988

Percentage

Domestic Policy

Foreign Policy

Defense Policy

Administration

	1971-76 (Nixon-Ford)	1977-80 (Carter)	1981-84 (Reagan)	1985-88 (Reagan)
Ns:				
Dom. Pol.	95	106	59	61
For. Pol.	11	47	13	13
Def. Pol.	38	21	55	70

reflecting the difference between divided versus united government on those matters, but there is little trend visible among the Republican presidents. Defense is the mirror image of domestic issues. Republican presidents had a low propensity to support amendments over time, and the proportion favored by Carter was twice that of any of the Republicans. In foreign policy, we are saddled with very few cases, except under Carter. Except in the second Reagan term, presidents supported only a relatively small percentage of amendments.[27] These data would seem to support the conclusion that Republican presidents were more satisfied with the committee bills dealing with defense (and generally with foreign policy as well) than with those on domestic issues. The reverse, however, was true for Carter.[28] Thus there appears to have been a Democratic presidential advantage within the committee system on foreign policy relative to domestic issues, and a Republican presidential advantage on defense. This is precisely what we would expect from the earlier theoretical discussion.

Parallel data that show which party provided greater support for amendments are presented in figure 3. If the proportion of Democrats voting aye is greater than the proportion of Republicans, we will term the amendment "Democrat favored," and the reverse situation will be "Republican favored."[29]

The proportion of domestic policy amendments that were Republican favored increased from the Nixon-Ford years to the Carter administration and stayed steady thereafter. On foreign policy, before the Reagan years, the Republican-favored proportion was even higher than on domestic issues. Indeed, under Carter, more than nine of ten foreign policy amendments had greater Republican support. Defense issues, however, show the reverse picture, as we would expect from the arguments above. The prodefense committees largely satisfied the Republicans, and it was usually the Democrats who had the incentive to try to change things. It is also worth noting the sharp changes in the number of amendments. Foreign policy amendments sharply increased in number under Carter (from about two per year to almost twelve) and then dropped back again under Reagan. For defense issues, on the other hand, the average annual number was steady under Carter (around six), and then it jumped sharply (to about fourteen per year, and then further to seventeen).

Next we turn to the question of presidential success on amendments (see figure 4). Not surprisingly, Carter was more successful than Nixon-Ford in both domestic and foreign policy, since the degree of shared preferences was greater between the president and the House majority. In Reagan's first term, the rate of success on both issues dropped somewhat, and then it dropped again substantially in the second term. With regard to defense, the president's success varied little from Nixon through Reagan's first four years, but here too success dropped in the second term. Two conclusions are warranted

Fig. 3. Proportion of Presidential-Position Amendments That Were Republican Favored, by Issue, 1971–1988

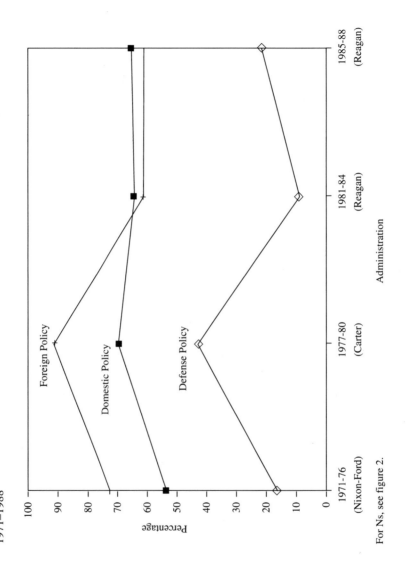

For Ns, see figure 2.

Fig. 4. Proportion of Presidential-Position Amendments on Which the President's Position Was Supported by a Majority of Members, by Issue, 1971–1988

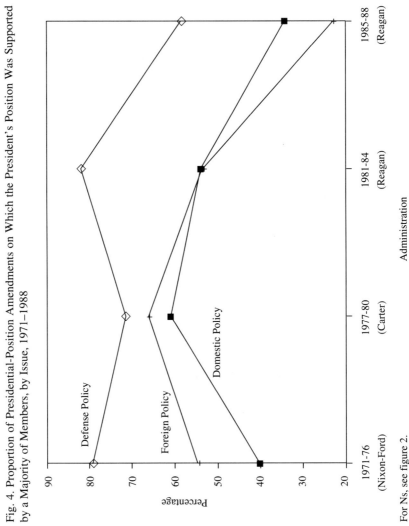

For Ns, see figure 2.

here. First, in all four periods presidents were more successful on defense than on the other issues, although the difference was small under Carter. Second, Reagan was much less successful in his second term in getting the House to respond to his preferences on amendments on all issues than he or his predecessors had been earlier.

These results are consistent with the earlier discussion of the impact of institutional and preference changes on the shaping of committee bills. I argued that a major development was the shifting preference patterns within and between the parties. Those changes are illustrated with respect to conflict about amendments in figures 5 and 6. Figure 5 shows the degree of partisan disagreement. It displays the average "party difference" (i.e., the absolute difference in the proportion of Democrats and Republicans voting aye) on amendments. There is no variation on domestic issues, but considerable change is apparent on foreign and defense issues. On the former, partisanship increased sharply under Carter, as the Republicans strongly attacked his internationalist policies,[30] and then it declined in Reagan's first term. In the next four years partisanship increased again as the content of the amendments shifted. For defense amendments, however, partisanship increased from the Carter era through the Reagan years. So across issues we see that partisanship was higher in the Nixon-Ford years on domestic issues than on foreign and defense policies, but by Reagan's second term the reverse was true.

In figure 6, we see the analogous data for sectional disagreement among Democrats: the average absolute difference in the percentage voting aye between northern and southern Democrats. On domestic issues, disagreement decreased between the Nixon-Ford years and the Carter administration, and then decreased again between the two Reagan terms. For foreign policy, the sectional difference declined in the Reagan years compared to the earlier period. Finally, on defense, the only notable change is from the first to the second Reagan term. So on all three issues there is a reduction of sectional disagreement across these administrations, but the timing is somewhat different, coming earlier on domestic issues and later on defense policy. In the context of this reduction, however, it still remained true in the second Reagan term that disagreement among Democrats was greater on defense than on other issues. Having examined these patterns of conflict over alternatives at the amendment stage, we can now turn to consider the corresponding evidence regarding bill passage.

Issues and Conflict on Bill Passage

Figure 7 shows the proportion of bills within each administration on which the president favored passage. As with amendments, bills passed by consensual votes must be excluded, which (as we saw from the data in fig. 1) wipes out almost all defense bills except under Reagan. Thus the figures will

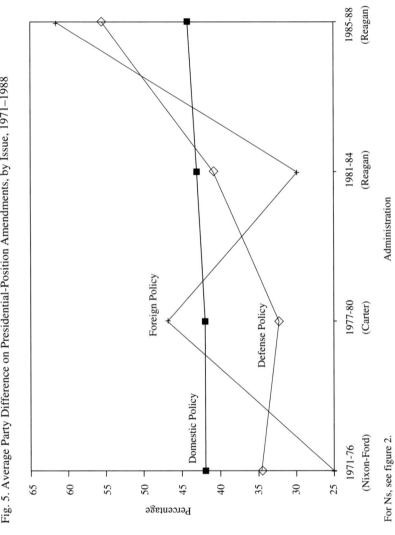

Fig. 5. Average Party Difference on Presidential-Position Amendments, by Issue, 1971–1988

For Ns, see figure 2.

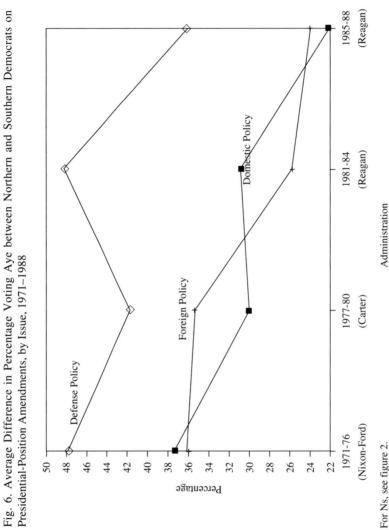

Fig. 6. Average Difference in Percentage Voting Aye between Northern and Southern Democrats on Presidential-Position Amendments, by Issue, 1971–1988

For Ns, see figure 2.

Fig. 7. Proportion of Presidential-Position Bills on Which the President Favored Passage, on Initial Passage, by Issue, 1955–1988

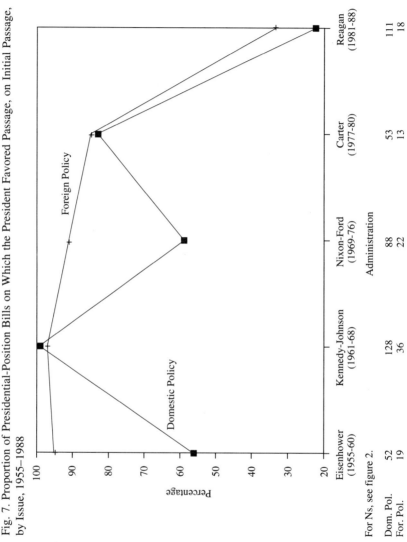

For Ns, see figure 2.

	Eisenhower (1955-60)	Kennedy-Johnson (1961-68)	Nixon-Ford (1969-76)	Carter (1977-80)	Reagan (1981-88)
Dom. Pol.	52	128	88	53	111
For. Pol.	19	36	22	13	18

display the data only for foreign and domestic issues, but I will contrast these with the Reagan defense data as we proceed.

The trends in presidential support on domestic bills match exactly what we would expect according to the shifts back and forth between divided and united government. Under Democratic presidents, almost all bills were endorsed, while under Eisenhower and Nixon-Ford, the president favored only somewhat more than half the bills. Then in the Reagan presidency, the rate of approval dropped below one in four. For foreign policy bills, on the other hand, both Democratic and Republican presidents supported the overwhelming proportion of bills until Reagan, who favored only one-third of them. In addition, Reagan supported passage of only half of the fourteen defense bills on which he took a position.[31] Clearly, before the Reagan presidency, partisan control of the presidency mattered significantly in the ability of the president to achieve what he wanted on domestic issues, but not on foreign policy and defense.

In figure 8, we see the trend in the share of bills that were Democrat favored. Under Eisenhower and Kennedy-Johnson, the share of foreign policy bills favored more by Democrats was markedly higher than for domestic bills, reflecting the greater coincidence of views among Democrats on foreign policy that we noted earlier. Also, in the Reagan administration the share of bills on *both* issues that was Democrat favored was almost as high as that under Democratic presidents.[32]

Figure 9 shows the average party difference among Democrats on the bill passage votes. On domestic issues, the degree of partisan division declined in the Nixon-Ford years, as issue preferences within the parties became more heterogeneous, but it climbed back to previous levels under Reagan. In contrast, before the Reagan years partisan differences were muted on foreign policy bills under Republicans, but they grew (although not to domestic policy levels) under Democrats. During Reagan's presidency, however, partisan division was as great on foreign policy as on domestic issues, and on defense it was were even greater still (56%). Thus the pattern of presidential-congressional interaction under divided government on foreign and defense bills appears to have shifted noticeably. Those issues had become more conflictual and more partisan.[33]

CONCLUSIONS

The literature on the two-presidencies hypothesis sought to ascertain whether the president had an advantage in the legislative process on foreign and defense policy issues relative to domestic matters. Most analysts agreed that if there was an advantage at one time, it had largely disappeared sometime between the beginning and the end of the Kennedy-Johnson years. Some researchers argued that the phenomenon did persist to a degree past that point, but that it was confined to Republican presidents and to less important

Fig. 8. Proportion of Presidential-Position Bills That Were Democrat Favored, on Initial Passage, by Issue, 1955–1988

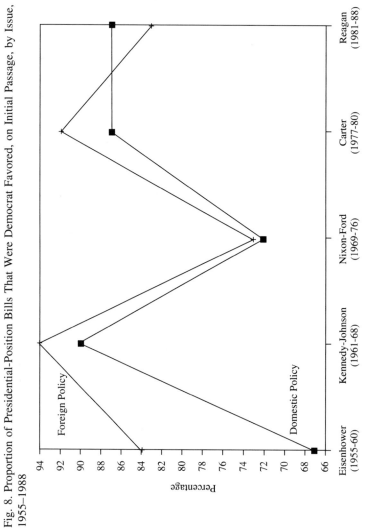

For Ns, see figure 7.

Fig. 9. Average Party Difference on Presidential-Position Bills, on Initial Passage, by Issue, 1955–1988

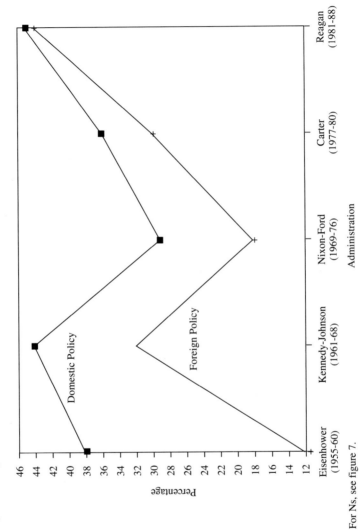

For Ns, see figure 7.

issues. In this analysis I sought to examine these questions from a somewhat different perspective, looking at the roll-call data in new ways and controlling for considerations that earlier researchers did not deal with. I will now summarize the conclusions that seem warranted by the analysis.

1. The evidence indicates that there was a presidential advantage on foreign and defense policy relative to domestic issues, and that the advantage persisted, to a degree, into the 1980s. The advantage was rooted in the organizational structure of the House (especially in the nature of the committee system), and in the degree of overlap of preferences between the president and the membership of relevant committees and of the House at large. During the terms of Presidents Eisenhower, Kennedy, and Johnson, committees were strong and there was substantial agreement between the president and the principal foreign and defense policy committees on matters within their jurisdictions. In addition, there was great consensus among the membership on defense matters. Although there was much less consensus on foreign policy, amendment rules and the power of committees and their leaders limited the ability to challenge decisions on the floor. As a consequence, the presidents generally got what they wanted on these issues. Virtually no conflict was visible on defense bills. On domestic issues, Eisenhower was less successful than on foreign and defense policy, because of the greater conflict rooted in partisan differences on those matters.

During the Nixon-Ford years, institutional arrangements changed in the House, and so did the distribution of preferences within and between the parties. Northern Democrats dropped out of the defense consensus and sought to use the revitalized floor amendment process to change policy. That was the arena where conflict occurred, because president-committee agreement remained high. Such agreement also remained substantial on foreign policy issues.

On some defense issues President Carter shared the views of conservative Democrats and Republicans, while on others he agreed with northern Democrats. Thus, since the armed services committee retained a conservative majority, Carter had more difficulty getting that committee to shape its bills in accordance with his positions than he did with committees dealing with foreign or domestic issues.

President Reagan's situation was largely the reverse of Carter's. It was *only* on defense matters that his views substantially overlapped with those of a majority on the committee of jurisdiction. Therefore he was less likely to support amendments in that area than in others, was more likely to have his position on amendments supported on the floor, and was more likely to be satisfied with the bills that resulted after the amendment process was completed. Reagan's advantage on defense was the result of the continuing sectional divisions among Democrats on that issue. As that division declined so did his advantage.

2. As the points just made and the earlier analysis indicate, there are noteworthy differences between defense and foreign policy, as well as between them and domestic issues. The differences spring partly from the makeup of the committees with primary jurisdiction in each area, and partly from the different degrees to which the preferences of particular presidents coincided with the preferences of committee members and of the House as a whole.

Eisenhower, Kennedy, and Johnson got the House to go along with what they wanted on foreign and defense policies not primarily because they had great information advantages or because they were superior leaders. Rather it was because their views were shared by the committees that controlled these areas and (to a lesser degree) by the membership of the House. When, under later presidents, the degree of agreement declined and committees became less dominant, presidents became less successful.

3. The impact of divided government on the existence of a presidential advantage in foreign and defense policy was not one-directional. That is, it was not the case that an advantage existed under divided government (or under Republican presidents, which was the same thing) and then disappeared when partisan control was unified. The data on bills from the era of strong committees indicate that presidential success on foreign and defense issues varied little between Eisenhower and the succeeding Democratic presidents. The amendment data from later years indicate that Carter maintained an advantage on foreign policy relative to domestic issues, but that he supported more attempts to change defense bills than he did in either of the other areas. Reagan, on the other hand, by his second term, exhibited more success on defense than on other issues, but no advantage on foreign policy relative to domestic matters.

These results suggest a more general point about divided government. Many analysts have decried the persistence of divided government in recent decades, arguing that it has undermined the federal government's ability to deal with national problems, leading to bitter conflict and policy stalemate.[34] The results presented here indicate that such consequences are neither theoretically automatic nor empirically inevitable. Instead, the impact of divided government depends on the kinds of policy preferences among government officials that are produced by the electoral decisions of voters.[35] If electoral forces produce consensus between the parties on issues (as used to be true on foreign and defense matters), divided government will not matter very much. If instead there is preference conflict across party lines (as has become true on international as well as domestic issues), then disagreement and stalemate will characterize divided government.[36]

4. Finally, it is appropriate to consider the relationship between this analysis and Paul Peterson's discussion in the first chapter in this volume. I agree that the United States provides a "hard test" of the version of

international relations theory he outlines, but I think there is potential compatibility at many points between his argument and mine. Nothing in my analysis disputes his view that "the international system greatly constrains the choices of the United States government," although clearly my results are incompatible with any suggestion that national choices are determined exclusively by the external environment, not also by domestic pressures. Moreover, it is true, as he points out, that majorities on the committees with the most direct focus on international issues have tended to have the greatest agreement with presidential viewpoints.

Where I do disagree with Peterson's analysis is with regard to his treatment of concepts like the "long-term interest of the nation." For example, he argues that under Carter and Reagan, Congress became critical because "the president's policy proposals constituted a dubious assessment of the country's long-term interest." These statements, and others like them, treat the "national interest" as some objective reality that some politicians accept and others ignore to pursue narrower selfish interests. To test international relations theory, as Peterson has outlined it, we would need to be able to specify—a priori and in some objective fashion—what is in the national interest and which policies involve a "realistic assessment of the international context." I do not believe that this is a feasible task. Rather I believe that my analysis indicates that disagreements about what is in the national interest and what is a realistic assessment of the world situation have become the stuff of partisan political conflict—within the Congress and in the country at large.

As with other political issues, these matters involve not only objective issues but value conflicts. If majorities of the committees of jurisdiction share the views of the president, this is owing to selection bias in choosing the membership, not because they have greater expertise. After all, these committees are internally divided on these issues. The president's dominance on defense and foreign policy declined over time (although it did not disappear) precisely because citizens and members of Congress were no longer willing to defer to the executive in the determination of what is in the national interest and which policies will protect that interest.

Chapter Six

★ ★ ★

CONGRESSIONAL
PARTY LEADERS

★ ★ ★

Steven S. Smith

Partisanship has been a common feature
of congressional voting alignments in the foreign and defense policy arena
since the 1960s. By January 1991, when voting on a resolution authorizing
the use of force in the Persian Gulf proved highly partisan, no one was
surprised. The fact that top leaders of the two parties took very different
points of view on such a salient issue in national security affairs was quite
unremarkable by that time.

In many respects, congressional party leaders are the missing link in recent
discussions of partisanship and interbranch relations in the field of foreign and
defense policy. Whole books on the congressional role in foreign policy making
have been written that scarcely mention central party leaders. This is unfortu-
nate and misleading. A growing gap in views between the branches or between the
parties is not reflected automatically in legislation or voting behavior. In most
cases, the forbearance, if not active support, of central party leaders is essential
to gaining a chamber or party response in opposition to presidential actions.

In this chapter I describe how the behavior of top congressional party
leaders has changed in response to the evolving context of foreign policy
decision making.[1] Important differences between House and Senate leaders
are uncovered, and, in general, it is found that party leaders have adopted
more partisan patterns of support for presidential positions in foreign policy,
assumed more prominent roles as party spokesmen in the foreign policy
arena, evolved more partisan patterns of consultation with presidents, and
sought to mobilize colleagues in the foreign policy arena more frequently.

THE LOGIC OF LEADERSHIP PARTICIPATION

I view congressional leaders as sophisticated individuals who, with certain
resources and under certain institutional rules, pursue deliberate strategies

designed to produce desirable outcomes.[2] The desirable outcomes are defined in terms of political interests. As elected party officials, congressional party leaders give high priority to maintaining or gaining majority status for their party and to public policies supported by their party colleagues. On the personal side, leaders may have personal policy or political goals to be served. Such goals may move leaders to resist or encourage actions supported by their party colleagues. We account for changes in leaders' behavior by noting changes in colleagues' demands, changes in leaders' resources and views, and changes in the formal rules of the legislative game.[3]

Central to leaders' strategies is the fact that they must often obtain the support of a majority of their chamber colleagues and the concurrence of the other chamber to exercise their potential influence over policy. But congressional leaders do not control their institution as well as presidents control the executive branch. Leaders cannot hire and fire their colleagues or unilaterally appoint committee and subcommittee leaders, and on most matters rank-and-file members may support competing policies without fear of retribution. Thus, while leaders generally are the most influential members of their parties, their control over the policy choices of their own institution is limited.

Furthermore, it is well understood that constraints on congressional party leaders are more severe in the area of foreign policy than in domestic policy. The president's advantages in formal powers and resources, as well as the public's expectations, put leaders in a more reactive and defensive posture in foreign affairs. Moreover, there is a fundamental difference between the strategic contexts common in domestic and foreign policy arenas. Simply put, the president is in a better position to mold the policy status quo in foreign policy than in domestic policy. Far more of domestic policy is codified in statutes and agency regulations and subject to relatively little direct manipulation by presidents. Changing domestic policy usually requires the approval of the Congress, where procedural biases favor the defenders of the status quo. But foreign policy is more readily manipulated by a president. Those who seek to modify the foreign policy status quo established by the president find procedural biases working against them.[4]

The open question is whether the demands placed on congressional leaders, leaders' resources, or the rules of the legislative game have changed. Relevant arguments about the changing political context of congressional party leaders now constitute a loosely structured story about the "resurgent Congress":

As television became the major source of news for Americans in the 1950s and 1960s, it brought the world into American living rooms, making the politicization of international affairs easier, if not inevitable.

In the same period, foreign policy attitudes in the mass public and policy elite began to align with domestic policy attitudes, which gave foreign policy divisions a more partisan cast.

Technological advances in transportation and communication furthered the integration of domestic and international affairs, and the number of organized interests with international agendas grew.

Local party organizations withered and legislators became more independent of party bosses, increasing legislators' electoral dependence on interest groups and encouraging legislators to pursue individually defined legislative agendas.

The democratization of Congress in the early 1970s—due primarily to weakening the autonomy of full committee chairs—gave rank-and-file members the resources and opportunities to pursue their own policy agendas.

The increasing demands of foreign policy on presidents, the increasing importance of foreign policy to presidents, and presidents' distrust of the foreign policy bureaucracy has led to a centralization of foreign policy decision making within the executive branch.

Prolonged divided government—a Democratic Congress with Republican presidents—has further intensified partisan motivations in foreign affairs and stimulated congressional activity.

Thus, a set of mutually reinforcing developments in and out of Congress led Congress to increase its potential influence over the direction of foreign policy by strengthening its oversight capacity and imposing new constraints on the executive branch during the 1970s.

If the hyperbole is forgiven (the model seems grossly overspecified), the resurgent Congress thesis makes sense. Descriptively, it seems accurate enough. Constitutional, institutional, and political obstacles to congressional effectiveness remain, as does congressional indifference in some areas of foreign policy, but meaningful involvement in the foreign policy arena is now a pursuit of many more members and committees of Congress.[5] Analytically, the resurgent Congress thesis challenges the "two-presidencies" view that congressional acquiescence in foreign policy is, or was, the product of inherent institutional disabilities and a strong prescriptive norm of deference to presidents. Rather, it suggests that policy preferences and political interests drive congressional activity in foreign policy as well as domestic policy (Oldfield and Wildavsky 1989, 54–59).

Four features of the resurgent Congress story suggest that the resurgence in congressional activity in foreign policy is associated, perhaps as both cause and effect, with more-assertive party leadership.

First, as foreign policy attitudes assumed a more partisan alignment, both congressional parties became more cohesive on foreign policy questions. What theory we have about congressional leadership suggests that strong party leadership flows from high party cohesiveness. Cohesive parties tend to empower their leaders to act on their behalf—leaders become more assertive and partisan (Cooper and Brady 1981). In contrast, members of an internally divided party tend not to trust strong leaders, and leaders themselves generally prefer not to intensify intraparty divisions by choosing sides. Parties that are more polarized in the foreign policy arena are expected to be associated with more assertiveness and partisanship on the part of their leaders.

Second, leaders may have filled the void created by the committee reforms of the early 1970s, which weakened full committee chairs. In the House, much of the power flowed to subcommittee chairmen and rank-and-file committee members, but they could not mobilize the same resources and exercise the same agenda control that full committee chairs once did. One result was greater committee vulnerability on the floor. The power vacuum created opportunities for the majority party leaders to exercise greater influence over policy outcomes. And in the House, the enhancement of the Speaker's control over committee assignments, bill referral, and the rules committee strengthened the majority party leadership's capacity to act.

Third, the strategic context in which some foreign policy is made has changed in an important way. Many of the new constraints imposed on the executive branch, particularly requirements for congressional approval (arms sales, use of military force, etc.), limited the president's ability to manipulate the policy status quo. Requests for congressional approval from the president give congressional party leaders, as gatekeepers for Congress's agenda, a source of leverage with the president they often lacked in the past.

And fourth, the centralization of foreign policy decision making within the executive branch has consequences for Congress. Interbranch relations operating at the level of subcommittee chairmen and deputy secretaries are less relevant. Only top party leaders are likely to regularly command the attention of presidents and their top advisers. As a result, rank-and-file members seeking to affect administration policy must work with central party leaders.

Before we get carried away with the logic of more-assertive party leadership, it is important to recognize that the resurgent Congress thesis actually has nothing explicit to say about congressional party leaders. In most accounts of Congress and foreign policy, central leaders are ignored and the emphasis is placed on the weakening of the conservative coalition and the old-guard, southern committee chairmen who acted as its enforcers. The associated empowerment of subcommittees and diffusion of staff resources represented a genuine decentralization of power. This version is not entirely consistent with a story about newly assertive central party leaders.

Moreover, discussions of the resurgent Congress thesis gloss over distinctions between the House and Senate. Traditionally, the Senate's constitutional role in treaty ratification and the confirmation of cabinet and ambassadorial appointees gave it a more central place in foreign policy making than the House. Further, the Senate's distinctive floor practices, which permit extended debate and nongermane amendments, require that its leaders be involved more frequently in floor consideration of controversial legislation, including measures related to foreign policy. And the Senate's higher public profile creates opportunities for its leaders to shape public opinion that often are not available to House leaders.

Yet many of the institutional changes that are noted, particularly the changing distribution of power within Congress, concern the House much more than the Senate. Given the traditional weaknesses of the House in foreign policy making, it might be that the expansion of oversight capacity and the addition of executive branch reporting and approval requirements improved the position of the House, relative to the president, even more than that of the Senate (Blechman 1990b, 112). And the stronger position of liberal Democrats in the House, particularly in the 1980s, made the House the more likely site for confrontations with the president on foreign policy matters.

The lesson is that change in the functions and influence of leadership in an institution as complex as Congress is often not unidirectional or uniform. Many possibilities are not realized and some are realized in one house but not the other. The distribution of power is somewhat fluid and contingent. Clearly, the strategies of party leaders in the resurgent Congress warrant closer examination.

Leaders' strategies can be treated as constituting *policy positions* and *modes* and *levels* of involvement. The logic of more-assertive party leaders implies that

congressional party leaders will show increasingly partisan patterns in their support for presidential foreign *policy positions*;

congressional party leaders will show increasing activity as *party spokesmen* in the foreign policy arena;

congressional party leaders will show increasingly partisan patterns of consultation with presidents, with opposition party leaders becoming less important as *intermediaries* between the White House and their Hill colleagues on foreign policy matters;

congressional party leaders will show increasing activity as *policy leaders* in the foreign policy arena; and

these changes will be greater in the House than in the Senate.

The following sections examine the pattern of change in leaders' positions and involvement since the mid-1950s.

LEADERS' POLICY POSITIONS

The degree of policy agreement between Congress and presidents is central to all arguments about a resurgent Congress, so it is appropriate to consider first the support congressional leaders have given presidents' foreign policy positions since the 1950s. Both the roll-call record and journalistic accounts of leaders' positions on the most important foreign policy questions confirm that leaders' policy positions have a strikingly partisan pattern in the period since the 1950s.

Leaders' voting records confirm the distinctive character of the foreign policy arena in the 1950s. Jon Bond and Richard Fleisher have calculated, for the 1953–88 period, the frequency that floor leaders supported the president on roll-call votes when the president's position was known to Congressional Quarterly (1990, 166–67).[6] Figure 1, derived from the Bond-Fleisher data, indicates the differences between the Democratic and Republican leaders' presidential support in the domestic and foreign policy arenas. The figure demonstrates that leaders of the president's congressional party have consistently provided more support than the opposition party's leaders in both foreign and domestic policy since the Eisenhower administration. However, during the Eisenhower administration, the difference between the two sets of leaders was quite small in the foreign policy arena. The difference in presidential support between Senate Democratic leader Lyndon Johnson and Republican leaders William Knowland and Everett Dirksen was only 11 percent, with Johnson supporting Eisenhower over three-fourths of the time.

The congruence of the parties' leaders on foreign policy evaporated the instant John Kennedy was sworn into office. The Senate's new majority leader, Mike Mansfield, gave Kennedy's foreign policy program substantial support, but Republican Dirksen's support dropped well below the level he provided Eisenhower. As the Vietnam War intensified during the Johnson administration, however, Mansfield's support declined and Dirksen's increased, yielding a smaller difference between the two leaders. But in the early 1970s, under Republican presidents Nixon and Ford, the foreign policy differences between the parties' leaders in the Senate became *even greater* than their domestic policy differences.

Partisan differences also grew among House party leaders, although the break with the past associated with the Kennedy administration was not as sharp as in the Senate. Democratic floor leader John McCormack differed from Republicans Martin and Halleck by only 13 percent in his support for Eisenhower. For no subsequent president was the difference between the two floor leaders nearly so small. The difference was greater in foreign policy than in domestic policy under only one administration, Jimmy Carter's, and then only by a trivial amount.

A similar pattern of change occurred on a very small set of major foreign policy issues. Table 1 indicates the apparent amount of agreement between

Fig. 1. Differences in Presidential Support between Democratic and Republican Leaders, 1955–1988

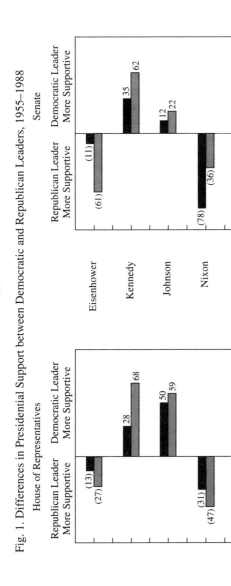

Data from Bond and Fleisher, 1990, 166–67. Each entry is the Democratic leader's presidential support score minus the Republican leader's presidential support score.

Table 1

Congressional Leaders' Agreement with the President's Position on Major Foreign Policy Issues, 1955–1987

| | Senate Leaders[a] | | | | House Leaders[b] | | | | |
| | President's Party | | Opposition Party | | President's Party | | Opposition Party | | No. of |
Congress	Agree	Disagree	Agree	Disagree	Agree	Disagree	Agree	Disagree	Major Issues
84th (1955–56)	9	1	6	1	1	0	6	1	14
86th (1959–60)	7	0	5	1	3	0	5	1	13
88th (1963–64)	6	2	5	3	5	0	1	4	13
90th (1967–68)	8	4	8	0	4	0	0	1	14
92nd (1971–72)	8	0	4	5	4	0	4	0	11
94th (1975–76)	8	0	3	3	4	0	4	0	11
96th (1979–80)	6	0	1	4	3	1	0	0	12
98th (1983–84)	4	0	2	3	6	0	2	4	11
100th (1987–88)	6	1	3	6	3	0	1	4	13
Totals	60	8	37	26	33	1	23	15	

Note: For every second Congress since 1955, the major foreign policy issues before the president were determined by examining the Department of State's Bulletin and Congressional Quarterly Weekly Report. A set of issues was identified, and congressional leaders' agreement or disagreement with the president was determined by scrutinizing the Weekly Report, the New York Times, and leaders' and presidents' biographies. More than half of the issues did not involve legislative action. Leaders' positions were not discernible for all issues, so the number of major issues does not equal the sum of agreements and disagreements for any leader. Agreement is indicated whenever there was at least partial agreement between the leader and the president.

[a]Senate majority leader and Senate minority leader.

[b]House Speaker and House minority leader.

congressional leaders and presidents on major issues, many of which did not involve legislative action. As the table indicates, general agreement with the president changed to substantial disagreement with him, particularly among leaders of the opposite party, during the 1960s. The contrasts are stark: whereas Johnson and Rayburn each agreed with Eisenhower on five of the six issues on which they had discernible views in 1959–60, Mansfield agreed with Nixon on only four of nine issues in 1971–72, and Byrd agreed with Reagan only partially on three of nine issues in 1987–88. But the pattern of change is uneven. Most noteworthy is that Senate Republican leader Dirksen gave his friend President Johnson substantial support in 1967–68.[7]

Underlying these changes in leaders' behavior are important changes in policy preferences. In the 1950s Senate Democratic leader Lyndon Johnson was a central figure in foreign and defense policy. While serving as his party's floor leader, he chaired an armed services subcommittee on preparedness and later chaired the defense appropriations subcommittee. Overall, he proved somewhat less supportive of Eisenhower's foreign policy than his Republican counterparts (Taft, Knowland, and Dirksen) by a margin of 76 percent to 87 percent, respectively, but the difference on domestic policy was much greater (Bond and Fleisher 1990). Johnson's views were in line with the conservative wing of his party, led by foreign relations chairman Walter George (D-Ga.), which constituted close to half the party in the mid-1950s. Johnson shared Eisenhower's view of the American role in the world and supported Eisenhower on nearly all major foreign policy questions. He supported a toothless alternative to the Bricker amendment designed to limit presidential treaty-making power, supported Eisenhower's free trade policies, worked hard to enact the administration's ambitious foreign aid program, endorsed anticommunist policies at least as strong as Eisenhower's, and was at least as eager as Eisenhower to employ military force as a tool of foreign policy when the occasion arose in the Middle East and elsewhere.

Senate Republican leaders Taft and Knowland were, like many Republicans, more isolationist and more fervently anticommunist than Eisenhower, creating problems for the president and providing a source of amusement for Johnson. Eisenhower is the only post–World War II Republican president whose Senate leaders were, overall, more supportive of his domestic policy positions than his foreign policy positions. Nevertheless, Taft and Knowland supported Eisenhower in foreign policy roll-call voting at a high rate, exceeding Johnson by a meaningful margin. By the time Everett Dirksen became the Republican leader in 1959, Senate Republicans and their leaders had joined Eisenhower in his internationalism, and Eisenhower had moved in their direction in his willingness to employ the military against Communist insurgencies. The net result was largely congruent policy preferences among Democratic and Republican congressional leaders and the Republican president.

Thus, leaders of both Senate parties were generally supportive of President Eisenhower's positions. But this should not taken as evidence for a nonpartisan atmosphere in foreign policy making. In fact, bipartisanship ran between congressional Democratic leaders and the White House more than across parties within Congress, where the political game was more zero-sum. Senate Democratic leaders, especially Johnson, frequently criticized the administration and the Republican party (though seldom Eisenhower personally) for its foreign policy and often used the differences between Eisenhower and Senate Republicans to score political points. For Johnson, the criticism of the Republican right wing appeared to be a coherent strategy of sabotaging Republicans without directly attacking Eisenhower (Evans and Novack, 1966, chap. 9). And Republican leaders Taft and Knowland passed up few opportunities to criticize Democrats. In the first few years of the Eisenhower administration, Republicans continued to rail against the policies of the Roosevelt and Truman administrations; they were only disappointed that Eisenhower failed to change those policies as quickly and as much as they preferred. And outside of Congress the partisan exchanges between officials of the national party committees over national security matters (the missile program, the Middle East, Eastern Europe) occasionally reached a fever pitch. At times, only Eisenhower's bilateral efforts with the congressional leaders of the two parties maintained some semblance of bipartisanship in the foreign policy arena. Partisanship flourished in the foreign policy arena of the 1950s, even though interbranch conflict, particularly among elected leaders, usually remained latent.

The pattern of presidential support was similar in the House. Democratic Speaker Sam Rayburn's presidential support in foreign policy mirrored Senator Johnson's. Rayburn supported Eisenhower slightly more than Johnson in percentage terms, and he differed with Eisenhower and Johnson on no major foreign policy issue. Rayburn, like Johnson, supported the administration much less frequently in the domestic arena than the foreign arena, but compared with Johnson he was less hawkish and substantially less prone to make partisan statements or threats. House Republican leaders Joe Martin and Charlie Halleck were more moderate and supported Eisenhower's foreign policy positions more frequently than their Senate counterparts, and showed the same shift toward a more internationalist perspective during the course of the 1950s. They seemed to follow Rayburn's lead in keeping partisan rhetoric to a minimum in the foreign policy arena.

Unfortunately, it is impossible to determine the extent to which Democratic leaders' support for Eisenhower turned on the president's popularity, their personal policy preferences, Eisenhower's willingness to adjust his policies to their concerns, or their commitment to the norm of institutional deference and bipartisanship. The conventional wisdom places substantial emphasis on leaders' institutional deference and insistence on bipartisanship in foreign policy making. Both Johnson and Rayburn spoke about bipartisanship on many occasions and even made public statements in 1956 warning presidential and congressional candidates not to politicize foreign policy. Biographers of both Johnson and Rayburn emphasize that bipartisanship was genuinely, even passionately, valued. Just how much that commitment altered their policy position and strategy is the open question.

The ascension of Senator Mike Mansfield and Congressman John McCormack to the top Democratic leadership posts in the early 1960s marked a substantial change in style and substance. Although these leaders proved to be very supportive of the Kennedy foreign policy program, Mansfield began to differ with the administration on a number of issues after Johnson assumed the presidency. Mansfield opposed the escalation of the Vietnam War, although he did little about it while Johnson was in office. Only after Nixon won the White House did Mansfield take a leading role in opposition to the war. Mansfield's support for presidential foreign policy positions fell to 13 percent, a post–World War II low for any congressional party leader.

House Speaker McCormack supported Johnson's war policies and refused to support the efforts of Democratic war opponents during the Nixon years. His majority leader and successor as Speaker, Carl Albert, also supported Johnson's and Nixon's Vietnam policies, although he eventually became less supportive by the end of the Nixon years. In contrast, his majority leader and successor as Speaker, Thomas "Tip" O'Neill, led the charge against the war as Democratic whip and majority leader in the early 1970s. By the mid-1970s Democratic leaders in both chambers were supporting the foreign policy positions of Presidents Nixon and Ford on roll-call votes far less than half of the time. The decline of bipartisanship was a common theme, and presidents began to assume that cooperation from congressional leaders of the opposite party was problematic at best.

Senate Republican leaders Dirksen and Scott supported the foreign policy positions of Democrats Kennedy and Johnson on about three out of five votes and provided support on about nine of ten votes to Republicans Nixon and Ford. The result, as Figure 1 shows for the Nixon and Ford administrations, was a polarization of the Democratic and Republican leaders. Because Democrats controlled both houses, the polarization took both a partisan and an institutional cast.

Substantial differences between presidents and opposition congressional leaders continued in the Carter and Reagan administrations, with one notable exception: Senate leadership during the Carter administration. Senate Majority Leader Robert Byrd proved somewhat less supportive of Carter on foreign policy votes than is typical of recent leaders of the president's party, while Minority Leader Howard Baker proved somewhat more supportive than is typical of recent opposition leaders. Baker, in fact, played a leading role in gaining Senate approval of the enabling legislation for the Panama

Canal treaties. His public stance was much like that of his father-in-law, Everett Dirksen—that is, support the president whenever you can in foreign affairs. Nevertheless, his support for Reagan was much greater than his support for Carter in this arena, typical of the pattern of the last two decades. For example, in mid-1979 he found that he could not support Carter on SALT II, perhaps because of his interest in securing conservative support for his presidential bid. By 1980 Baker was delivering broadsides at Carter's foreign policy competence, hardly compatible with the Dirksen model.

Of course, bipartisanship continues to be a theme in leaders' rhetoric and can often be found in their behavior. For example, following the deployment of troops to Lebanon in 1983, Speaker O'Neill insisted on negotiating a resolution to implement the War Powers Act that would satisfy President Reagan, in spite of harsh criticism from fellow liberals. O'Neill insisted that the patriotic position was for Congress to work with the president to find a mutually acceptable policy, although he later changed his position on the grounds that Reagan's diplomatic efforts were inadequate. Similarly, Senate Democratic leader Byrd resisted the enactment of SALT II compliance requirements on the grounds that it should not be done without bipartisan support. He, too, changed his mind—this time after fellow Democrats protested that he was not adequately representing his party colleagues' views. The O'Neill and Byrd episodes suggest that party leaders now find it more difficult to resist rank-and-file demands for more partisan leadership than many of their predecessors did.

SERVICE AS OPINION LEADERS

All leaders since the 1950s have made interaction with the press an important part of their leadership activities. In the House, all speakers have held brief press conferences before each daily session of the House since Rayburn's era. Rayburn's successors, McCormack and Albert, refused to appear on television interview programs, although O'Neill and Wright did so selectively. Each House Republican leader has promised to gain attention to Republican views and has devised new strategies to do so. Halleck joined with Senate Republican leader Dirksen in a press conference—the "Ev and Charlie Show"—following their weekly leadership meeting, a practice that continued after Ford took over for Halleck in 1964. The joint conference was discontinued when the next Republican president was elected in 1968. House Republican leaders Rhodes and Michel were more willing to defer to other party and committee leaders to take the point in public relations; Michel seems to have allowed Newt Gingrich, his whip, to take over the function nearly entirely.

In the Senate of the mid-1950s, Democratic leader Johnson actively courted the press, applying heavy doses of the "Johnson treatment" in private interviews. He followed Rayburn's lead by instituting daily briefings before the start of each day's session and called frequent press conferences in his office as well. Republican Knowland was sometimes openly hostile to the press and had little time for regular press conferences. Dirksen started his own weekly press conferences upon assuming the floor leadership in 1959 and proved to be President Eisenhower's chief defender against the charges of Democratic critics. He became a television celebrity during the 1960s. Subsequent Senate leaders have held the daily briefings, although they have varied in their use of press conferences. Senate leaders have refused invitations to appear on television interview programs far less frequently than their House counterparts.

In the 1950s leaders' relations with the press and media appeared to serve personal rather than party purposes. Robert Peabody's 1976 examination of leadership contests, *Leadership in Congress*, makes plain that service as a party spokesman was seldom a major consideration in leadership selection in the 1950s, 1960s, and early 1970s. Service to colleagues, mastery of the mechanics of the legislative game, and position among party factions were given greater weight. Perhaps because of their weak institutional position and lack of national media coverage, only House Republicans made media skills much of an issue in leadership contests. In general, party leaders took a back seat to committee leaders as opinion leaders on matters of policy. In fact, the leading studies on party leadership of the 1960s did not catalog service as party spokesman or anything similar among the major functions or techniques of leaders (Ripley 1967, chaps. 3, 5; 1969a, 44–45; 1969b, 24).

Nevertheless, perhaps with increasing frequency, leaders have been subject to criticism for their ineffectiveness as party spokesmen. The increasing importance of television as a medium of political communication, presidents' domination of television news, and the increasing number of news programs seem to have increased the demand for telegenic leaders. Since the mid-1960s, opposition congressional leaders have sought and have been granted time on the television networks to respond to presidential addresses (Foote 1990, 33ff.). In the 1970s, differences in public relations skill were noted about Senate Republican leaders Scott and Baker and about House Democratic leaders Albert and O'Neill, as were the contrasts between Congressmen O'Neill and Wright and Senators Byrd and Mitchell in the 1980s. Again, House Republicans have been the most concerned of the four congressional parties in recent years about the media presence of their leaders. And in all four parties more leadership aides have been appointed with journalistic, media, or speech-writing expertise. By the early 1980s the spokesman's role had become so prominent as to warrant listing it among leaders' primary responsibilities (Sinclair 1983, 40–41; Davidson 1985, 236).

What leaders want most from the interaction with the press and the electronic media is favorable coverage of themselves and their party. Regrettably, I do not have a way to assess how favorable the coverage is or to apportion the influence of leaders' efforts and other factors on the nature of the coverage. But the volume of coverage is measurable, thanks to indexes of newspapers and television news broadcasts. The volume of coverage reflects leaders' efforts and newsworthiness, as well as the judgments of reporters, editors, and directors about what is newsworthy. It yields a picture of the attention gained or granted to leaders and the policy content of the coverage.

The *New York Times* is the only national newspaper with a quality index for the entire period under study. It has the additional advantage of giving substantial emphasis to foreign policy issues. The *Times*'s shortcoming as an indicator of change over time is that it altered its reporting practices in the late 1970s to include fewer but larger stories on Congress, reducing the number of stories in which leaders could be mentioned.[8] Other papers also have shifted reporting practices, resulting in a smaller number of mentions of all leaders and limiting their opportunities to influence opinion through the press. However, the *Times* index allows for an assessment of the relative standing of leaders and the relative importance of foreign policy in leaders' coverage.

Television must be considered as well. The Vanderbilt News Archive has assembled indexes and abstracts of the evening news programs of the three television broadcast networks since 1968. It should be noted that television became the major source of news for Americans only in the mid-1960s, so data on the frequency and policy context of leaders' appearances or mentions are available for most of the period in which television was a critical outlet for opinion leaders. Systematic data on newscasts other than the evening news, television interview programs, news specials, and documentaries are not available.

Change in the relative importance of foreign policy in stories mentioning congressional leaders is visible in figure 2. Before the late 1970s, the proportion of *Times* mentions involving foreign policy was higher for Senate leaders than House leaders, consistent with the traditional foreign policy roles of the two chambers. It was common for a majority of Senate leaders' coverage to be related to foreign policy, while House leaders' foreign policy coverage seldom exceeded one-third of their coverage on policy matters. Of course, leaders show great variation, with Knowland and Mansfield predictably leading other leaders in their emphasis on foreign policy.

Not until the late 1970s did a House leader—Speaker O'Neill—regularly exceed a Senate leader in foreign policy emphasis. Although he averaged fewer stories, O'Neill exceeded both Senators Byrd and Baker in the proportion of stories devoted to foreign policy issues. He attracted coverage on a number of issues: legislation to implement to the Panama Canal treaties, the deployment of troops to Lebanon, aid to El Salvador and the Nicaraguan contras, and others. Nearly all of the coverage concerned House legislative activity. But it is Speaker Jim Wright who stands out. Wright took charge of

Fig. 2. Percentage of *New York Times* Stories on Foreign Policy That Mention
Leaders, 1955–1991

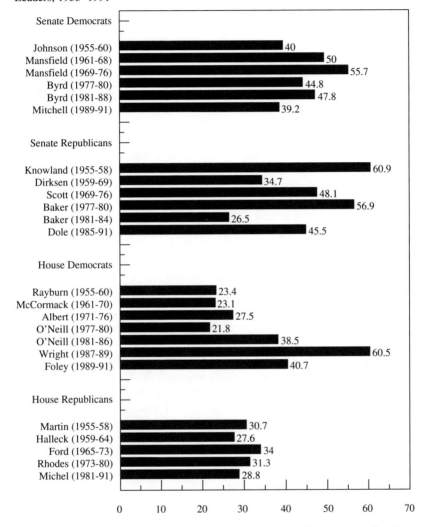

Data from New York Times Index. Each entry is the annual average of all policy-
related stories.

Central American issues for his party and, owing primarily to Central American issues, surpassed both Senate leaders in the proportion of *Times* coverage involving foreign policy.

The pattern of coverage on network news programs is not quite so clear, as figure 3 indicates. Until Senator Howard Baker's emphasis on foreign policy dipped during the first Reagan term in the early 1980s, both Senate leaders outpaced House leaders in their foreign policy emphasis. Newscast coverage of O'Neill and Baker showed nearly equal emphasis on foreign affairs during the early 1980s. But, as with the *Times*, Speaker Wright's foreign policy efforts are reflected in his appearances and mentions on the network news programs.

Even more impressive is the fact that during the 1980s the absolute number of television news stories mentioning the Speaker in a foreign policy context exploded, as figure 4 illustrates. During most of the 1980s, House leaders were more prominent than they had been previously, and when House activity on a variety of Middle East and Central American issues was salient in the mid-1980s, House leaders gained a significant presence on the network news programs. In some years Speaker O'Neill's foreign policy count exceeded the combined total for the Senate's two party leaders.

Judging from the *New York Times* and television newscasts, then, Senate leaders' distinctive position as opinion leaders in foreign affairs weakened as House leaders, particularly the Speaker, gained more prominence. The foreign policy emphasis of Senate leaders' coverage has not changed systematically since the 1950s. But House leaders have come to look more like Senate leaders in the emphasis they place on foreign policy. These changes appear to correspond with the rise of the House as a player in foreign policy making and the partisan character of House participation in that arena.

SERVICE AS INTERMEDIARIES

One of congressional leaders' special responsibilities is to serve as intermediaries between Capitol Hill and the White House. The specific nature of the relationship between presidents and leaders is a function of choices made by each participant, although the initiative in this relationship generally rests with the president. No congressional leader has been unwilling to consult with the president, although presidents have sometimes preferred to avoid or ignore congressional leaders. And, of course, the relationship between presidents and Hill leaders develops within a web of relationships between the two branches. Other members of Congress interact with the president and administration officials, usually in a manner not controlled by party leaders, creating opportunities and constraints for the top leaders. The attitudes and functions of cabinet officers and presidential assistants influence the relationship between leaders and presidents as well.

Unfortunately, mapping the relationships between presidents and Hill leaders is difficult. The relationships are often quite personal, and good

Fig. 3. Percentage of Network Television Evening News Stories on Foreign Policy
That Mention Leaders, 1968–1991

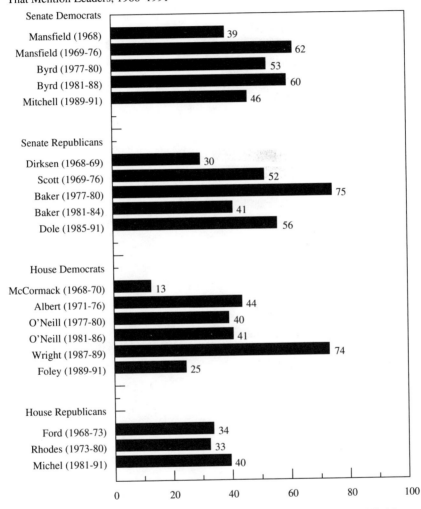

Data from *Television News Index and Abstracts* (Nashville, Tenn: Vanderbilt News
Archives). Each entry is the annual average of all policy-related stories.

Fig. 4. Number of Network Television Evening News Stories on Foreign Policy That
Mention Leaders, 1968–1991

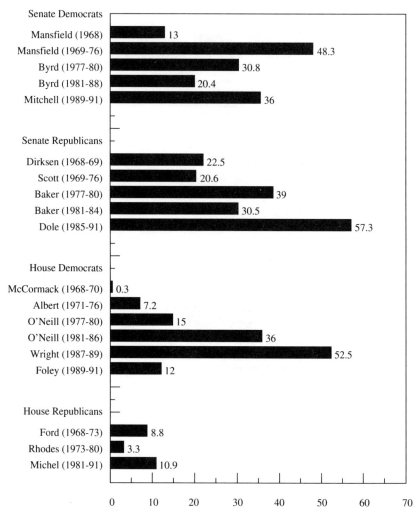

Data from *Television News Index and Abstracts*s (Nashville, Tenn: Vanderbilt News
Archives). Each entry is the annual average of all policy-related stories.

records of meetings and phone conversations often do not exist. In the absence of a thorough search of presidential libraries, only a few generalizations can be offered with much confidence. The most important of which is that consultation between presidents and leaders is now more highly structured by party than it was in the 1950s and 1960s.

Eisenhower's relationship with congressional leaders is often touted as the model of bipartisan cooperation. During his two terms, he held two hundred weekly breakfast meetings with his own party's leaders while Congress was in session.[9] These involved the top two or three leaders from each chamber, with a committee leader joining the group on occasion as the agenda warranted.[10] The agenda usually involved both domestic and foreign policy matters, with 75 percent of the meetings including discussion of at least one foreign policy issue. Frank discussion often took place at these meetings, but the quality of the discussion seemed to decline over the years. Eisenhower grew tired of listening to Knowland lecture him, particularly on policy toward Communist China. By the time Knowland left the Senate in 1958, according to one historian, Eisenhower had turned many of these meetings into "pep talks on holding down spending" (Ambrose 1984, 549).

Eisenhower's more informal contact with Republican leaders exhibited great variation (Ambrose 1984; Burns 1963; Donovan 1956; Greenstein 1982; MacNeil 1966). Senate leader Taft was granted open access to the White House and used it extensively to push his orthodox Republican views on budgetary and other domestic matters. Taft's death left a vacuum. Knowland and House leader Martin did not have nearly as much legislative influence as Taft and, perhaps in part for that reason, did not consult Eisenhower as frequently on a private basis in the realm of foreign policy. On Senate matters, Knowland's whip, Everett Dirksen, became Eisenhower's most important lieutenant. Dirksen towed the line on foreign policy requests from the president, began to have personal breakfasts with him with some frequency, and became an important consultant of Eisenhower's, at least with respect to the legislative implications of policy options. In the House, Republican whip Charles Halleck appears to have played a similar role. The relationship blossomed further after the 1958 elections, when Dirksen and Halleck became their parties' floor leaders.

Eisenhower did not invite Democratic leaders Johnson and Rayburn while Taft was majority leader in 1953, but began to hold formal and informal meetings with them thereafter. Between early 1954, after Knowland took over for Taft, and the end of his second term in 1960, Eisenhower called nineteen formal bipartisan leadership meetings (*President Eisenhower's Meetings*). The first of these meetings was called to stem sharp partisan exchanges about China policy and administration leaking of the Yalta papers. The bipartisan meetings were devoted almost exclusively to foreign and defense policy matters (the exception concerned the constitutional amendment on presidential succession). The setting was not conducive to personal consultation and candid exchange. The meetings took place over lunch, and the usual format was a briefing, normally by cabinet officers, followed by legislators' comments and questions. And the mean number of attendees from Congress was 21.9, reflecting the presence of leaders from the appropriations, foreign policy, and armed services committees as well as top party leaders. Informative exchanges occurred at these meetings, but it was not the best forum for Johnson and Rayburn to consult with Eisenhower.

After the Democrats regained majority status in both houses in the 1954 elections, Eisenhower began to cultivate the good will of Johnson and Rayburn in evening get-togethers over cocktails. According to one report, the threesome eventually met this way at least once a month (Evans and Novak 1966, 168–69). These sessions were sometimes supplemented with meetings that included foreign policy committee leaders, particularly Senators Walter George and William Fulbright. Genuine consultation appears to have occurred at these meetings: there is evidence that Eisenhower was influenced by what he learned from time to time. The interparty, interbranch relationship appeared to be a truly cooperative, consultative one.

Beginning in 1957 a series of foreign developments occasioned objections to Eisenhower's policies from Johnson and even from the more deferential Rayburn.[11] Middle East policy was the most important sticking point, but policies concerning the Soviet Union and its actions also were subject to disagreement. A biographer noted that "whenever Rayburn offered objections in foreign matters, Eisenhower showed displeasure as if he was violating the rules" (Steinberg 1975, 318). By late 1958, the relationship between Eisenhower and the Democratic leaders had lost much of its warmth, and the number of personal meetings declined. Eisenhower contributed to the deterioration by becoming more partisan in the 1958 election campaign. Despite Eisenhower's and Johnson's rhetoric about reestablishing bipartisanship in foreign policy, Eisenhower appeared to become more assertive and partisan during the next two years, when he called only one formal bipartisan leadership meeting.[12] The more highly charged political atmosphere following the 1958 Republican election debacle, the strengthened congressional ranks and increasing boisterousness of liberal Democrats, and partisan maneuvering in advance of the 1960 presidential election contributed to cooler relations. Thus, after a period in which Eisenhower consulted with Democratic leaders at least as frequently as with Republican leaders, his administration ended with a more partisan pattern of rhetoric and consultation.

All presidents since the 1950s have scheduled weekly meetings, usually breakfast meetings, with leaders of their own party while Congress was in session. These weekly meetings generally concerned legislation currently before Congress and so tended to emphasize domestic policy. These meetings were a well-established norm, the violation of which would risk the wrath of congressional leaders whose support is vital to the success of the president's legislative program. The nature of the weekly meetings has varied, as has the frequency of special meetings and phone conversations with party leaders. Meetings with opposition leaders, usually jointly with leaders of their own party, also is a regular feature in presidents' schedules in recent decades, although there is great variation in the frequency of these meetings. But as with Eisenhower, Johnson, and Rayburn, the relationship between presidents and Hill leaders has often turned on more private and informal relations. It is in this area that the decline of bipartisan consultation is most notable.

Kennedy's bipartisan leadership meetings were more frequent than Eisenhower's. In less than three years, Kennedy convened at least sixteen bipartisan meetings. His daily schedules and the identity of the committee leaders attending some of these sessions suggest that most of the bipartisan meetings were called for the purpose of briefing leaders on a foreign policy matter—the Cuban crises, the situation in Laos, the Berlin crisis, and so forth. Kennedy invited Senate Republican leader Dirksen for a private meeting about once a month (MacNeil 1966, 281). The Kennedy-Dirksen sessions were not as focused on foreign policy matters as the Eisenhower-Johnson-Rayburn sessions had been. Kennedy met with Halleck less often, and their relationship remained less personal.

Johnson continued the usual meetings, but his relationship with Dirksen was extraordinary. Congressional reporter and Dirksen biographer Neil MacNeil explains:

The very frequency with which Johnson and Dirksen conferred let Dirksen speak with confidence on how the President stood on almost any public question and encouraged the view that they worked out their differences in private. Where President Kennedy invited Dirksen to the White House perhaps once a month and telephoned him only a little more frequently, President Johnson was constantly talking to Dirksen, to the extent that he seemed to depend on Dirksen for advice. Johnson asked Dirksen to the White House two or three times a week in normal times and even more frequently at times of travail. His telephone calls to Dirksen were numberless, sometimes as many as ten in a single day. (1966, 281)

Dirksen appears to have consulted with Johnson much more frequently than did either the Democratic leader or the House minority leaders Halleck and Gerald Ford, the House Republican leader during most of Johnson's presidency. Dirksen, much to the chagrin of many fellow Republicans, particularly Ford, supported Johnson's Vietnam War policies and was seldom critical. Dirksen's 1964 charge, made in a joint statement with Halleck, that Johnson was concealing the extent of U.S. involvement in Vietnam was the exception to the rule for the Senate leader. He generally intimated that he had the inside track to Johnson's thoughts and refused to bow to Republican pressure to be more partisan in foreign affairs.

President Richard Nixon maintained quite cool relations with congressional leaders. He began in the usual pattern by conducting weekly meetings with his party's leaders, but little consultation appears to have taken place at these sessions.[13] Senate Republican leader Hugh Scott, Dirksen's successor, has been listed among Senate liberals whom Nixon "reviled," even though Scott appeared to become a loyal party soldier when he joined the leadership (Evans and Novak 1971, 108; Rae 1989, 106).[14] Instead, in both domestic and foreign affairs, Nixon preferred to work with nonleaders on the Hill who were ideological or personal friends (Jones 1983, 117). But even these meetings lost some of their regularity, as table 2 suggests. Other meetings and phone conversations did not compensate. The last year of Nixon's first term and his brief second term represent the nadir of leaderhsip consultation with the president on all matters, including foreign policy.

Proportionately, Nixon held about as many bipartisan leadership meetings as Kennedy and Johnson did. As with his predecessors, these dealt with foreign policy almost exclusively. However, Nixon's meetings appear to have been more superficial, often just briefings following one of his international trips. Nixon attempted to establish a more meaningful, private relationship with Mansfield, inviting Mansfield to breakfast once a month, and sometimes more frequently, for discussions about foreign affairs during his first term (Baker 1990, 45).[15] But the relationship between Nixon and Mansfield was nothing like the Eisenhower and Johnson relationships with opposition leaders (Evans and Novak 1971, 106–7). The two men disagreed on a number of basic foreign policy issues, and Mansfield was less willing or able to act aggressively on behalf of the president when they were in agreement. Nixon held few bipartisan leadership meetings during the last half of his administration and did not consult with opposition leaders before implementing most important foreign policy decisions. The shrinkage of his legislative agenda

Table 2
President Nixon's Meetings with Members of Congress, 1969–1972

Type of Meeting	1969	1970	1971	1972
Republican leadership	24	16	13	15
Bipartisan leadership	10	4	9	5
Individuals or groups of members	227	275	172	53
Telephone conversations	204	140	180	61

Source: Adapted Ehrlichman 1982, 203.

and the increasing emphasis on vetoes led Nixon to operate more and more without consulting Hill leaders of either party.

After ascending to the presidency, Gerald Ford reestablished relations with his party's elected congressional leaders as his primary conduit to the Hill and kept his commitment to hold weekly meetings with them (Ford 1979, 140). He also held many bipartisan leadership meetings — at least twenty-five during his thirty months in office — most of which were devoted to foreign policy (Kravitz 1977, 129). Democratic leaders were pleased with the turnaround in their relations with Republican presidents, although Ford did not have special private rendezvous with any opposition leader as his four predecessors did. Moreover, Ford shared Nixon's views about the obstructionist Congress in international affairs and the inappropriateness of consulting congressional leaders before making certain military decisions.[16]

President Jimmy Carter's problems with his own party's congressional leaders are now infamous (Jones 1981, 240; Peabody 1981, 94–95). Troubles stemmed from a lack of consultation on major legislative proposals, distrust of established insiders on Capitol Hill, inattentiveness to — and sometimes disdain for — the courtesies usually extended to members of Congress, and the lack of White House support for leaders' efforts to enact Carter's legislation. Relations did improve considerably during Carter's term in office. To the chagrin of Speaker O'Neill, Carter spent far too much of the leadership breakfasts on foreign policy matters at the expense of pressing domestic issues (O'Neill 1987, 316). Senator Byrd came to develop a quite effective working relationship with Carter, particularly on foreign policy matters, and the two men consulted privately on substance and process from time to time.[17] But Senator Byrd's support was not automatic, even on the Panama Canal treaties and SALT II. Carter's relations with his party's leaders remained quite businesslike.

On the one military deployment for which Carter could have consulted with Hill leaders in advance — the hostage rescue in Iran — the subject had arisen at one or two leadership breakfasts. But Carter did not advise members of his plans. He apparently intended to inform congressional leaders after the rescue team was positioned in Iran. Just before the operation took place he consulted with Byrd (whom he considered quite trustworthy) about who should be notified, telling Byrd that a rescue attempt was imminent. No member, including Byrd, was advised about the actual plan before the results were known (Carter 1982, 513–14; O'Neill 1987, 328).

Carter's relations with House Republican leader John Rhodes were almost nonexistent beyond a few bipartisan leadership sessions, but a more extensive relationship developed with Senate Republican leader Howard Baker. Carter recorded in his diary that Baker "wants to work closer with me, as did his father-in-law, Senator Dirksen, with Presidents" (1982, 224). The occasion was Baker's announcement a year into the Carter term that he intended to support the Panama Canal treaties, and his support proved pivotal. And Baker helped Carter on controversial Middle East arms sales and ending the Turkish arms embargo. But the Carter-Baker relationship never approached the strength of the Dirksen-Kennedy or Dirksen-Johnson relationships. Baker was not invited to the White House for private consultations very often and opposed Carter on some important foreign policy matters. In fact, in mid-1979 Baker followed conservative Republicans in opposition to the SALT II treaty.

President Reagan maintained the established pattern of regular sessions with his party's Hill leaders and continued the practice of occasional meetings with opposition leaders. He held proportionately more domestic policy sessions, but the balance remained in favor of foreign policy sessions that took the form of briefings. The Iran-contra investigations exposed a pattern of avoided congressional consultations on Central America and the Middle East, which was made easy by President Reagan's lack of control over his foreign policy machinery.

In summary, it appears that since the Nixon administration, presidential relations with opposition leaders have been more circumscribed and formal. The private bonds that Eisenhower, Kennedy, and Johnson shared with at least some opposition leaders were not present in subsequent administrations. Relative dependence on formal meetings increased, and the frequency of meaningful consultation, including consultation on foreign affairs, was much lower after the Johnson administration.

The pattern demonstrates the difficulty of connecting the policy preferences of the congressional parties with the behavior of congressional party leaders. Leaders Johnson, Rayburn, and Dirksen, and to a lesser degree Baker, all consorted with an opposition president at times when such collaboration was contrary to the wishes of substantial, and probably majority, blocs of their congressional parties. These leaders were willing to take calculated risks in their leadership roles. But there are limits. Consultative relationships with opposition presidents were restricted when leaders' parties clearly differed with the administration on important issues. The frequency and depth of such differences in the last two decades may account for the tendency of Hill leaders not to establish intimate consultative relations with opposition presidents in the first place.

Nevertheless, it appears that consultation did contribute to bipartisanship in important ways during the 1950s and 1960s, independent of the reciprocal effect of party preferences on leaders' and presidents' behavior. The agenda control Johnson and Rayburn were able to exercise reduced the opportunities for partisan differences to emerge, which achieved what Eisenhower was after—congressional acquiescence and the appearance of broad domestic support for his foreign policies.

SERVICE AS POLICY LEADERS

During the middle decades of this century, elected congressional party leaders were characterized as managers, facilitators, negotiators, and middlemen in the legislative game (Truman 1959, 104–6). Their chief function was to service the parliamentary needs of the real policy leaders found in congressional committees, executive agencies, and organized private groups. Such a leadership style was not adopted by all leaders on all issues, but it does seem to have been the modal pattern. The pattern was consistent with a decentralized legislative process dominated by committee specialists, one in which the congressional party organizations played little role.

I have reviewed journalistic and biographical accounts for indications that leaders played an active role on major foreign policy issues.[18] Table 3 records the frequency with which leaders sponsored legislation or amendments, led the effort to attract votes, or negotiated legislative provisions.

The record since the 1950s shows that active participation in foreign policy matters was more common among Senate leaders than House leaders until recently, when House leaders, particularly the Speaker, became nearly as active as Senate leaders. In the six Congresses between 1955 and 1976 for which evidence was gathered, the Senate majority leader was active on four times as many major foreign policy issues than the House Speaker. But for the three post-1979 Congresses indicated in table 3, the issues on which the Senate majority leader was active outnumbers those for the House Speaker by only fifteen to twelve.

Table 3
Congressional Leaders' Activity on Major Foreign Policy Issues, 1955–1987

| Congress | Senate | | House | | | No. of Major Issues |
	Majority Leader	Minority Leader	Speaker	Majority Leader	Minority Leader	
84th (1955–56)	4	4	3	0	2	14
86th (1959–60)	3	2	1	0	0	13
88th (1963–64)	3	4	1	0	0	13
90th (1967–68)	5	2	2	0	0	14
92nd (1971–72)	4	4	0	0	1	11
94th (1975–76)	5	1	0	1	1	11
96th (1979–80)	5	2	3	0	0	12
98th (1983–84)	3	2	5	3	3	11
100th (1987–88)	7	5	4	3	3	13

Note: For every second Congress since 1955, the major foreign policy issues before the president were determined by examining the Department of State's *Bulletin* and *Congressional Quarterly Weekly Report*. A list of 12–15 issues was identified, and congressional leaders' activity was determined by scrutinizing the *Weekly Report*, the *New York Times*, and leaders' and presidents' biographies.

The pattern for House leaders conforms to the expectation that party leaders have become more active in the foreign policy arena. But the Senate pattern does not. Little systematic change has occurred in the frequency of active participation by Senate leaders, who have regularly been actively involved in one-third to one-half of major foreign policy issues.

Institutional differences underlie the level of participation by House and Senate leaders. One reason for the different rates of participation is that treaties go to the Senate and usually do not involve the House, giving Senate leaders more opportunities than House leaders. The Senate majority leader, for example, was actively involved in seven of the twelve treaties among the major foreign policy issues examined. But this accounts for only about a third of the cases in which the Senate majority leader was active and the House Speaker was not. Most of the difference is due to the distinctive parliamentary functions of party leaders in their respective houses.

House and Senate floor procedures differ in vital ways. The ability of any senator to offer nongermane amendments and to conduct extended debate (filibuster) on most legislation preserves the power of individual senators to obstruct Senate action. Large minorities, of course, can prevent cloture from being invoked, killing legislation altogether. The unpredictability of Senate floor activity puts a premium on gaining consent to limit, or at least schedule, amendments and debate, which in most circumstances can be done only by unanimous consent. Obtaining unanimous consent for time limitation agreements, which is a central function of the floor leaders, often requires negotiation with senators who do not want their side disadvantaged. These negotiations involve floor leaders in discussions that are necessarily about both process and policy substance.

In contrast, House rules prohibit nongermane amendments and limit debate. Majority party leaders still have incentives to further structure floor consideration of controversial legislation, but any further structuring is accomplished by special rules that require only majority approval. Consequently, House leaders are less frequently involved in the detailed negotiations over substance than are entailed by Senate leaders' negotiation of unanimous consent agreements in their chamber. And House leaders' detailed involvement in policy matters is more likely to be limited to matters of partisan importance.

These differences account for the relatively high and stable level of participation of Senate leaders and make the record of House leaders since the late 1970s all the more remarkable.

LEADERS IN A NEW ERA

The behavior of congressional party leaders since the 1950s supports the propositions drawn from the resurgent Congress thesis. In the foreign policy arena, leaders show increasingly partisan patterns in their support for presidential positions, increasing activity as party spokesmen, increasingly partisan patterns of consultation with presidents, and increasing activity as policy leaders. And with respect to leaders' performance as spokesmen and policy leaders, the observed changes have been greater in the House than in the Senate.

These propositions about the direction of change must not be taken as claims about the absolute degree of leadership involvement or influence in the foreign policy arena. Committees remain the center of congressional action on most foreign policy matters. In most cases, committee members are the effective policy leaders and committees are the point of origin for the vast majority of legislative measures shaping foreign policy.

Moreover, much of the change of the last three decades goes beyond committees and leaders. Rank-and-file members became more active in both domestic and foreign policy making. Indeed, some of the same factors that led to greater leadership activity in this arena—all a part of the resurgent Congress thesis described at the outset—fostered broad participation and stimulated demands for new avenues of participation. One leadership response has been to channel rank-and-file members into party committees and task forces. All four congressional parties have relied on task forces to devise party policy proposals and tactics. House Democrats have used task forces more than the other parties, employing them to design policy on Central America and conduct oversight of the executive branch with respect to Lebanon, among other things.

The parties also reactivated their caucuses. Table 4 reports the frequency of formal policy actions by party caucuses and their policy committees that were discernible in *Congressional Quarterly Weekly Report* for the period since 1955. In the late 1950s and early 1960s, the party units exhibited little policy activity worthy of note. Perhaps contrary to expectation, however, what little activity there was involved foreign and defense policy.

In the mid-1960s, House Republicans led the way in using party units to make policy pronouncements. Resolutions or reports critical of the Democratic administration on Vietnam, NATO, and the general defense posture of the United States were issued. Democrats in both houses became more active during the Nixon and Ford administrations, paused during the Carter administration, and gained new life during the Reagan administration. In fact, the general pattern is for the out-party—the party not controlling the White House—to have more-active party caucuses. Of the seventy cases of party policy action counted in table 4, fifty-five, or about 79 percent, were actions of an out-party. Out-party members appear to see party units as vehicles for criticizing the opposition president, reestablishing a party identity after a presidential election defeat, countering the legislative influence of the president, and circumventing committees that are perceived to be too sympathetic with administration views. In contrast, in-party activity is

Table 4
Frequency of Policy Resolutions Adopted by Party Caucuses and Policy Committees, by Policy Type, 1955–1988

| | House | | | | Senate | | | | Total | |
| | Democrats | | Republicans | | Democrats | | Republicans | | | |
Congress	Dom[a]	For[b]	Dom	For	Dom	For	Dom	For	Dom	For
Eisenhower Congresses										
84th (1955–56)	0	0	0	0	0	1	0	2	0	3
85th (1957–58)	0	0	0	0	0	1	0	0	0	1
86th (1959–60)	0	0	0	1	0	0	0	0	0	1
Kennedy-Johnson Congresses										
87th (1961–62)	0	0	0	0	0	0	0	0	0	0
88th (1963–64)	0	0	0	1	0	0	0	0	0	1
89th (1965–66)	0	0	0	2	0	1	2	0	2	3
90th (1967–68)	0	0	1	1	0	0	0	0	1	1
Nixon-Ford Congresses										
91st (1969–70)	2	0	0	0	0	2	0	0	2	2
92nd (1971–72)	0	2	0	0	0	1	0	0	0	1
93rd (1973–74)	2	1	0	1	1	0	0	1	3	3
94th (1975–76)	5	1	4	0	3	2	1	0	13	3
Carter Congresses										
95th (1977–78)	1	0	0	2	0	0	1	1	2	3
96th (1979–80)	4	0	1	0	0	0	0	0	5	0
Reagan Congresses										
97th (1981–82)	3	1	0	0	2	0	0	0	5	0
98th (1983–84)	2	1	0	0	2	1	0	0	4	2
99th (1985–86)	0	2	0	0	2	1	0	0	2	3
100th (1987–88)	0	2	0	1	0	0	0	0	0	3
Totals	19	10	6	8	10	9	4	4	39	31

Source: Party resolutions, statements, studies, reports, or other vehicles for adopting party policy positions mentioned Congressional Quarterly Weekly Report for the period. Included are the statements of party caucuses, party policy committees, and party task forces, without double-counting statements recommended by committees and task forces that were approved by caucuses. Party actions on procedural reform and routine scheduling matters are excluded.

[a]Domestic policy.

[b]Foreign and defense policy.

usually avoided because it tends either to create problems for the party's president or to make little contribution to enacting the president's program.

Nevertheless, resistance to party activity has produced a pattern of intermittent policy action, even for out-parties. In only five instances did a party take more than three formal policy actions that warranted reporting in any two-year Congress, and three of those five instances occurred during the Ford administration. Committee members often resent the intrusion of party units into their jurisdictions. Party leaders often prefer to avoid situations that might exacerbate intraparty tensions on controversial issues. And some leaders, most notably Senate Democratic leader Robert Byrd, preferred to maintain personal control over party policy positions and public relations.

Yet the overall pattern is consistent with the propositions drawn from the resurgent Congress thesis. In the realm of foreign policy, congressional leaders and their parties have become more active in foreign affairs, changing the identity of the players in the legislative game and making the legislative game more partisan in process as well as outcome.

Part IV

THE POLICY
ARENAS

Chapter Seven

★ ★ ★

BUDGETING
FOR DEFENSE

★ ★ ★

Ralph G. Carter

INTRODUCTION

When interacting with the executive in
foreign policy making, one of the key strengths of Congress is its constitutional "power of the purse" (Carroll 1958). Nowhere is this power more
potentially significant than in the annual budget process, where the participants never forget that each year's relative "victories" and "losses" will
affect the process the following year. Yet in defense spending, influence
varies situationally. Members of Congress find it easier to cut the president's
defense spending requests than to force him to spend more than he wants.
Given the president's need for the annual defense appropriation, it is unlikely
he would veto the entire defense appropriations bill owing to insufficient
funding for only a small part of it (Wildavsky 1988). The only exception
comes when the specific item underfunded by Congress is symbolically
important to the president. Yet even in these cases, as long as Congress
provides some funds for the contested items, it is politically easier for the
president to try for additional funding next year than to veto the entire
defense budget this year.

On the other hand, when Congress tries to force higher spending upon the
president, the situation changes. Members must show they are in a better
position to assess external risks facing the country than is the president,
aided by his national security advisers. Consequently, forcing a president to
spend more when his heels are truly "dug in" is difficult for Congress.

With this asymmetry in influence relationships, how have congressional-
executive defense spending interactions changed over time? Most would
agree that defense spending jumped with the Korean War rearmament and
continued to increase each year thereafter. Bruce Russett described the pre-
Vietnam period by saying, "Once the executive branch has reached agree-

ment on its defense request from Congress, not once in the past quarter-century has the legislature voted down a major weapons system proposal. It has always provided virtually everything asked of it" (1970, 26). Most observers agree that congressional passivity in defense spending ended with the downturn of U.S. involvement in Vietnam (Bax 1977; Blechman 1990b; Frye 1975; Russett 1990). The questions are how, and to what extent, did it change.

ANNUAL DEFENSE SPENDING

Annual Totals

Table 1 shows postwar U.S. defense spending in both current and constant dollars. Both the constant dollar amounts, and figure 1's illustration of defense spending as a percentage of GNP, show that *real* levels of defense spending have been quite volatile since the Korean War. Table 2 shows the average annual percentage change in real defense spending by administration and time period. As the conventional wisdom suggests, the greatest percentage increases occurred before the downturn in Vietnam. However, most of those increases came in Truman's second term, as a result of the Korean War and the institutionalization of the cold war. Otherwise, considerable variation is seen across different administrations. These fluctuations in real defense spending levels generally follow the fluctuations in superpower relations. Real spending sharply decreased after the Korean War, stabilized then rose slightly during the Sputnik period of the late 1950s, fell until the U.S. reaction to the 1964 Tonkin Gulf incident "Americanized" the Vietnam War, then decreased during the détente period of the 1970s, only to rise again after the Soviet invasion of Afghanistan and then fall again in the latter 1980s. Thus, real defense spending has been driven by important changes or events in the international system.

Congressional Responses to Administrative Requests

But do members of Congress always agree with administration assessments of the international system? To what extent does Congress change administrative defense spending requests? Table 3 shows the annual percentage change made by Congress in the administration's real defense spending requests. Reflecting its traditional desire to discourage waste and increase efficiency, Congress cut the administration's requests far more often than it increased them (Fenno 1966; McNaugher 1989). However, the degree of annual change is important. Generally, congressional changes must exceed 5 percent to be significant (Fenno 1966; Korb 1973). According to table 3, Congress made changes in excess of 5 percent twenty times in forty-five years, or 44 percent of the time. Most of those instances of significant change came after the downturn in Vietnam.[1] Between fiscal years 1946 and 1968,

Table 1
U.S. Defense Spending Outlays in Current and Constant Dollars,
Fiscal Years 1947–1991 (in billions of dollars)

Fiscal Year	Current Dollars	Constant Dollars[a]	Fiscal Year	Current Dollars	Constant Dollars[a]
1947	12.8	89.9	1970	81.7	225.6
1948	9.1	55.8	1971	78.9	202.7
1949	13.2	77.4	1972	79.2	190.9
1950	13.7	83.9	1973	76.7	175.1
1951	23.6	150.3	1974	79.3	163.3
1952	46.1	258.9	1975	86.5	159.8
1953	52.8	271.5	1976	89.6	153.6
1954	49.3	250.0	1977	97.2	154.3
1955	42.7	211.0	1978	104.5	155.0
1956	42.5	198.5	1979	116.3	159.1
1957	45.4	203.5	1980	134.0	164.0
1958	46.8	198.3	1981	157.5	171.4
1959	49.0	196.0	1982	185.3	185.3
1960	48.1	192.1	1983	209.9	201.3
1961	49.6	195.2	1984	227.4	211.3
1962	52.3	202.2	1985	252.7	230.0
1963	53.4	197.1	1986	273.4	243.7
1964	54.8	198.8	1987	282.0	250.3
1965	50.6	181.4	1988	290.4	252.9
1966	58.1	197.9	1989	298.3	250.0
1967	71.4	235.1	1990	299.3	247.0
1968	81.9	254.8	1991[b]	298.9	235.9
1969	82.5	243.4			

Sources: Data from *Historical Tables, Budget of the United States Government, Fiscal Year 1990*, 123–30; *Historical Tables, Budget of the United States Government, Fiscal Year 1992*, 70.

[a]The constant dollars are FY1982 dollars.

[b]FY1991 outlays are estimates.

Congress made annual changes in excess of 5 percent only 32 percent of the time. Between fiscal years 1969 and 1989, Congress made changes of this magnitude 57 percent of the time.

The differences before and after Vietnam are confirmed by table 4. With the exception of those of Carter and Bush, each administration after Johnson's suffered annual defense spending cuts that averaged approximately 5 percent or more for the entire administration. Further, the Carter and Bush exceptions are easily explainable. Before Bill Clinton's election, Jimmy Carter was the only post-Vietnam president whose party controlled both chambers of Congress, while George Bush is the only postwar president to

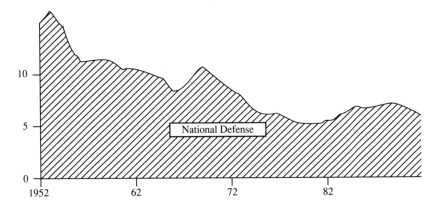

Fig. 1. Defense Spending as a Percentage of GNP.

Source: *Historical Tables, Budget of the United States Government. Fiscal Year 1990, 12.*

Table 2
Average Annual Percentage Change in Constant Dollar Defense Spending,
by Time Period

Time Period	Percentage Change
Administrations	
Truman I	0.4
Truman II	41.2
Eisenhower I	− 6.7
Eisenhower II	− 1.0
Kennedy	0.6
Johnson	4.6
Nixon I	− 7.9
Nixon II	− 4.4
Ford	− 1.7
Carter	2.7
Reagan I	7.6
Reagan II	2.1
Bush	− 3.0
Fiscal Years	
1947–68	7.8
1969–91	− .5

Source: Calculated from table 1.

Note: FY1982 constant dollars.

Table 3

Congressional Changes in Major Defense Spending Requests, Fiscal Years 1947–91
(in billions of FY1982 dollars)

Fiscal Year	Request	Appro-priation	Percentage Change	Fiscal Year	Request	Appro-priation	Percentage Change
1947	103.2	80.1	− 22.4	1970	213.7	197.2	− 7.7
1948	70.5	54.6	− 22.6	1971	182.7	176.8	− 3.2
1949	75.6	68.6	− 9.3	1972	194.7	186.8	− 4.1
1950	81.5	79.6	− 2.3	1973	181.7	169.8	− 6.5
1951	305.7	307.6	.6	1974	175.4	165.2	− 5.8
1952	361.1	350.4	− 3.0	1975	167.6	157.8	− 5.8
1953	284.9	251.4	− 11.8	1976	176.1	160.6	− 8.8
1954	183.6	175.5	− 4.4	1977	177.0	171.3	− 3.2
1955	153.7	146.8	− 4.5	1978	175.3	168.6	− 3.8
1956	146.7	149.0	1.6	1979	174.8	170.7	− 2.3
1957	157.8	162.3	2.9	1980	166.9	165.1	− 1.1
1958	166.5	155.1	− 6.8	1981	187.9	192.2	2.3
1959	155.2	164.8	6.2	1982	210.6	207.2	− 1.6
1960	162.9	162.1	− .5	1983	247.7	229.3	− 7.4
1961	160.6	162.5	1.2	1984	250.9	238.3	− 5.0
1962	169.3	184.4	8.9	1985	275.3	257.4	− 6.5
1963	183.8	183.4	− .2	1986	280.2	258.2	− 7.9
1964	188.6	180.7	− 4.2	1987	281.3	251.5	− 10.6
1965	180.3	176.7	− 2.0	1988	264.5	250.2	− 5.4
1966	205.7	210.5	2.3	1989	244.7	244.0	− .3
1967	234.8	235.4	.3	1990a	223.4	223.3	0.0
1968	244.5	236.1	− 3.4	1991	210.8	196.5	− 6.8
1969	238.7	221.6	− 7.2				

Sources: Calculated from data in *Congressional Quarterly Almanacs*, 1946–90. Conversions to FY1982 constant dollars for fiscal years 1947–89 were calculated from ratios in table 1. Conversions for fiscal years 1990–91 were calculated with conversion factors from *Budget of the United States Government, Fiscal Year 1991*, A-283.

Note: Major defense spending includes the annual defense, military construction, and supplemental defense appropriations bills. Not included are appropriations bills for foreign military aid, veterans affairs, or Army civil functions (i.e., Corps of Engineers).

aBecause of a noncomparable reporting format for FY1990 appropriations in *Congressional Quarterly Almanac 1989*, FY1990 data reflects funds authorized, not appropriated.

have had a formal budget agreement with congressional leadership specifying the overall amount of military spending before the budget process began. So those exceptions aside, the post-Vietnam period shows an important shift in congressional willingness to make significant changes in the administration's overall defense spending requests. By the early 1970s, any congressional reluctance to challenge the presidency over military policy had disappeared.

Table 4

Average Annual Percentage Change by Congress in Administrative Constant Dollar
Requests for Major Defense Spending, by Time Period

Time Period	Percentage Change
Administrations	
Truman I	− 18.2
Truman II	− 4.1
Eisenhower I	− 1.1
Eisenhower II	0.0
Kennedy	1.4
Johnson	− 2.0
Nixon I	− 5.4
Nixon II	− 4.8
Ford	− 6.0
Carter	− 1.3
Reagan I	− 5.1
Reagan II	− 6.0
Bush	− 3.4
Fiscal Years	
1947–68	− 3.4
1969–91	− 4.7

Source: Calculated from table 3.

Notes: FY1982 constant dollars.

Major defense spending includes the annual defense, military construction, and supplemental defense appropriations bills. Not included are appropriations bills for foreign military aid, veterans affairs, or Army civil functions (i.e., Corps of Engineers).

PATTERNS OF CONGRESSIONAL ASSERTIVENESS

Has congressional willingness to challenge administrative spending requests been uniform, or has it varied by the type of defense spending involved? Beginning with FY1960, data on military expenditures by appropriation title are available, and the percentage changes Congress made in administrative requests are displayed in table 5. In the area of military personnel, congressional changes exceeded the 5 percent threshold eight times in thirty-two years. All those instances occurred after the downturn in Vietnam. Similarly, congressional changes in operations and maintenance spending exceeded the 5 percent threshold six times in thirty-two years. Again, all six instances came after the downturn in Vietnam.

Congressional changes are much more common in the area of military procurement. In nineteen of thirty-two years, Congress made procurement changes exceeding the 5 percent threshold, and only one of these instances occurred before 1968. Moreover, large congressional procurement cuts, ranging from 7 to 16 percent, were the norm from fiscal years 1969 to 1979

Table 5
Congressional Percentage Changes in Administrative Budget Requests by
Appropriation Titles, FY1960–1991

Fiscal Year	Military Personnel	Operations & Maintenance	Procurement	Research & Design[a]
1960	.1	− .7	− .1	1.2
1961	.2	− .6	3.3	6.9
1962	− .5	− .5	− 1.1	9.5
1963	− 1.1	0.0	1.2	2.6
1964	− 2.9	− .7	− 6.1	− 4.3
1965	− .1	− .7	− 2.4	− 4.1
1966	.3	.2	− .1	− 2.1
1967	.3	.2	1.4	1.1
1968	− 1.0	− 1.5	− 4.0	− 2.3
1969	− 1.9	− 4.5	− 14.1	− 5.7
1970	− 3.3	− 4.3	− 14.6	− 10.4
1971	6.5	3.1	− 7.7	− 4.7
1972	7.9	− .5	− .7	− 5.4
1973	.3	− .8	− 15.9	− 9.2
1974	6.5	4.2	− 7.3	− 3.8
1975	.7	− 4.4	− 13.9	− 8.0
1976	1.5	− 3.2	− 13.4	− 7.2
1977	2.6	− .7	− 8.7	− 5.6
1978	− .3	− 2.5	− 8.7	− 3.3
1979	− .2	− .1	− 5.3	− 2.5
1980	5.5	7.0	.3	− .7
1981	15.0	9.4	18.2	− 3.0
1982	9.6	.1	1.2	− 6.9
1983	− 5.8	− 5.3	− 10.4	− 7.0
1984	− 1.3	− 3.3	− 7.6	− 6.3
1985	− 1.3	− 4.2	− 9.8	− 8.2
1986	− 7.5	− 4.6	− 8.8	− 10.2
1987	− 2.0	− 9.0	− 11.3	− 14.6
1988	− 1.3	− 6.7	.4	− 15.1
1989	.1	− .4	− .1	− 1.3
1990	− .5	− 4.4	8.2	− 3.6
1991	− 1.3	− 6.0	− 13.1	− 5.5
1960–68	− .5	− .5	− .9	.9
1969–91	1.3	− 1.8	− 6.2	− 6.4

Sources: Kanter 1972 for FY1960–70, Handberg and Bledsoe 1979 for FY1971–79, Bledsoe 1983 for FY1980–82, and *Congressional Quarterly Almanacs*, 1982–90 for FY1983–91.

[a]More accurately referred to as research, design, testing, and evaluation (RDT&E).

and from fiscal years 1983 to 1987. Had it not been for the 18 percent increase in procurement spending imposed on the Carter administration in FY1981 (after the Soviet invasion of Afghanistan), the post-Vietnam period would have averaged annual congressional cuts of 7 percent. Even with this 18 percent outlier included, the average annual congressional cut in procurement expenditures exceeded 6 percent.

A more striking indicator of procurement assertiveness involves the congressional termination of major weapons systems. Congress has killed the Army's Mauler surface-to-air missile, main battle tank (MBT-70), and division air defense weapon (DIVAD); the Navy's F-111B (TFX) fighter, "fast deployment logistics" ships (FDLs), and Condor medium-range cruise missile; and the Air Force's Safeguard ABM system. Only the Mauler's termination occurred before 1968.

In the post-Vietnam period, Congress has been aggressive regarding procurement funding when its members feel the White House is misreading the international environment. Striking illustrations come from the Reagan administration. Many in Congress felt the president's strident anticommunism was preventing the country from taking advantage of opportunities for significant nuclear arms control agreements with the Soviets. Thus they began to "appropriate arms control."[2] Because they were seen as destabilizing, "first-strike" weapons, the administration got only half the MX missiles it desired (fifty rather than a hundred), and those were permitted only after the administration agreed to make concessions in the START talks with the Soviets. The administration was also forced to delay its deployment of Pershing II intermediate-range missiles for over two years. Again, critics said that putting such highly accurate nuclear missiles only a few air minutes away from Soviet targets would only escalate the arms race. This congressional delay provided the time for the generation of political pressures, which ultimately produced the 1985 Intermediate Nuclear Forces Treaty between Reagan and Gorbachev (Blechman 1990b).

It would be difficult for Congress to have an impact on procurement spending without similarly affecting research, design, testing, and evaluation (RDT&E) expenditures. Table 5 also reflects congressional activism regarding RDT&E expenditures. The 5 percent threshold of significant change was exceeded in seventeen of thirty-two years. The importance of Vietnam as a turning point is again reaffirmed. After the downturn in Vietnam, congressional cuts in the annual RDT&E budget have averaged more than 6 percent. Significant for the short-term future are the large cuts, ranging from 10 to 15 percent, made by Congress in RDT&E in the FY1986–88 budgets. Thus the development process for weapons sought by the Reagan administration for deployment in the 1990s was significantly slowed, again reflecting how sharply congressional perceptions of the external environment differed from Reagan's.

REASONS FOR CONGRESSIONAL ASSERTIVENESS

Policy Disputes

At the heart of the most important congressional-executive disputes over the shape of the defense budget lies a fundamental difference of opinion over how best to protect the nation's national security interests. As an institution of 535 members, some of whom change every two years, Congress has a difficult time achieving a broad and lasting policy consensus regarding national security issues (Huntington 1957). For members of Congress, the easy route is to respond to presidential national security initiatives. Yet it is inevitable that presidents and congressional majorities will at times disagree over the specifics of our defense requirements, at least in part because of differing estimates of the external threats facing the United States. At such times of policy disequilibrium, the political incentives for members of Congress to get more highly involved in defense budgeting sharply increase (Huntington 1961). Four major examples of such policy disequilibrium can be identified.

The first major policy disequilibrium came as a result of the Vietnam War's impact on the cold war consensus. Although one prescient representative saw this disequilibrium coming as early as 1954, his colleagues did not address it until the latter 1960s.[3] Growing domestic antiwar protests and the shock of the 1968 Tet Offensive made many in Congress increasingly critical of administration policy, and they turned to the authorization/appropriations process as a vehicle for expressing their policy concerns. In 1969 the Cooper-Church amendment was added to the FY1970 defense appropriations bill, prohibiting the introduction of U.S. ground combat forces in Laos or Thailand. In 1970 this prohibition in the FY1971 defense appropriations bill was extended to include not only the use of money to support U.S. ground troops in Cambodia but also the use of U.S. funds to support South Vietnamese or other allied troops fighting in Laos, Thailand, or Cambodia. In 1973 the second FY1973 supplemental appropriations bill contained a ban on any U.S. ground or air combat operations in Indochina after 15 August 1973. These attempts to use defense appropriations to limit the president's options as commander-in-chief were unprecedented.

A second, related episode of policy disequilibrium involved the general issue of U.S. forces overseas, whether overt or covert. In 1973 an amendment to the FY1974 defense procurement bill required our NATO allies to pay more to offset the cost of U.S. troops stationed on their soil, linking each country's payment to the U.S. balance of payments deficit with that country. The administration unsuccessfully opposed the amendment. The FY1975 defense appropriations bill included another "anti-NATO" amendment requiring 12,500 U.S. troops stationed overseas to be brought home by 31 May 1975. The administration lost in this case too. However, the most significant such congressional challenge to the executive branch came in 1975. An amendment to the FY1976 defense appropriations bill prohibited the use of any funds in the bill to support combat operations in Angola, thereby terminating CIA support of the "anti-Marxist" factions in the Angolan civil war.

A third example of policy disequilibrium is represented by the congressional effort to "appropriate arms control" when serious disagreements on this issue exist between the White House and Capitol Hill. The previously noted restrictions on the MX and Pershing II missiles fit in this category, as do broader policy prescriptions.

While Congress took a preliminary step in this direction in 1976 (by requiring separate authorization for any civil defense fund after FY1977), the practice of enacting broad arms control policy prescriptions via the authorization/appropriations process was most prevalent in the 1980s, beginning with the nuclear freeze movement. In 1982 the House rejected a tough nuclear freeze amendment to the FY1983 defense authorization bill by a two-vote margin, accepting an administration substitute that called for a weapons freeze at "equal and substantially reduced levels" instead (*Congressional Quarterly Almanac* 1982, 113). The next year, the House passed a nuclear freeze amendment to the FY1984 defense appropriations bill. This one was so heavily diluted that both hawks and doves in the House could claim victory with its passage. The Senate, however, refused to pass it.

After the passion for a nuclear freeze had cooled, congressional arms controllers switched their attention to delaying the new Strategic Defense Initiative (SDI), or "Star Wars" defense system, and had greater success. In the FY1985 defense appropriations bill, they inserted a moratorium on testing of an antisatellite (or ASAT) missile, one of the elements of the program most likely for quick deployment. The moratorium was extended again in the FY1986 defense appropriations bill and the FY1987 defense authorization bill, specifically denying any testing of an ASAT weapon against a target in space. Moreover, in that FY1987 defense authorization bill, a House prohibition against all but the smallest of underground nuclear weapons tests was deleted from the bill only after the Reagan administration agreed to seek Senate approval of two 1970s-era treaties limiting the size of nuclear weapons tests. Finally, the defense authorization bills for both FY1988 and FY1989 contained amendments that barred any SDI-related tests in space that would violate the traditional interpretation of the 1972 ABM Treaty. In short, if Congress did not have the votes to stop basic research on SDI, the votes were available to slow its deployment by denying any realistic testing of its early components.

All three of these examples of policy disequilibrium involved differing congressional and administrative assessments of the external environment and the national security spending levels thus required. The final example of

Congress using its power of the purse to address a major policy disequilibrium concerns an internal matter—domestic military procurement practices. Led by the members of the House appropriations committee, Congress has always been quick to criticize what it sees as wasteful spending, often cutting procurement dollars by 1 to 3 percent across the board in hopes of encouraging thrift (Fenno 1966). As early as 1954, the Senate included a provision to its version of the FY1955 defense appropriations bill calling for strict reliance on competitive bidding in the awarding of defense contracts. Congressional alarm at the apparent mismanagement of procurement funds in 1969 led it to amend the FY1970 defense appropriations bill, directing the secretary of defense and the budget director to identify all procurement funds unexpended after three fiscal years, and all shipbuilding funds unexpended after five fiscal years, so Congress could rescind them. Congressional trust continued to deteriorate, and the FY1974 defense procurement authorization bill prohibited the Defense Department from entering into any contract in excess of $25 million without prior approval of the armed services committees.

Despite this continual evolution of congressional concern about the way procurement dollars were spent, it took sensational scandals in the Reagan administration to prompt more assertive action. Incensed by Air Force purchases of $7,000 coffee pots and $640 toilet seats, Congress included procurement reforms in the FY1986 defense authorization bill. These provisions prohibited Pentagon reimbursement to contractors for payment of entertainment, lobbying, and contract-related legal fees; required the secretary of defense to plan for "multiple sourcing" of all research and procurement for major weapons systems—a provision that could be waived if national security grounds so dictated; and prohibited Pentagon officials from negotiating with defense contractors with whom they had discussed future employment. In the FY1987 defense authorization bill, Congress went further. It tried to make one person ultimately responsible for Pentagon procurement by creating a new "procurement czar" position, the under secretary for defense acquisition, who outranked everyone in the Defense Department except the secretary and his deputy. The bill also required that at least two competing contractors build prototypes of any new major weapon, and realistic combat testing of such weaponry was mandated before procurement could begin. Finally, it banned Pentagon officials from going to work for contractors with whom they had worked closely until two years had elapsed since leaving the department.

The above examples demonstrate the congressional penchant for using the annual authorization/appropriations process to deny the president his preferred options when important policy disputes exist between the branches. These policy disputes provide the incentives, the "will," for Congress to challenge the administration over defense spending.

Increased Congressional Expertise

If policy disputes provide the "will" to challenge the president, increased congressional access to expertise in the post-Vietnam era has provided the "way." Congressional reforms led personal and committee staffs to increase sharply in the early 1970s, as shown in figure 2, giving members the ability to probe defense issues in much more depth. The staffs of each chamber's appropriations and armed services committees have also increased dramatically over time (table 6). Further new institutions, such as the Congressional Budget Office and the Office of Technology Assessment, provided additional investigative resources to members of Congress, as did the increased staffs of existing institutions like the General Accounting Office and the Congressional Research Service of the Library of Congress. New budget committees forced members of Congress to be explicit in linking domestic and foreign policy expenditures (Blechman 1990b; Davidson and Oleszek 1981). Thus by the 1980s, there were those in Congress, often chairmen or ranking minority members of the relevant committees or professional staffers, who had as much or more defense expertise as the administration officials with whom they dealt (Blechman 1990b). The 1981 creation of the Military Reform Caucus was an important manifestation of this growing sense of confidence in congressional military expertise (Reed 1984). With such institutional changes in the context of congressional defense spending behavior, it is not surprising that members of Congress were becoming much more assertive in putting their policy imprint on the defense budget.

With more staff help available, members of Congress can get more involved in the details of defense spending. The degree to which they have done so has led to the charge of congressional "micromanagement" of the defense budget. Having the staff to read them, the relevant committees can

Table 6
Growth in Committee Staff Personnel over Time

Year	House Appropriations	Senate Appropriations	House Armed Services	Senate Armed Services
1947	29	23	10	10
1960	59	31	15	23
1970	71	42	37	19
1975	98	72	38	30
1979	129	80	48	31
1985	182	82	64	48
1987	188	81	70	49

Source: Data from Ornstein, Mann, and Malbin 1990, 137–38.

Fig. 2. Growth in Congressional Staff over Time.

Number of employees

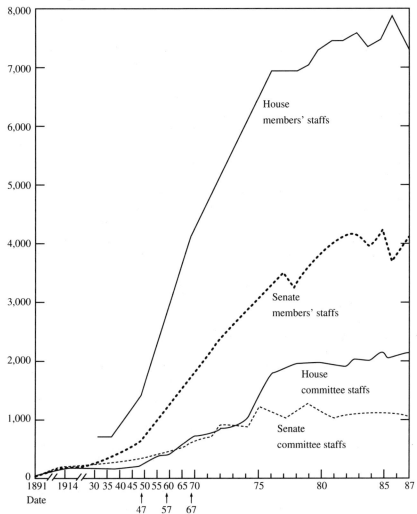

Source: Ornstein, Mann, and Malbin 1990, 133.

demand increasingly detailed reports from the Defense Department. The number of such reports jumped from 36 in 1970 to 719 in 1988, a twentyfold increase. Partially as a result of such studies, the number of congressionally mandated actions required of the Defense Department increased from eighteen in 1970 to the low two hundreds by the 1980s (Blechman 1990b, 41).

With increased staff personnel, committee hearings lengthened. The hearings by the armed services committees and subcommittees increased from approximately sixty days a year in the 1960s to roughly a hundred days a year in the 1980s. Now approximately two hundred executive branch officials are required to make between three hundred and four hundred appearances yearly before the armed services and appropriations committees, and, not surprisingly, the annual reports of these committees have grown from about a hundred pages in length to over a thousand (Blechman 1990b, 40–41).

Perhaps the heart of the "micromanagement" charge has been the congressional desire to make changes in specific budgetary line items. Where once attention was paid primarily to budgetary totals and subtotals, such is no longer the case. In 1970 Congress made changes in 180 authorization line items and in 650 appropriation line items. By 1985 the number of line items changed had grown to 1,315 and 1,848, respectively (Blechman 1990b, 41). Between fiscal years 1976 and 1983, the armed services and appropriations committees made a total of over 10,000 line item changes in the defense budgets submitted to them, averaging over 1,250 changes per year (Bledsoe 1983).

Partisanship

When Congress makes policy, partisanship matters, and defense spending is no exception to this rule (Fenno 1966, 1973; Wildavsky 1988). Table 7 reports the average annual congressional change in the administration's budget requests for overall defense spending and for the four major titles of the annual defense appropriation bills by partisan configuration. The importance of partisanship is pronounced. When one party controlled both chambers of Congress and the presidency, the 5 percent threshold was never approached, much less surpassed. Yet when one party controlled both chambers of Congress and the other party controlled the presidency, the 5 percent threshold was approached for post-Vietnam overall spending and surpassed for post-Vietnam procurement and RDT&E spending. In the 1981–86 period, when each party controlled one chamber of Congress, the 5 percent threshold was surpassed in the overall spending, procurement, and RDT&E categories and was approached in terms of operations and maintenance. In every case, the average annual cuts were greater with split partisan control of Congress than when one party controlled Congress and the other had the presidency. Thus when at least one chamber of Congress is controlled by the nonpresidential party, partisanship becomes an important factor in explaining congressional changes in presidential defense spending requests.

Table 7
Average Annual Percentage Change by Congress in Administrative Requests by
Expenditure Type, Fiscal Year Time Period, and Partisanship

Spending Type and Period	Single Party Control	Dual Party Control	Split Control
Major defense spending[a]			
1947–68	− 3.3	− 3.4	NA
1969–91	− 2.4	− 4.8	− 6.5
Military personnel			
1960–68	− .7	.2	NA
1969–91	3.6	1.6	− 1.4
Operations and maintenance			
1960–68	− .4	− .7	NA
1969–91	1.9	− 2.0	− 4.4
Procurement			
1960–68	− 1.6	1.6	NA
1969–91	− 1.9	− 7.2	− 7.8
Research and design			
1960–68	.1	4.1	NA
1969–91	− 3.0	− 6.7	− 8.9

Sources: Calculated from tables 3 and 7.

Notes: Single party control = The same party controlled both chambers of Congress and the presidency when the budgets for the relevant fiscal years were passed, i.e., fiscal years 1947, 1950–55, 1962–69, and 1978–81. Dual party control = Both chambers of Congress were controlled by one party and the presidency was controlled by the other when the budgets for the relevant fiscal years were passed, i.e., fiscal years 1948–49, 1956–61, 1970–77, and 1988–91. Split control = One party controlled one chamber of Congress and the other party controlled the other chamber when the budgets for the relevant fiscal years were passed, i.e., fiscal years 1982–87. NA = Not applicable; these cases came in the 1980s.

[a]Major defense spending includes the annual defense, military construction, and supplemental defense appropriations bills. Not included are appropriations bills for foreign military aid, veterans affairs, or Army civil functions (i.e., Corps of Engineers).

Changes in Senate Roles

Like partisanship, another important aspect of Congress is the institutional interaction between House and Senate. In the pre-Vietnam era, it commonly happened that the House appropriations committee would cut defense spending for the sake of efficiency and fiscal prudence, the losers in this cutting would then seek relief from the Senate appropriations committee, and the Senate would often restore part of the funds cut. Thus, the Senate acted as a court of last resort for those whose oxen had been gored (Fenno 1966, 1973). This practice generally diminished after Vietnam (see table 8).

Although the frequency of Senate restoration actually increased for the years of single party control of both Congress and the presidency after Vietnam, the drop in Senate restoration was precipitous during the post-Vietnam period when Congress was controlled by one party and the presidency by the other.[4]

CONCLUSION

Before 1968 Congress rarely made major challenges to the administration's defense spending requests. However, this longitudinal examination of congressional defense spending behavior shows that congressional assertiveness toward the executive branch became much more common after the downturn in the war in Vietnam. Over the last twenty-five years, multiple internal and external factors have prompted Congress to challenge the executive branch on defense spending issues.

As Kenneth Shepsle (1989) notes, the old "textbook Congress" was one marked by committee dominance over constituency or partisan concerns. According to Shepsle, the demise of this "textbook Congress" began with the 1958 congressional elections, elections that coincided with dramatic external challenges to U.S. military policy. How to respond to the increased Soviet military threat, embodied in the successful Sputnik launch, became a matter of public and partisan debate. Members of Congress responded by getting more involved in military policy, particularly by requiring more and more of the defense budget to be subject to annual congressional authorization. In 1959 Congress made all procurement of aircraft, missiles, and naval vessels subject to the annual congressional authorization process. In 1962 RDT&E on missiles, aircraft, and naval vessels was made subject to the annual

Table 8

Frequency of Partial Senate Restoration of House Cuts in Major Defense Spending Requests by Time Period and Partisanship

	Fiscal Years	
	1947–68 (%)	1969–91 (%)
All cases	77	65
Single party control	64	80
Dual party control	100	42
Split control	NA	100

Sources: Congressional Quarterly Almanacs, 1946–90.

Notes: Major defense spending includes the annual defense, military construction, and supplemental defense appropriations bills. Not included are appropriations bills for foreign military aid, veterans affairs, or Army civil functions (i.e., Corps of Engineers).

For definition of terms, see note to table 7.

authorization process. The next year, Congress broadened that requirement to include all Defense Department RDT&E. In 1965 this requirement was extended to the procurement of all tracked combat vehicles (Art 1985).

Then came the Tet Offensive of February 1968, an enemy attack of such political significance it discredited President Johnson and his war policy. Thereafter, many members of Congress felt increasingly qualified to put their mark on both the "macro" and the "micro" dimensions of military policy. Efforts to shape military policy at the "macro" level had been made before; now they occurred more often.

The willingness to "micromanage" the defense budget, however, was a sharp departure from earlier practice, as the number of changed line items, reports demanded of the executive branch, and other such indicators demonstrate. Further illustration comes from the increasing specificity of congressional authorization requirements. In 1969 congressional authorization was extended to the procurement of "other weapons"—defined as artillery, rifles, machine guns, mortars, small arms, and any crew-fired piece using fixed ammunition. The next year, the procurement of torpedoes and related equipment also became subject to the annual authorization process. Finally, in 1983 this requirement was extended to "other procurement"—such as trucks and electronic gear affecting the military's combat readiness (Art 1985).

Changes in the context of congressional policy making accompanied and facilitated these policy challenges. Members of the armed services and appropriations committees had long wanted to "micromanage" the defense budget when their policy preferences differed from those of the administration, but it took the dramatic expansion in institutional expertise in the 1970s to make it easier. For its part, the Watergate scandal added partisan reasons to stand up to the president, regardless of the policy dimension.

In sum, the pattern in congressional defense spending behavior shows an important change in the last twenty-five years. While congressional challenges did at times occur before the Vietnam War, they escalated markedly thereafter. While post-Vietnam internal reforms and institutional changes made challenging the White House easier for Congress, the will to challenge the administration over defense spending came primarily from policy disputes regarding the level of threat present in the external environment. Members of Congress felt such threats were less severe than did the Nixon and Ford administrations and more severe than did the Carter administration. Also, Congress was quicker to recognize the reduction in international threats posed by the Gorbachev regime than was the Reagan administration.

Perhaps the most important key to change has been the role played by the armed services committees. By increasing the share of the defense budget requiring annual congressional authorization, the armed services committees gave Congress a procedural avenue to challenge any administration when basic differences in military policy arise. With such policy differences, a heightened sense of partisanship, and increased military expertise, Congress now has both the will and the way to challenge the administration's defense policy preferences.

However, the historical record strongly suggests that these committees will continue to prefer presidential leadership in the defense spending area, challenging the president only when he seems to perceive the external threats facing the country incorrectly. These committees led Congress to be even more "cold warriorish" than the president in responding to the Sputnik challenge, and followed presidential leadership in the "Americanization" of the Vietnam War. However, they later pushed the executive branch to disengage from Vietnam sooner than desired. On Capitol Hill as throughout the land, the burning question was, how can we oppose communism in Indochina while pursuing détente with the Soviet Union? Similarly, these committees led Congress to force greater spending on the Carter administration after the Soviet invasion of Afghanistan, and they endorsed the early spending requests of the Reagan administration. After all, it seemed the Soviets were on an expansionist march. However, once the Soviets bogged down in Afghanistan, and particularly after Mikhail Gorbachev came to power, these committees held back the defense spending desires of the Reagan administration. Both Congress and the public had determined that the threat from Moscow had significantly diminished.

In all these examples, congressional defense spending shows a consistent sensitivity to the security concerns in the international environment. When the administration seems to respond correctly to such stimuli, Congress follows its lead; yet Congress will balk when the administration seems to have read the international situation incorrectly. Further, post-Vietnam changes in the congressional policy-making process have made such challenges easier than they were before. Thus it is imperative that the president and Congress share in a consensus regarding the national security environment facing the country. Otherwise, presidents will learn it is impossible to lead Congress where it refuses to go, at least in the area of defense spending.

Chapter Eight

★ ★ ★

SEARCHING
FOR ARMS CONTROL

★ ★ ★

Alton Frye

Of the many prisms through which to
view contemporary changes in executive-legislative relations, few are more
revealing than one focused on security and arms control policy. Recent years
have seen remarkable developments in the character and intensity of interactions between the branches on issues of strategy and diplomacy. The relative
passivity that long marked congressional attitudes toward these arcane
subjects has been succeeded by a persistent activism that touches virtually
every aspect of this policy domain, from the choice of strategic weapons to
the framing of negotiating positions (Blechman 1990, 3–22, 63–111, 201–18;
also Mann 1990).

These patterns qualify substantially the central tenet of the two-presidency theory, that is, that presidential autonomy in foreign policy is the norm.
They also indicate the shortcomings of any theory of state behavior that does
not consider the ways in which domestic political dynamics, no less than
external factors, constrain a government's international conduct.

A compartmentalized theory that emphasizes constraints imposed by the
international system on rational actors pursuing national interests oversimplifies reality. It overlooks the importance of domestic political processes in
defining what actions and policies are rational expressions of the national
interest. It takes too little account of the ways in which the weight accorded
external constraints is determined by interaction of internal political forces.
It underestimates the degree to which a national leader may engage in less
rational behavior from an international standpoint in order to accommodate
domestic political requirements.

In the United States instances abound in which the executive has altered
the country's foreign policy — sometimes toward greater rationality, sometimes toward less — as a function of judgments about what the political

market would bear in the Congress and in the country. It was not, for example, international strategy that prompted Gerald Ford to ban the word *détente* from his 1976 presidential campaign and to delay conclusion of the SALT II treaty, to his later regret; it was his wariness of Ronald Reagan's challenge for the Republican nomination and the prospect of a bruising congressional battle over ratification. This chapter does not offer a systematic theory of how legislative-executive relations shape American foreign and security policy. It seeks only to demonstrate that no theory can explain American behavior in international politics unless it recognizes the centrality of interbranch dynamics.

The impact of congressional activism is manifest in contemporary strategic policy, to the frequent distress of executive officials and often to the discomfort of legislators themselves. "Micromanagement" is a common epithet in executive descriptions of congressional intrusions into management of defense affairs and in portrayals of members' involvement in diplomatic staffing and operations as well. A tinge of ambivalence is evident in many members, not only those of the president's party, who worry that Congress as a body is too fractured and unwieldy to function coherently on complicated matters of security. Had it not been for repeated shortcomings in executive performance and chronic condescension by high officials toward congressional prerogatives, that ambivalence would probably have preserved the legislature's longtime habit of intermittent engagement on these fronts.

In this field, as in so many others, Congress is a house of mixed emotions. It reflects the multiple impulses of the American public, favoring active efforts to achieve military modernization but also supporting negotiated restraints that might provide an escape from the nuclear peril. Yet the fact that attitudes on issues of high policy vary widely is not unique to this realm, nor are the contradictions so acute that public sentiments are of no value as guides to policy.

Rather, this dispersion of opinion about the best way to maintain national security is a normal trait of a pluralistic society. It imposes a demand on the legislature to balance contending considerations on strategy and arms control, just as it must on other policy questions. Congress has both stimulated and reacted to periodic surges of public concern about weaponry and arms diplomacy, particularly those with a nuclear dimension. Presumably, that is what representative government is supposed to do.

When the balance of congressional-executive relations shifts in any policy domain, two fundamental questions arise. Does the change produce better or poorer policy than the arrangements previously prevailing? And is the change healthy for the American constitutional system? Few questions are so simple and yet so contentious. Close observers differ in their judgments but the case argued here is emphatic: the greater engagement of Congress in security and arms control has improved the policy performance of the American government and has shored up eroding constitutional safeguards.

Time and again, on crucial decisions, Congress has offered useful course corrections to executive policies. It has spurred laggard administrations to negotiate more vigorously, cautioned others to take due care for the maintenance of sound defense programs, tempered the tendency of some in both branches to abandon pragmatism in favor of ideological excursions. To be sure, the legislature has also at times hampered executive initiatives that were constructive and pressed for courses based on parochial calculations.

We are dealing here not with claims of unique virtue on the part of Congress but with a dynamic pattern in which the legislature's role has been to compensate for executive error or excess, or to stimulate consideration of neglected problems or alternative approaches. The pattern has not produced a dominant Congress overawing the executive in national security policy, but it has altered the habitual deference legislators generally paid to executives in strategic matters. Presidential preferences still tend to prevail in this field, but they are more often moderated by awareness that an alert Congress will scrutinize proposals thoroughly. What now seems guaranteed, in contrast to earlier generations, is a Congress prone to engage in the intimate details of national security. The analysis that follows points toward a more energetic application of checks and balances in strategic policy than was the norm for most of the postwar period.

LEARNING FROM EXPERIENCE

One must not overinterpret every tendency in legislative-executive affairs as a reaction to the experience of Vietnam. The disillusionment stemming from that tragedy permeated most dealings between the branches on issues of national security and foreign policy. Certainly as a symbol and as a record of failure, the calamities in Southeast Asia stripped away the aura of executive superiority in analyzing international requirements and defining policies to meet them. The loss of that mystique cost the presidency its claim to dominate foreign policy in the way that it had during and after World War II.

But in the realm of arms control and strategy a number of specific factors reinforced doubts about the executive's comparative advantage in formulating wise policy. During the 1970s and 1980s, a group of leaders emerged in Congress whose expertise matched or exceeded that of executive officials. Decentralization of authority in Congress affected many issues, but the rise of such figures as John Tower, Sam Nunn, William Cohen, and John Warner in the Senate, and Les Aspin, Dante Fascell, and Richard Cheney in the House, helped to compensate for weakened powers at the center by providing focal points for winning coalitions.[1] Through long service and close attention to the subject, these members gained considerable influence with their colleagues, which in turn gave them substantial leverage in dealing with an executive branch that could not afford to alienate them. Political calculations reinforced the regard many military officers and others in the national security establishment came to have for the knowledge and dedication of key legislators. This did not guarantee agreement, but it made disagreements less easy to dismiss as the product of congressional incompetence.

A more general phenomenon was the development of confidence in Congress that legislators were as qualified as those in the other branch to judge the principal elements of strategic policy. This trend was partly a reaction to perceived mistakes in the executive; some members wondered if they could really do worse than the president's men. One senator, young but experienced, caught this spirit at an off-the-record meeting of foreign policy professionals in 1984: "When I came to the Senate, I thought foreign policy and national security were too complicated for amateurs," he said, "but now I realize that I've been at this just as long as you guys."

The statement conveyed more than ego. It was an accurate summary of the spreading conviction on the Hill that excessive deference to executive judgment in these matters was neither wise nor necessary. Although understandable in the years of cold war anxiety, allowing the president's team exclusive sway over these sensitive affairs had not served the country well.

As the 1970s progressed, the lore of Capitol Hill taught that lesson in several ways. Dismaying revelations of certain government intelligence activities heightened a sense of sinister policy and operational bumbling in executive quarters. More pertinent to Congress's budding role in strategic policy, however, was the perception that executive management of strategic policy and arms diplomacy had contributed to the deterioration of America's geostrategic position. Here the legacy of the 1968–72 debates over the ABM (antiballistic missile) system and MIRV (multiple independently targetable reentry vehicles) was formative. As the Soviet-American competition evolved, lessons from those debates took root and sprouted.

Looking back to the late sixties, members of Congress could see that if the Johnson administration's recommendations had been accepted, the United States would have deployed a multibillion dollar, nationwide system of antiballistic missiles too primitive to protect against a Soviet attack but too large to be compatible with major offensive force limitations. If the Nixon administration's recommendation had been accepted, the country would have deployed the same technology to protect missile silos only to find that rampant growth in Soviet capabilities could overwhelm it.[2] If Congress had not slowed the movement toward ABM deployment, the strategic competitors would have lost the opportunity to devise the 1972 ABM Treaty, the cornerstone of subsequent attempts to reduce offensive forces.

Still more sobering was the realization that on the other premier strategic choice of the age, the introduction of MIRV, the executive branch had blundered by ignoring the clear advice tendered by the Senate. Instead of seeking to head off MIRV testing and deployment, the administration had played for short-term advantage by fielding the system. It calculated that the threat of MIRV would keep the heat on Moscow to come to terms on ABM limits and that deployment of MIRV would maintain American technological superiority for years to come. Within months of that action and in the immediate aftermath of the SALT I agreements, National Security Adviser Henry Kissinger was lamenting that no one had warned him of the dangers a MIRVed world would create for strategic stability (Newhouse 1989, 11, 30, 123–30, 133–34; Frye 1975, 47–96).

The belated acknowledgment of MIRV's potential for disaster caused the Senate's collective chin to drop; by a vote of 72 to 6, senators had sent that exact warning in April 1970, weeks before the first Minuteman III became operational. Crossing the MIRV threshold compounded the conundrum that planners and negotiators had to face. The technology triggered a severalfold expansion in the arsenals of both sides, and, of special significance, it permitted the Soviet Union to exploit the payload of its larger missiles to mount a steadily increasing threat to U.S. strategic forces.

To members of Congress evaluating military and diplomatic options, the MIRV commitment loomed as a colossal misjudgment. The decision looked worse and worse as each passing year added hundreds and then thousands of Soviet warheads targeted on the United States. Members might be hesitant to believe that Congress was a wiser strategic policy maker than the executive, but bowing to the administration on that great issue had cost the nation dearly in both dollars and security. This awareness inclined a growing number of members to skepticism regarding claims of superior executive judgment in such matters. From that skepticism germinated wholesale congressional intervention in the strategic policy decisions of later years.

ENERGIZING DIPLOMACY

The bittersweet memory of congressional advice ignored by the executive but vindicated by history was not the only factor working to change relations between the branches. The results of the SALT I negotiations, especially the interim agreement on offensive forces that was supposed to pave the way for a treaty limiting such weapons, persuaded members, led by Senator Henry Jackson, that Congress had to inject itself more directly into diplomatic operations, including personnel decisions. Jackson's long service on the armed services committee and the joint committee on atomic energy had made him one of the premier legislators on defense issues, and he was a valued administration ally in pressing strategic modernization. His sharp critique of the substance and procedure of the SALT I deal was intimidating enough to force major changes in the role and staffing of the Arms Control and Disarmament Agency (ACDA).

The Washington Democrat wrought more than a shake-up in arms control personnel, however. He drew the basic guidelines for subsequent negotiations by the Nixon, Ford, and Carter administrations. Jackson set the standard for SALT II in an amendment to the resolution by which Congress approved the interim agreement of 1972.[3] Negotiators were on notice not to bring home any deal that did not provide for "equal" limits on Soviet and American forces. There were to be no future arrangements that accepted Soviet advantages denied to the United States, as Jackson felt SALT I had done in regard to heavy ballistic missiles and numbers of submarine-launched ballistic missiles.

Arms control proponents in both branches feared that Jackson's rule would rob U.S. diplomats of needed flexibility in striking reasonable balances between the very different forces deployed by the two nations. That may have been the intention of some Jackson aides and supporters, but the effect of the provision seems to have been more benign. As Carter succeeded Ford and SALT negotiations proceeded into the late 1970s, ACDA Director Paul Warnke—the target of fierce personal attacks from the Jackson forces—found it useful to remind the Soviets that Congress had insisted on equal limits. The Soviets, no less than U.S. officials, were on notice that any agreement would have to satisfy the Jackson requirements in order to be ratified.

The SALT II treaty owed much of its eventual complexity to concern about likely congressional reaction. During its negotiation (1972–79) problems of verification, noncircumvention, and qualitative arms control, that is, restraints on technological modernization, all grew prominent in legislative discussions of the impending agreement. These issues were intrinsic to the negotiations, but, as they were amplified in feedback from congressional channels, the SALT II team gave special attention to them. Furthermore, to smooth passage of the treaty, Warnke resigned before it was submitted for ratification, in order to reduce the personal frictions with the Jackson group that had blighted the ACDA chief's tenure.

Whether the SALT II treaty would have been ratified no one knows (Caldwell 1991).[4] It embodied many features that advanced the process of verifiable strategic restraint and opened the door to far-reaching accords in the future. Jackson and his associates verged from skepticism to hostility, even though the pact reflected earnest efforts to accommodate congressional perspectives. In the verdict of the Joint Chiefs of Staff, the agreement was "modest, but useful," best considered a building block for more-comprehensive arrangements still to be devised.

Factors extrinsic to its own terms sealed the treaty's fate. The Soviet invasion of Afghanistan in December 1979 prompted President Carter to suspend Senate consideration of the treaty. Well before that disruption, however, the treaty's political difficulties had grown severe. They were due in large part to the inept domestic strategy of a well-meaning administration. The SALT treaty was the president's avowed priority, but he concentrated initially on ratifying the Panama Canal Treaty, a battle that simultaneously sapped his political capital and made it harder for an indispensable ally, Minority Leader Howard Baker, to join forces with him on the arms control front. Sharp attacks on Baker by Republicans opposed to his leadership on the Panama treaty demonstrated that politicians do not prosper by repeatedly leading the charge for their opponents' controversial initiatives. The administration's treaty sequence, placing Panama ahead of SALT, worked to the disadvantage of arms control.

Another element of the administration's record was even more lethal to the treaty. President Carter's performance on a number of defense-related issues had undermined confidence in his stewardship of national security. Public sentiment favored active diplomacy to limit arms, but it also mistrusted the Soviets to abide by agreements and supported substantial funds for defense. Yet Carter shut off the country's only open production line for ICBMs, canceled the B-1 bomber, and stretched out the Trident program. There were good arguments for each of those decisions, but they added up to a large question mark about Carter's commitment to a vigorous national defense. His belated increases in the defense budget and other course corrections to demonstrate that he was sound on these matters proved ineffective in overcoming that apprehension. This factor formed another barrier to SALT ratification (Frye and Rogers 1979).

CONGRESSIONAL DAMPENING OF THE REAGAN REACTION
With the arrival of Ronald Reagan at 1600 Pennsylvania Avenue, arms control reached its nadir. The Reagan team brought to power many of those who were most contemptuous of arms control, including the president himself. One result was a noticeable reversal of roles between the branches. The Congress whose ambivalence had delayed ratification of SALT II now became the political counterbalance to the new administration's impulses to do away with the entire enterprise. The Congress that had dragged its feet to compensate for what it feared was an overeager embrace of arms control by Jimmy Carter now found it necessary to press his successor to the bargaining table.

Anxieties about Carter's diplomacy with the Soviets gave way to anxieties about Reagan's lack of it. As a ranking senator put it in 1983, "Half the people up here don't trust the Russians—and the other half don't trust Reagan to negotiate seriously" (pers. com.). Even while supporting a shift in emphasis to new defense spending, the public and Congress became alarmed at the administration's casual references to the possibility that nuclear war might actually have to be fought. Partly because he believed that the Soviets were dedicated to a so-called war-fighting strategy, the President himself had mused about fighting and winning a nuclear exchange. Secretary of Defense Caspar Weinberger spoke of "prevailing" against the Soviet Union, a speculation capped by the statement of his deputy undersecretary T. K. Jones that "if there are enough shovels to go around, everybody's going to make it. It's the dirt that does it" (qtd. in Talbott 1984, 287).[5]

That kind of rhetoric fed a grassroots movement for a "nuclear freeze" that eventually won considerable sympathy in Congress. In 1982 opinion surveys showed 83 percent of the public favoring a freeze on testing and deployment of nuclear weapons, and the next year the House of Representatives endorsed a profreeze resolution.[6] Although the Senate appeared ambivalent on that proposition, it had called for a deployment freeze even before completion of SALT I; its anti-MIRV resolution of 1970 urged "an immediate suspension by the United States and by the Union of Soviet Socialist Republics of the further deployment of all offensive and defensive nuclear strategic weapons systems."

The tilt in executive attitudes and performance provoked congressional intervention on the twin agendas of strategic weapons and strategic arms control. A focal point of contention was the future of the land-based missile force, specifically the large MIRVed system known as the MX. In 1976 an amendment authored by Senator Thomas McIntyre, chairman of the armed services subcommittee on research and development, had set a precise requirement for the system. The weapon could only be deployed if the government could make it survivable. Although the Air Force originally proposed to field three hundred MX with three thousand warheads in silos, it quickly came to share McIntyre's verdict that such bases would be vulnerable to the mounting Soviet threat. Accordingly, after many false starts, the service contrived a multiple protective shelter (MPS) scheme to assure survivability by moving the missiles around among several thousand shelters. Carter worried about deploying such a formidable system, but he won congressional approval for the plan (J. Edwards 1982; Frye 1986).

Reagan liked the missile but, in the course of his campaign, had opposed the deployment mode on the advice of close associates Paul Laxalt and Jake Garn, senators from states (Nevada and Utah) scheduled to receive MX bases. After ten months in office, he urged Congress to proceed with the deployment but reverted to the plan for basing the missiles in silos. The irony was exquisite: a president deeply torn about the system's destabilizing properties had won support for it; a president vocally committed to the weapon had abandoned the only basing mode with the demonstrated capacity to win majority approval. In doing so he provoked the outrage of such key allies as Senate armed services committee chairman John Tower, who described the MX as "a textbook case of how not to manage an important national-security issue" (pers. com.).

Reagan's October 1981 decision on the MX set the stage for a series of struggles in Congress that would reverberate powerfully in arms control policy. The president's determination to go forward with the program led key members to hold the system hostage for more forthcoming administration action on the diplomatic front. Republican senators William Cohen and Warren Rudman warned the administration that the necessary votes would not be found unless the MX was part of a coherent package blending strategic programs and arms control policy. From that premise emerged the so-called Scowcroft Commission, appointed by Reagan in early 1983. The commission's report provided a transitional rationale for MX but concluded that strategic stability would best be approached by de-MIRVing the missile forces on both sides. The commission also endorsed the general logic of the "strategic build-down" concept being advocated by Cohen, Nunn, and foreign relations committee chairman Charles Percy (*Report of the President's Commission*).

Bolstered by the commission's finding, the senators joined congressmen Les Aspin, Albert Gore, and Norman Dicks in an effort to alter the administration's strategic line.[7] By conditioning their votes on the MX, the "gang of six" succeeded in convincing the administration that it had no alternative but to change its policy in two basic respects. To facilitate de-MIRVing, it committed itself to begin work on a single-warhead ICBM, nicknamed the "Midgetman." And the president agreed in October 1983 to incorporate essential features of the build-down proposal in the U.S. START position, offering a comprehensive trade-off between American advantages in bombers and Soviet advantages in ballistic missiles.[8] This legislative intervention laid the foundation for balanced reductions in the START agreement that brought ultimate success under George Bush.

The MX controversy was one of two major strategic programs that figured in the observable shift in legislative-executive equilibrium during the Reagan era. Strategic defense was the other and, in several respects, the more crucial. The search for protection against intercontinental ballistic missiles had languished for a decade, discouraged by the restraints of the ABM Treaty and the sharp escalation in the offensive threat. Both philosophical and political inclinations were to change the situation. Reagan's faith in the technological ingenuity of American scientists mingled with skepticism about managing the nuclear threat through a combination of deterrence and arms control. The president also came under mounting pressure, from both the American people and foreign allies, to do something more than say no to arms control and yes to new weapons.

By spring of 1983 the president's instinct for the dramatic brought forth a new rallying cry in the debate over national security. He proposed an ambitious, space-based system of defenses against missile attack, officially known as the Strategic Defense Initiative (SDI) and disparagingly dubbed "Star Wars." It was an unsettling break with the pattern of Soviet-American stability, but it was also a remarkable feat of political jujitsu. Coupled with

his call for deep cuts in nuclear weapons—envisaging their ultimate elimination—the SDI commitment offered a technological response to popular
demands for safety from the nuclear menace. It tapped and redirected many
of the anxieties from which the nuclear freeze movement had sprung.

For knowledgeable experts in Congress and elsewhere, however, the
promise of SDI was by no means so clear. The concept had not been reviewed
thoroughly within the administration itself, nor had legislators or European
allies been consulted. In many respects the venture seemed a form of
technological escapism rather than a credible approach to the excruciating
dilemmas posed by nuclear weapons. The Congress did approve increased
funding for the programs consolidated under the SDI rubric, but opinion ran
strongly against precipitate action that would undermine the ABM Treaty or
frustrate negotiated limitations on offensive forces. Much the same view
prevailed in NATO circles, where British prime minister Margaret Thatcher
and German chancellor Helmut Kohl coaxed the president to state explicitly
that the SDI program would abide by the ABM Treaty provisions.

Through years of growing skepticism about the president's initial notion of
an "astrodome" defense, Congress trimmed, shaded, and contained SDI. As
in the Nixon period, the legislature was not rejecting the president's desire to
explore defenses, but it was modulating the endeavor so as to buy time and
maneuvering room for the negotiations to which it gave priority. By midterm
in the Bush years Congress had substantially reoriented SDI toward modest,
but achievable, ground-based systems and away from problematic space-
based weapons aimed at intercepting ballistic missiles during their boost
phase.[9] In May 1993 the Clinton administration officially buried SDI,
shifting resources and emphasis to work on theater missile defenses.

INNOVATING INSTITUTIONALLY

The mounting involvement of legislators in strategic policy brought several
innovations that strengthened Congress's capacity and confidence. One was
the development of informed staff and members on both the House and
Senate intelligence committees. A major focus of those committees has
become surveillance and verification technologies, which are central to
implementation of arms control agreements. The Senate intelligence com-
mitee participated actively in analyzing the SALT II treaty, which reached
the Senate at the very time when the Shah's fall in Iran disrupted operations
critical to monitoring Soviet missile tests.

Senator John Glenn, in particular, grew more worried about the treaty's
verification provisions as he studied the gap in capabilities caused by the loss
of Iranian cooperation before other systems were on line. His reluctance to
endorse the agreement was a serious obstacle to the administration. Over the
next few years, Glenn and other intelligence committee members tracked
U.S. verification systems closely to assure themselves that impending deals

could be monitored satisfactorily. In both houses, the intelligence committees became training grounds for members interested in these sensitive matters and, as in the case of Albert Gore, gave them the grounding to reach firmer judgments about strategic issues.

Evasive Soviet behavior and noncompliance with previous agreements — Soviet construction of a large radar in violation of the ABM Treaty was the primary instance — confirmed the committees' insistence on thorough verification. The verdicts rendered by the intelligence committees were more temperate than the campaign by some administration officials and senators who exploited the compliance issue as a weapon against the arms control process itself. The anti–arms controllers engineered a requirement for annual reports by the administration on Soviet compliance with existing agreements, a reasonable concept that in application tended to portray ambiguities as conclusive evidence of Soviet perfidy (Krepon 1989, xi–xxvii, 137–62).

Together with the administration's firm line, strong congressional pressure on these issues helped to keep the heat on Moscow to redress real problems. That proved true most vividly when the Soviet foreign minister publicly acknowledged the illegality of the radar at Krasnoyarsk and the Soviets undertook to correct the violation. This dramatic denouement followed a visit by a group of House members and staff to Krasnoyarsk, an inspection arranged by the Soviets to demonstrate that the radar was far from operational and in some respects beginning to deteriorate. Commotions over compliance were not always wholesome, but they ultimately became less a barrier to arms control than a boost for verification procedures that served the cause.

A surprising innovation that strengthened congressional involvement in arms negotiations came at the outset of Reagan's second term: the creation of the Senate Arms Control Observer Group. There has always been a variety of views regarding the proper role for sitting legislators in ongoing diplomacy. While Senators Jackson and John Sherman Cooper had managed to keep themselves close to the SALT process, some members felt that the wiser constitutional practice was to maintain a certain distance from the process in order to avoid being co-opted. They worried that proximity to the diplomacy would erode the independence of senatorial judgment in appraising a treaty.

These concerns pitted classical separation-of-powers doctrine against the practical requirement for the two branches to share power in shaping the content of treaties. Separation-of-powers logic argued for senators to maintain an arms-length relationship to the negotiations until the executive presented results for pristine review in the upper chamber. According to this contention, close senatorial engagement in ongoing negotiations ran the risk both of corrupting the diplomatic process and of contaminating the Senate's independent evaluation of treaties. Executive officials frequently emphasized the constitutional strictures against congressional presence, much less participation, in negotiating sessions.

Increasingly, however, members of Congress came to see active monitoring of major negotiations as proper and wise. They argued that the involvement of legislative observers in arms negotiations offered three decisive advantages: it helped educate members to complex issues on which they would later be called to pass judgment; it sensitized negotiators to legislative concerns that, unless addressed carefully, might lead to an agreement's rejection; and it signaled to foreign diplomats that Congress was a major party whose approval of any bargain was essential. This rationale extended the familiar theme articulated by Senator Arthur Vandenberg and others, namely, that Congress had better be in on the "takeoff" if it was going to be in on the "landing."

The disappointing experience of the abortive SALT II treaty changed the attitude of a number of senators, notably Democratic leader Robert Byrd. As the START and Intermediate Nuclear Forces (INF) negotiations lumbered into the mid-eighties, Byrd and Republican leader Robert Dole found themselves in agreement that more-systematic arrangements were needed to ensure that the Senate could exercise the "advice" component of its treaty powers. After a Soviet walkout disrupted the talks from late 1983 until early 1985, Byrd and Dole persuaded Secretary of State George Shultz to embrace a novel link to the Senate, the Arms Control Observer Group created at the beginning of the 99th Congress. The stated goal was "to avoid a recurrence of the problems of the 1970's, when three successive arms control treaties, signed by three Presidents, were never approved for ratification by the Senate."[10]

The group proved to be a significant two-way bridge between the branches. The administration offered full briefings about the content and status of the negotiations, regular access to the American negotiating teams, and informal contacts with the Soviet diplomats as well. The group encompassed a wide spectrum of opinion, including Republican whip Ted Stevens, Richard Lugar, John Warner, and Malcolm Wallop, along with Democrats Nunn, Gore, Edward Kennedy, and Daniel Moynihan. It became a valuable learning experience for the senators, and a useful sounding board for U.S. negotiators Max Kampelman, Paul Nitze, and others. Equally important, the group conveyed directly to the Soviets both strong support for a mutually advantageous deal and the full force of legislative concern about Moscow's violations of past accords.

Group members became regular attendees at START and INF working groups and were occasionally present at plenary sessions of those negotiations. The group also conducted independent inquiries of its own. At critical moments in the negotiations the group convened with outside experts to canvass for ideas that might be explored, either informally by group members or officially by U.S. negotiators themselves. The Observer Group served both as a monitor, tracking the course of the talks, and as a counselor, alerting the executive to aspects of the negotiations that might cause problems for eventual ratification. Not only did the members become familiar with the substance of arms diplomacy, they also gained standing for later debates with their colleagues. The group's operations worked to build mutual confidence between Congress and the executive, as it demonstrated that legislators were capable of handling sensitive diplomatic details responsibly.

The Observer Group's evolution was in sharp contrast to earlier efforts by senators trying to keep abreast of arms talks. Senator Cooper, for example, was a leading watchdog of the SALT negotiations from his vantage point on the foreign relations committee, but he enjoyed little access to the process even when he traveled to Vienna or Helsinki. He was excluded from the plenary discussions and was granted no official connection to the delegation. So eager was Henry Kissinger to fend off congressional involvement that he reportedly vetoed a plan for Senate leaders Mike Mansfield and Hugh Scott, as well as Cooper, to accompany President Nixon to the 1972 Moscow summit. Where Kissinger saw only trouble in an active Senate role, George Shultz recognized an opportunity. To be sure, Shultz had the benefit of much sad intervening experience, but it is remarkable that the most conservative administration of modern times showed flexibility on such an innovation.

The Observer Group's central achievement has been to establish a new standard on the perennial question of shared authority. It underscores the insight that separation of powers does not mean segregation of information. Unless the information essential to decision making is shared, the system of checks and balances is doomed either to paralysis or to evisceration. Few developments have contributed as much to a constructive working relationship on arms control.

As Ambassador Max Kampelman has emphasized, the relationship is one of rather subtle, mutual influence, as both legislators and negotiators overcome their initial stiffness and come to see each other as colleagues in a shared enterprise, albeit one in which they bear distinctive responsibilities.[11] By and large, the senators refrained from "grandstanding" to garner publicity, and the diplomats were more forthcoming in sharing access to information and to Soviet negotiating teams. The collaboration proved useful in ironing out wrinkles during the final bargaining and ratification of the Treaty on Intermediate Nuclear Forces, and promised to be of further value in the larger bargains scheduled to follow.

RECALIBRATING THE CONSTITUTIONAL BALANCE

The arms control process has been a source of serious constitutional tension. It has generated two broad classes of conflicts touching the Senate's treaty power. One class grows out of a spreading tendency to observe *unratified* treaties over lengthy periods. The second and more serious class stems from radical new claims by some executive officials to a sweeping power to alter the interpretations of treaties presented to the Senate in support of ratification. These developments represent differing threats to the integrity of republican government, and they deserve assessment primarily in constitutional terms, rather than in terms of the policies embodied in particular treaties.

SALT AND NUCLEAR TESTS: TREATIES UNRATIFIED
BUT OBSERVED

After the mid-1970s the United States found itself respecting major accords that it had never ratified or that had expired. In one case, the 1972 Interim Agreement on Strategic Offensive Forces was approved by both houses of Congress. It was to run for five years, with the expectation that a longer-term treaty would be completed in that time. With SALT II negotiations continuing, the Carter administration decided to remain in compliance with the interim accord after its scheduled expiration in October 1977. The decision went beyond the general international practice of adhering to negotiated agreements pending ratification.

Since the interim agreement was to be superseded by the more stringent provisions of SALT II, there was a convincing rationale for the policy, and it elicited little criticism in the Senate. Even though the 1972 resolution of approval had assumed only a five-year life for the pact, various legislative declarations encouraged continued adherence while the search went on for a more comprehensive SALT package. It took slight reflection, however, to see that the indefinite extension of the policy would tend to subvert the Senate's authority. The effect would be to substitute vague strategic standards approved by simple majorities in hortatory resolutions of both houses for the rigorous evaluation and two-thirds Senate majority prescribed for treaty ratification.

A similar pattern unfolded with regard to pacts restricting nuclear testing, but the status of those agreements was quite different. As part of the long-running attempt to reach a comprehensive ban on nuclear testing, the United States and the Soviet Union followed up the 1963 treaty confining tests to underground by agreeing to prohibit tests above 150 kilotons in yield (Threshold Test Ban Treaty or TTBT) and to regulate so-called peaceful nuclear explosions (Peaceful Nuclear Explosions Treaty or PNET). After those accords were signed in 1974 and 1976, respectively, both governments constrained their test activities in anticipation that the treaties would be ratified. For a time in the Carter administration, there were also negotiations to build upon the achievements of Presidents Nixon and Ford by completing a comprehensive test ban (CTB). The CTB discussions, however, were suspended for most of the next decade, as the Reagan administration deferred any consideration of such a pact until a distant future when the United States would no longer rely on nuclear weapons for deterrence. Meanwhile, for a variety of reasons, no president pressed forward to seek Senate concurrence in the TTBT and PNET—Nixon and Ford because of the inner turmoil and political distractions of their tenures, Carter because he had more ambitious priorities, Reagan because his advisers insisted on stronger verification provisions.

The TTBT and the PNET languished for more than a decade, respected but unratified—indeed, not even submitted for Senate action. This bred rising exasperation in Congress, where both the Senate and House repeatedly urged the president to submit the two agreements for advice and consent. Proponents pointed out that the accords provided significant verification arrangements that would not be implemented until final ratification. They stressed the value of ratification as a means of imparting momentum to the glacial negotiations on other issues. And many members worried about the constitutional implications of habitual compliance with agreements that had never received definitive evaluation by the Senate. For the congressional majorities favoring test limitations, approval of the TTBT and PNET was an essential step toward the larger goal of a comprehensive, verifiable prohibition on all tests.

On the eve of Reagan's meeting with Mikhail Gorbachev at Reykjavík in October 1986, Congress and the president struck a bargain regarding these pacts. The White House agreed to submit them for Senate action, along with recommendations to enhance their verification provisions. In exchange, Congress deleted a number of arms control provisions from the conference version of the fiscal 1987 defense authorization bill. The deal was designed to liberate the president from constraints he found objectionable as he met with the Soviet leader. But it also aimed to end the protracted wrangling over the TTBT and PNET, to clear the decks for the next phase in arms control diplomacy.

The deal broke down amid charges of bad faith when the administration presented the treaties in a manner that would encumber them with a double ratification scheme. Though the Senate might offer advice and consent to the basic treaties, the president proposed to defer implementing the accords until completion of new verification negotiations, which would then require a second action by the Senate. To Senator Nunn and others who had worked to give Reagan maximum leeway at Reykjavík, this procedure amounted to breaking a solemn pledge. They had expected the administration to state its verification requirements so that the Senate could incorporate them, as precedents permitted, in reservations or understandings attached to a single resolution of ratification. The alternative approach now proposed would make any initial Senate vote futile.

What had been conceived as an equitable settlement of interbranch discord was now perceived as one-sided manipulation by the executive branch.

Opinion in the Senate foreign relations committee divided. Some members favored blanket ratification of the agreements with authority for the president to refine their verification provisions without further reference to the Senate; others preferred to delay advice and consent until the submission of final verification language. There was virtually no sentiment for the "twice-through-the-gate" scenario concocted by the administration. Thus, the constitutional anomaly persisted. The nuclear test restraints remained in effect de facto without benefit of formal blessing by the Senate until George Bush succeeded to the Oval Office and concluded additional verification arrangements that brought easy ratification. On 25 September 1990 the Senate voted 98–0 for both treaties and their protocols; accompanying declarations endorsed continuing "safeguards" and further efforts to achieve a comprehensive ban. Two years later Congress would press still harder for a CTB by imposing a moratorium on U.S. tests.

Related concerns arose in a case of far greater import, the SALT II treaty of 1979. Although President Carter withdrew the pact from consideration, he and his successor nonetheless adhered to its principal provisions. Ronald Reagan's denunciation of the treaty as "fatally flawed" did not prompt him to abandon it. As he launched his own initiatives to achieve "real arms control," which he defined as deep cuts in offensive forces, Reagan found it expedient not to undercut the SALT II provisions. That attitude changed in 1986, when the United States for the first time actually approached some of the agreement's ceilings. At that time the president took note that the treaty had never been ratified and in any case would have expired in December 1985. Apparently hoping to put greater pressure on the Soviets to accommodate his proposals, on 27 May 1986 Reagan announced that future decisions on U.S. strategic forces would not be guided by the SALT II standards.[12]

The alarm in Congress and among American allies was palpable. Many saw the Reagan decision to shift course on SALT II as prejudicing the chances for more-satisfactory arms accords. Legislative demands to retain the SALT II limits burst out immediately. In the next several months solid majorities in both houses advanced measures either mandating or admonishing the administration to extend compliance with the treaty, especially its numerical sublimits on multiple-warhead missiles and bombers equipped to carry cruise missiles.

There was a distressing confusion of roles here. Senators and their House colleagues found themselves endorsing U.S. self-restraint, provided the Soviet Union matched it, in several areas that would normally require ratification of treaties to establish constitutional legitimacy. Presidents, one of them avowedly skeptical of arms control, followed as policy treaties that in some respects lacked such legitimacy. Reagan's decision to edge beyond SALT II placed many legislators in the position of urging respect for the agreement, even if it meant nominally less respect for their own constitutional prerogatives.

Troublesome precedents, these. Yet one can comprehend them only as part of a chronic struggle through which the political branches of government strive to fit divergent policy preferences into appropriate constitutional niches. The higher logic of the Constitution does not preclude the Senate from yielding form to assure substance, so long as there are safeguards to prevent permanent deformation of the political structure. It is the gravity of arms diplomacy in the nuclear age that persuaded senators to grant so much leeway in support of negotiations to protect national security. They have done so out of a broad consensus that allowing discretion to the executive offered the best hope of producing agreements on which the Senate could eventually pass judgment. Patience is seldom the child of anxiety, but in the legislature's posture toward executive behavior in the nuclear negotiations, it has been. Nevertheless, when the most profound issues of strategic diplomacy linger for so long in a state not congruent with constitutional practice, Congress must finally act to forestall perpetuation of that misalignment.

One possibility for doing so emerged rather belatedly in Congress, namely, recourse to other powers to ensure that legislative policy prevails on matters that become hostage to slow-motion diplomacy or executive manipulation of the treaty process. As a constitutional matter, Congress did not have to await the presentation of a negotiated agreement to bring U.S. strategic programs and deployments into conformity with standards it believed the Soviet Union was prepared to respect. It had ample authority to determine the size and character of American forces, and there was no constitutional obstacle to statutes setting numbers and types of strategic forces, or the scale and frequency of weapons tests the executive branch may perform. These options flowed from specific congressional powers to raise and equip the nation's armed forces and to control federal expenditures. To paraphrase Justice Jackson's famous formulation, the commander-in-chief may command only those forces Congress places at his disposal.

Legislators have shown great reluctance to employ such powers in the context of ongoing negotiations. No member wants "to do the Russians' work for them," that is, to stipulate by law force restraints for which an adversary should have to bargain. The president's associates constantly play upon apprehension that Congress may weaken the president's hand in negotiations. Yet executive recalcitrance sometimes drives members to reassess their usual reticence on this point. Those who doubted that the Reagan administration was pursuing arms control in earnest took steps that once would have seemed too drastic.

There thus unfolded a game of chicken in which many in Congress tried to throw the burden of choice back to the president. He could have more of the defense spending he wanted if he accepted statutory strictures holding the United States to SALT II deployment levels and severely limiting nuclear tests (always predicated on Soviet reciprocity). Alternatively, he could veto defense bills and, at the price of lower defense spending, ward off arms control provisions to which he objected. For example, following similar action by the House, in October 1987 the Senate voted 57 to 41 to enforce adherence to SALT II limitations as part of the defense authorization bill. Faced with vehement veto threats, the conference committee worked its will by denying funds to overhaul a submarine that would have moved U.S. force levels beyond the SALT II range (Bumpers, Chafee, and Leahy, 1987). These tensions stemmed from the extraordinary collapse of confidence between the branches, brought on in large degree by ideological strains between Hill and White House.

This contest to shape American policy on fundamental strategic questions involved judgments of prudence more than of principle. So far as the Constitution is concerned, there is no reason why Congress should not counter the president's assertive approach to treaties by invoking other powers to protect its own role. Guerrilla warfare between the branches is hardly wholesome, but neither is surrender of Congress's responsibility for the substantive policies intended to be governed by the treaty power. The Reagan administration labored under a cloud of suspicion that it was indifferent to arms control and agreeable to deceiving Congress, when convenient. In the defense authorization bills of the mid-eighties it faced recurrent attempts to impose strategic restraints aimed at preserving the arms control framework for which it had produced no replacement.

THE ABM TREATY REINTERPRETATION DISPUTE

Overriding all other contemporary disputes about arms control treaties was the unprecedented furor surrounding interpretation of the 1972 ABM Treaty. Thirteen years after the treaty received Senate concurrence, officials of the Departments of Defense and State put forward the view that the treaty in fact permitted development and testing of defensive technologies that every administration, including President Reagan's, had consistently said it prohibited.[13] A reinterpretation propounded by State Department Legal Adviser Abraham Sofaer in October 1985 claimed that secret negotiating records, not disclosed to the Senate at the time of ratification, revealed that U.S. negotiators had failed to gain Soviet acceptance of interpretations offered by the executive branch to win advice and consent.

This remarkable assertion was embedded in perhaps the most divisive debate in American strategic history, one provoked by President Reagan's call to shift away from deterrence based on the threat of retaliation to deterrence based on the so-called Strategic Defense Initiative, SDI (Nolan 1989, 1–33, 183–285). At the outset the president had portrayed SDI as purely a research program to be conducted within limits set by the ABM Treaty. Now, however, by reinterpretation of an ambiguous negotiating record, those limits were described as elastic in the extreme.

Without discussing the purported ambiguities with the treaty's American negotiators or with the Soviet Union, the administration asserted the right to proceed with SDI under what it termed "the legally correct interpretation" (LCI). Reeling under the criticisms of leading congressmen, as well as those of Prime Minister Thatcher and Chancellor Kohl, the president was induced by Secretary Shultz to announce that he would hew to the original interpretation merely as a matter of policy.

The claimed right to reinterpret a treaty in direct contradiction of understandings on which the executive branch won ratification elicited vigorous rebukes on constitutional grounds. Even some Republican senators felt that the administration's doctrine would not only weaken relations between the Senate and executive, but could make the Senate irrelevant to the treaty-making process.

Administration spokesmen contended that there was no constitutional crisis. They tried to center the discussion on international, rather than domestic, legal issues. State Department studies were countered by perhaps the most intensive and authoritative treaty assessments ever prepared by individual senators. The independent analyses of Sam Nunn, supplemented by the work of Carl Levin and others, persuaded most observers that the reinterpretation was insupportable as a constitutional matter and implausible as an international one.[14]

The heart of the dispute lay in the administration's bald assertion that the so-called negotiating record, rather than the record of treaty ratification, is the supreme source for determining a treaty's meaning. In fact, the "negotiating record"—the myriad notes, memoranda, cables, and miscellaneous jottings generated through the lengthy ABM Treaty discussions—did not exist in any accessible form when the administration concocted its broad interpretation. These materials included countless internal contradictions that were ironed out by the conclusions incorporated in the treaty itself. The idea of constructing a negotiating record post facto meant that an agreement would be vulnerable to changing interpretation whenever a bureaucrat stumbled across one more misplaced file. Meanwhile, the Soviet Union publicly professed to have accepted the original interpretation and urged negotiations to define more precisely the types of development and testing that would be lawful under the treaty.

The first fact to consider is the fundamental contradiction between an executive claim that the amorphous negotiating record is determinative and the constitutional requirement for Senate advice and consent. The administration's view stood out starkly in testimony by Judge Sofaer: "When it gives its advice and consent to a treaty, it is to the treaty that was made, irrespective of the explanations it is provided"—a statement destined to become notorious in the history of legislative-executive struggle[15] (U.S. House 1985, 130).

The problems with Sofaer's formulation are manifold. Former foreign relations committee chairman J. William Fulbright, who managed the ABM Treaty debate, declared that he would have opposed the agreement or offered reservations to it if he had ever thought it could be radically reinterpreted. He made the point bluntly: "A law means what its framers intended it to mean and not what a later generation of policymakers would like it to mean."[16] Belatedly, the administration conceded that it had omitted from its analyses elements in the ratification proceedings that confirmed the original interpretation. It also acknowledged that the omissions may have a bearing on the president's obligations to the Senate.

A major argument advanced by the reinterpreters held that subordination of the negotiating record to the ratification record as an interpretive standard could destroy the essential "mutuality of obligation" in international agreements. There could well be problems if another party to a treaty has not in fact accepted the interpretations offered to the Senate. The constitutional solution, however, is not to abandon the American interpretation but to pursue its enforcement. If revelations of this nature were discovered in the negotiating files after a treaty was ratified, proper procedure would be to consult with the Senate to determine whether the United States should exercise its right to seek amendments or to withdraw from the treaty.

What unfolded in the ABM Treaty case, however, is something quite different. When the Senate finally extracted portions of the negotiating record from a reluctant executive, exhaustive study by Senator Nunn found far more ambiguity in the negotiating materials than in the ratification proceedings. The diplomatic papers provided nothing approaching the definitive case to which the administration alluded, and the ratification history left little doubt that the senators who addressed the question—among them Henry Jackson and James Buckley—understood the original interpretation to govern. The administration's ardent advocacy strained both records beyond reason. The collective impact of these congressional studies was to shred the administration's credibility.

The episode raised serious problems of a practical nature. If senators cannot rely on the forthrightness of executive testimony, they will have to ferret out the vast and messy reams of material that constitute the negotiating record. That is a prescription for stymieing approval of any treaty. Bureaucratic saboteurs could be tempted to seed the record with documents having no weight at the time but great potential for undermining the accord later. So far as negotiators themselves are concerned, these prospects cripple their capacity to convey credible commitments to foreign interlocutors and to deal with Congress. These implications are quite as perplexing for the executive branch as for the Congress.

In Nunn's analysis, the administration's argument was tantamount to holding that there may be two "contracts" in a single treaty, one between the executive branch and a foreign government, and another between the executive and the Senate. The senator questioned that logic, since there can be no treaty made with a foreign power until the Senate acts. But even under its own terms, the two-contract theory has a one-Constitution prerequisite: if the two contracts are in conflict, the one with the Senate must prevail.

The administration had moved, inch by inch, from what may have seemed a clever ploy to accommodate the president's ambitions for SDI to a profoundly anticonstitutional revision of treaty powers in general. Comments made at a February 1987 meeting of the National Security Council reveal an instinct to interpret treaty obligations as matters of unilateral convenience. Minutes of the session, leaked to ABM Treaty opponents, quoted the president himself as asking, "Why don't we just go ahead on the assumption that this is what we're doing and it's right? Don't ask the Soviets. Tell them. . . . I'll say I've re-evaluated" (Fossedal 1987).

For a number of reasons, the dispute gradually lost its intensity. While the executive branch continued to flirt with the broad interpretation, Congress eviscerated the more expansive conception of the Strategic Defense Initiative, trimming billion of dollars every year from administration requests and redirecting the program away from ventures that would strain treaty limits. By 1991 Republicans Cohen, Lugar, and Warner advised President Bush that the Senate would not support hasty movement toward space-based defenses favored by SDI proponents. They urged him to concentrate on more-modest, ground-based systems and to respect the ABM Treaty while exploring with Moscow possible amendments to allow more than the single-site deployment now permitted.

The transformation of East-West relations in the late eighties gave renewed impetus to arms control as the preferred instrument for mutual security. There was no valid reason to pursue strategic defenses so far as to disrupt cooperative restraints on Russian and American offensive forces. The focus was shifting to other threats, particularly missile strikes against forces in the field, which less demanding technologies might effectively counter. Along that line lay the prospect not only of achievable defenses but also of a workable consensus between Congress and president.

REVIVING A VITAL PRECEDENT: SHARED INFORMATION

If budget cuts and the reorientation of Soviet-American strategic cooperation did not finally resolve the conflict over interpretation of the ABM Treaty, the episode did settle the argument over senators' access to negotiating records. Nunn and others used their leverage over SDI and other strategic programs to compel the administration to supply the voluminous documents that allegedly supported the reinterpreters' claims. With the negotiating record in hand, the senators were able to argue with the administration on an equal footing. This gave them added authority to impose their differing interpretation.

Far from setting a dubious precedent, the Senate's success in obtaining the negotiating record actually revived the original practice established by George Washington. The importance of the Senate's firm posture on the matter became clearer during the Iran-contra affair, when Lt. Col. Oliver North invoked a widespread myth by asserting that the first president had refused to turn over treaty negotiating records to Congress. Indeed, Washington had declined to provide the House of Representatives with materials relating to negotiation of the Jay Treaty, stating that he would do so only if the House request were framed in terms of a constitutional function allocated to that body, such as impeachment. The relevant precedent, however, had been set months before, when the Senate considered and recommended ratification of the controversial accord, the first treaty negotiated under the Constitution. Although the treaty was an embarrassment to the Washington administration, and although Jay had exceeded his instructions on some points, the president had conveyed the negotiating records to the Senate for its confidential review (Sofaer 1976, 85–93; Frye 1987). North, like those arguing that only executive officials could see and interpret the ABM Treaty negotiating records, was advocating a constitutional aberration that would render meaningless the Senate's role in ratification.

Thus, in protecting its prerogative to receive and evaluate the ABM Treaty records, the Senate was providing an indispensable balance between the branches. That it intended to maintain that balance became clearer when the Treaty on Intermediate Nuclear Forces (INF) was concluded in 1987. The Senate insisted on timely submission of the relevant negotiating materials, subject to appropriate safeguards, and the administration reluctantly complied. While a few senators exploited the records in an effort to block ratification, the availability of the records undoubtedly smoothed Senate approval by confirming the president's good faith. After the flap over the ABM Treaty, many members needed reassurance that future confrontations were not hiding among the negotiating files. Close Senate scrutiny helped identify a small number of ambiguities and open questions, mainly bearing on verification, which deserved further discussion with Moscow before ratification. Secretary of State George Shultz saw to it that these problems were resolved in short order, and the Senate tendered its advice and consent with but trivial opposition (Nolan 1991).

Members used the INF proceeding to signal that stringent verification arrangements would be necessary for the Senate to approve major reductions in strategic forces. The debate on that topic fortified an executive branch already committed to intrusive inspection as a prerequisite to a START agreement.

The INF Treaty review also caused tendencies of quite a contradictory sort to surface. After years of demands for on-site inspection and access to the most intimate details of Soviet military capabilities, the United States had second thoughts. The Joint Chiefs of Staff and some military industrialists came to fear the loss of technological intelligence to Soviet inspectors. American corporations were quite concerned about the loss of proprietary information and the impact on future government contracts if the Defense Department found it advisable to favor firms not subject to inspection. These considerations played back into the INF debate and produced some safeguards in the resolution of approval, which, inter alia, prohibited discrimination against inspected facilities in government contract decisions.

CONCLUSION

This essay has drawn only a few illustrations of the remarkable changes that characterize legislative-executive relations in security policy and arms control. The pattern depicted here—one of mounting congressional engagement on issues long considered primarily an executive preserve—holds on many other fronts.

Item: Pressing for negotiations on chemical weapons, for several years a moderate majority in Congress delayed funding for so-called binary munitions. By 1991 older chemical weapons were coming out of Europe, and the United States helped lead the way to conclusion of a multilateral convention banning such weapons.

Item: While arms control initiatives to ban antisatellite weapons (ASAT) foundered, congressional restraints on ASAT tests prevented premature experiments in that field from undercutting related negotiations on strategic defenses and, not incidentally, avoided commitment to technologies that would be inadequate if ASAT eventually proves necessary.

Item: Despite pro forma executive declarations of interest in a comprehensive nuclear test ban (CTB) as an ultimate objective, it was active congressional support for a CTB that kept the issue alive in U.S. policy. Beyond repeated reminders that the United States is committed by treaty to pursue a verifiable CTB, Congress on its own initiative mandated a "test ban readiness" program to ensure that, in the event of a CTB, American nuclear weapons would remain safe and reliable. In 1992 it imposed a moratorium on U.S. tests and set strict guidelines for any resumption.

By no means do these interventions signify that Congress is the sole fount of wisdom on the nation's security. Nor do they indicate that Congress has decisively taken charge to set the arms control agenda for the nation. What they do demonstrate is that a legislature once inclined to doubt its capacity to deal with the arcana of strategy and arms control has found the means and the self-confidence to enter the field with vigor and determination. The scope and detail of such congressional intervention, as well as the diverse range of legislative participants, mark a sharp contrast between earlier decades and the period since the late 1960s.

Notably, leaders in both branches have often shifted position on arms control questions. Those shifts respond to a changing policy context — negotiating positions for dealing with Joseph Stalin or Leonid Brezhnev were inappropriate for dealing with Mikhail Gorbachev or Boris Yeltsin — and to evolving ideological preferences among leaders of Congress and the executive. The main constant in the institutional equation is the Capitol's tendency to resist excesses in executive policy, whether overexuberance in arms control or overeagerness in arms deployments.

It is also notable that congressional action on these issues has been largely free of sustained interest-group pressure for arms control. Grassroots movements have generated recurrent campaigns — for the nuclear test ban in 1961–63, against the ABM programs of 1968–72, for the nuclear freeze in 1981–83 — but they have not established the kind of potent lobbying forces associated with many other interests. Because arms control campaigns peak and fade, the persistent congressional attention to these issues depends on the recognition by elites within Congress of their vital importance. By and large, legislative action on arms control is policy driven rather than interest group driven.

In my opinion, recent struggles over arms control and security policy have arrested several pernicious tendencies that had crept into legislative-executive practice. In some respects the executive has been obliged to accommodate the legislature's insistence on sharing responsibility for strategic policy and nuclear diplomacy.

Indisputably, the president remains the principal in the process. Congress acts most often by qualifying executive proposals it is reluctant to reject. It constrains the president's options, rather than denying them flatly. Arms control proponents in Congress can at most encourage a president to negotiate with a foreign power. At times, however, a persuaded majority can maximize the executive's incentives to negotiate by linking diplomatic effort to approval of weapons programs sought by the administration. That Congress has shown itself willing to exploit that linkage on MX, SDI, chemical weapons, and antisatellite systems is a clear measure of the activist role it has assumed.

There is little evidence that the altered balance of influence on these delicate matters has undermined U.S. effectiveness in coping with these matters. On the contrary, it has tempered more extreme impulses in executive behavior, while adding some leverage to American negotiators dealing with other nations. Fears that legislative involvement in arms negotiations or strategic decisions would imperil the nation have turned out to be misplaced.

On the overriding questions of high policy, the interbranch frictions and diversions and procrastinations have worked over time to encourage a national security posture that combines preparedness with restraint. Congress and the president have agreed to field a robust nuclear and conventional force, but they have also kept alive the negotiating process that has at long last yielded historic results. Far from disrupting this endeavor, Congress has sometimes shown strategic foresight, as on the MIRV question, and diplomatic imagination, as in its initiatives to preserve the ABM Treaty and to spur a strategic build-down. Some will contend that these efforts shackled an executive who would have produced better and quicker results if left to its own devices. Evidence for such claims does not leap spontaneously from the record of recent administrations.

Haltingly, selectively, erratically, Congress has reinvigorated the founders' design. Even the most farsighted presidents benefit from the discipline of accountability, in matters of arms control no less than in other fields. That discipline has increased during the last two decades. Sustaining it will be vital to the quality and consistency of American security policy in the decades to come.

Chapter Nine

★ ★ ★

DISAGREEING
ON LATIN AMERICA

★ ★ ★

Robert A. Pastor

THE BALANCE OF INTERBRANCH POWER:
CYCLICAL, SECULAR, OR SIMILAR?

From Alexis de Tocqueville through George F. Kennan, most students of American government and diplomacy have argued that the U.S. president is and should be preeminent in foreign affairs and that congressional assertiveness in this area is worrisome.[1] The collision in the 1980s between President Ronald Reagan and Congress on aid to the contras was a wrenching example of how interbranch disagreement can handicap U.S. policy, although analysts differ on the cause of that conflict and its long-term implications.[2] Is conflict between the branches increasing? Is there a trend of congressional assertiveness, and is this a *cyclical* phenomenon in U.S. history? Or do structural changes portend a *secular* trend and a permanent increase in congressional power? Or is the current relationship basically *similar* to that of the past?

To answer these questions, I will examine U.S. foreign policy toward Latin America and the Caribbean during the last thirty years, when the pendulum of power swung, or at least was perceived to have swung, from the president to Congress and back again. In 1960, when presidential power and the cold war were unquestioned, Fidel Castro's invitation to the Soviet Union to establish a close relationship with Cuba evoked an arsenal of U.S. initiatives ranging from a covert attack at the Bay of Pigs to the Alliance for Progress. By the early 1970s, the "imperial presidency" came under attack. "Vietnam," wrote Arthur M. Schlesinger, "discredited executive control of foreign relations as profoundly as Versailles and mandatory neutrality had discredited congressional control" (1973, 283). By the late 1970s, complaints arrived from the opposite direction: the pendulum had swung too far toward congressional assertiveness (Franck and Weisband 1979). Finally, the reelection of Ronald Reagan in 1984 and his apparent skill in manipulating Congress led some to believe that the pendulum had swung back again to presidential power. In brief, the last thirty years offer a good field for examining whether the balance of power between the two branches has been subject to a cyclical pattern, whether there has been a secular trend in favor of increasing congressional power, or whether the relationship between the two branches has not changed very much.

At the same time, U.S. policy toward Latin America offers a particularly good test of the thesis of presidential preeminence in foreign policy, since so much of the policy seems to have been made by the president. From the Monroe Doctrine to the Reagan doctrine, from McKinley's Spanish-American War to Bush's invasion of Panama, from the building of the Panama Canal by Theodore Roosevelt to its "giveaway" by Jimmy Carter, from FDR's Good Neighbor policy to JFK's Alliance for Progress, from Kennedy's Bay of Pigs to Reagan's contra scandal — U.S. policy toward the region has been identified with presidents and sculpted by their interventions.

It would be tempting to trace the role of Congress in the formulation of these landmark initiatives, but that would require a volume. Indeed, even a comprehensive examination of U.S. policy toward Latin America during the last thirty years is beyond the scope of this work. I will have to restrict myself to a few cases, and I have selected the following: (1) The Alliance for Progress, 1961–69; (2) U.S. policy on human rights, 1975–85; (3) negotiation and ratification of the Panama Canal treaties from Lyndon Johnson to Jimmy Carter; (4) the long battle over Nicaragua that preoccupied Presidents Carter, Reagan, and Bush and the Congress in the 1980s; and (5) the U.S. invasion of Panama, December 1989.

These cases were chosen using the "structured, focused comparison" method to test several sets of hypotheses (George 1979). To assess whether the balance of power between the branches has remained the same or been subject to a cyclical pattern or a secular trend, the cases had to span the whole time period. If the "cyclical theory" is correct, one would expect presidential dominance on the Alliance for Progress, the contras, and the invasion of Panama, and congressional assertiveness on human rights and the Panama Canal Treaties. If the "secular trend theory" is correct, one would expect presidential dominance only on the alliance, with increasing congressional power in the latter four cases. If the relationship between the branches is basically unchanged, one would expect that the two branches would have interacted in similar ways in all five cases.

That explains the need for cases that span the thirty-year period, but it doesn't explain why these specific cases were selected. There are many potential cases, but these five were pivotal moments in U.S. policy toward Latin America during the past thirty years. Throughout the 1960s the

Alliance for Progress was the defining element of U.S. policy; it represented a reaction to Castro's support for revolution and a positive effort to promote development. Although the human rights program has been identified with Jimmy Carter, it actually began during the Nixon-Ford administrations and continued to evolve through the Reagan administration. The policy had a profound impact on the region during the 1970s. The Panama Canal treaties were the most controversial and difficult that the president and the United States Senate had faced since the Treaty of Versailles. In the 1980s President Reagan's commitment to the contras was the issue that engaged his attention most fully, and the invasion of Panama to replace General Noriega was President Bush's rite of passage. In brief, the five cases were defining moments in U.S. policy during the last thirty years.

The five issues were also representative of U.S. foreign policies toward Latin America. Aid has long been a central element in U.S. policy, and the alliance was the largest foreign aid program. The human rights policy has much in common with U.S. efforts to promote democracy and project its domestic concerns and values in the region. The Panama Canal has probably been the single most treasured American asset in Latin America and also the most controversial Latin American issue ever debated in the U.S. Senate. The contras were the most recent of a large number of covert actions—in Guatemala, Cuba, the Dominican Republic, Chile—aimed at undermining unfriendly governments in the region. And the decision to use force in Panama has a similarly large number of precedents, especially, but not only, during the first three decades of the twentieth century.

The five cases also demonstrate five kinds of state instruments in which different actors are involved. The alliance represents a transfer of taxpayer resources to the region; human rights is often a matter of routine diplomacy; the Panama Canal issue was settled by a treaty that required a two-thirds vote of the Senate; the contras were a covert action; and the Panama invasion represented the first overt use of unilateral force by the United States for over sixty years. If all five cases were treaties or covert actions, we would only be able to test the nature of the interbranch relationship for treaties or covert actions. Since the cases reflect the full spectrum of foreign and defense policies, we are better positioned to judge the hypotheses on the balance of institutional power and the utility of analyzing U.S. foreign policy solely from a presidential perspective.

Our purpose in examining these cases is to understand the nature of the interaction between the two branches and the process by which U.S. policy is made. There are a "thicket of theories" for explaining U.S. foreign policy; most tend to focus on the bureaucratic crevices or the organizational routines of the executive branch or on the psychological dysfunctions of executive decision makers (Kurth 1989). Although there are numerous theories of congressional policy, few have focused on Congress's role in foreign policy making, perhaps because of the assumption that its role is minor. In this chapter, I will not try to test different theories of U.S. foreign policy making; rather, I will assess the utility of an executive-dominant or an interbranch politics perspective.

The premise of the executive-dominant approach is that all one needs to do to understand the process and outcome of U.S. foreign policy is to study the executive branch. The interbranch politics approach, on the contrary, defines U.S. foreign policy as the product of a subtle and dynamic process of interaction between the two branches; the principal hypothesis is that foreign policy differs importantly from the president's preferences, and the variance can be explained by the influence or the decisions of Congress. Executive-dominant perspectives on U.S. foreign policy assume that the president initiates foreign policies and Congress impedes or obstructs. Interbranch politics suggests that the roles can be reversed, with Congress initiating and the president blocking.[3] For clues on the evolution and nature of foreign policies, executive theories focus on the struggle within the executive branch, while interbranch politics looks to the signals that are sent from one end of Pennsylvania Avenue to the other. While some suggest that differences in the foreign policy process might be due to the nature of the issue (Lowi 1964; Evangelista 1989), the interbranch lens suggests that the key distinction is the instrument of policy—that is, law, treaty, appointment, diplomacy, or war.

In the next section, I will offer an overview of U.S. policy toward Latin America. Then, I will develop the five cases, discuss the questions related to the supposed shift in the balance of institutional power and the roots of interbranch conflict, and, finally, offer some thoughts on an interbranch politics perspective and on its usefulness in explaining the U.S. foreign policy process.

MOTIVES VIVENDI

Since independence, U.S. foreign policy has been torn between realistic calculations of national security and idealistic aspirations for a democratic world community. Toward no region has this tension been more evident than Latin America, where U.S. policy makers have wrestled with the contradictions between James Monroe's dictum to exclude foreign rivals and Woodrow Wilson's dream to respect self-determination and defend human rights. The dilemma has usually been resolved by an interbranch compromise between security and values.

Beginning with the Monroe Doctrine, virtually every important U.S. policy has included both a moral and a realistic dimension. Monroe declared that the Western Hemisphere's promise of republican government made it separate and better than Europe, but he also warned the Europeans not to try to gain a new foothold in the New World. The doctrine combined the idealistic voice of Henry Clay, Speaker of the House, who advocated a ringing declaration of solidarity with worldwide democratic revolution, and the realist voice of Secretary of State John Quincy Adams, who argued that U.S. security could best be defended by keeping Europe out of the Americas and the United States out of Europe.[4] Some have charged that the idealistic component was just rhetoric, but such views neglect the influence of the moral argument in the American debate, and the "distinctive cast," in Samuel Huntington's phrase, that these values inject in U.S. foreign policy (1989, 239).

For most of the nineteenth century, the United States concentrated on continental expansion, industrial consolidation, internal division over slavery, and then national unification. The constraint on U.S. expansion into Latin America was not the power of Europe or the nationalism of Latin America, but reservations within the United States itself. Before the Civil War, northerners impeded expansion for fear that it would mean more slave states. After the Civil War, the country debated whether to be imperialistic like Europe, but until the century turned, the answer was negative.

The Spanish-American War marked not only the division between the centuries but also America's changed role in the hemisphere. In the nineteenth century, the United States was unconcerned with the chronic instability in Central America and the Caribbean, but in the twentieth century, the United States was often obsessed with these countries' internal affairs. What changed was that the United States now had a larger stake in the region — primarily because of the Panama Canal — and a growing fear that Germany and Japan would take advantage of the region's instability to gain a foothold.

In 1898 Congress pressed President William McKinley into war, but, paradoxically, it also limited his objectives. The Teller amendment to the declaration of war was uniquely American in its pledge not to annex the war's main prize, Cuba. The president resisted the amendment, but Congress compelled him to accept it. The United States fought to free Cuba, not enslave or annex it, but it was also not willing to let Cuba be completely free. In 1901 Congress passed the Platt amendment giving the United States the right to intervene in Cuba's affairs, and Cuba was obliged to insert the amendment into its constitution. Together, the Teller and Platt amendments defined the nation's distaste for imperialism but also its unwillingness to accept equality with small, unstable neighbors. The compromise was an American variation of imperialism, a new kind of relationship that would permit Cuba to have a circumscribed independence. This "protectorate" policy characterized U.S. relations with several governments in the Caribbean during the first three decades of the twentieth century.

The United States turned inward after World War I, and by the late 1920s it began to withdraw its marines from the entire region. Franklin Roosevelt's Good Neighbor policy formally dismantled the last vestiges of the previous era—withdrawing marines, repealing Platt amendments, and accepting the principle of nonintervention. Roosevelt deliberately fashioned new, respectful relationships with Latin America that paid a handsome dividend when the United States went to war against Germany and Japan.

The United States did not turn inward after World War II as it had done before. It organized new global political and economic institutions. As tensions with the Soviet Union increased, the United States developed a global strategy aimed at containing Soviet expansionism. The principal threats were in Europe and Asia. In the early postwar period, the prospects for a Communist takeover in the hemisphere were judged by the CIA as small.

President Dwight D. Eisenhower and his secretary of state John Foster Dulles saw the threat more intensely then President Truman and Dean Acheson had done, and approved a program to overturn the leftist regime in Guatemala in 1954. By then, the dominant motive guiding U.S. foreign policy toward Latin America was a fear of Soviet expansion through Communist subversion. When the threat was perceived as remote, the United States, by and large, concentrated on other regions or issues. But when it was viewed as more immediate, the United States employed a wide range of economic, political, diplomatic, and military instruments to counter the threat and alleviate the root causes of instability. No threat was viewed more seriously than the decision by Fidel Castro in 1960 to establish a close relationship with the Soviet Union. This was considered a flagrant violation of the Monroe Doctrine.

THE ALLIANCE FOR PROGRESS
The Bay of Pigs invasion and the Alliance for Progress were the two Janus faces of the classic American strategy: a covert intervention to overthrow Castro and a Pan American initiative to promote economic development. On 13 March 1961, while Cuban exiles were making final preparations for their invasion, President Kennedy unveiled his ten-year, $10 billion aid plan for the Alliance for Progress. He requested $3 billion for the first three years so as to permit the Latin Americans to make long-term development plans. Congress applauded the program and then reduced it by $600 million and insisted that the president would have to request appropriations annually. This was not the first time, nor would it be the last, that the president would ask for multiyear appropriations and Congress would reject the request and reduce the amount (Pastor 1980, chap. 9).

Several years before, Congress had recommended to the Eisenhower administration that it shift its foreign policy emphasis to economic aid and increase it, and at the initiative of Senator Mike Monroney, Congress passed a resolution urging the establishment of the International Development Association (IDA) to make low-interest concessional loans to the developing world. In August 1958 eight members of the Senate foreign relations committee, including Senator John F. Kennedy, followed up this congressional initiative with a letter to the president decrying his misplaced priorities and recommending a renewed emphasis on economic aid to the developing world. As president, Kennedy was better positioned to implement this new priority, but he was met by a new Congress that did not want to do as much as it had proposed when faced with a more niggardly Eisenhower administration.

Not only was Congress intent on reducing the size of the alliance and keeping the president on a short leash, it had some of its own ideas on directions the program should take. The first important disagreement between the branches occurred on the issue of how the United States should respond to expropriations of U.S. businesses in Latin America. Since the Marshall Plan, both Congress and the president had viewed foreign investment as an important component of the U.S. foreign aid package: public funds were considered insufficient and private enterprise thought to be the best instrument to stimulate economic growth.

Castro's expropriations of U.S. companies caused many in Congress to fear that other governments would repeat his actions, and when a governor of a Brazilian state expropriated a U.S. power company in 1959, two senators introduced an amendment to put a halt to the trend. They proposed to deny foreign aid to a government that expropriated American property without "adequate, effective, and prompt compensation." The State Department argued strongly against the amendment, and it was narrowly defeated.

Three years later, in 1962, as Congress debated the alliance and after another Brazilian governor had expropriated a subsidiary of Internationl Telephone and Telegraph Corporation (ITT), Senator Bourke Hickenlooper introduced a similar amendment. The Kennedy administration took the same negative stance as its predecessor had. In a press conference President Kennedy called the amendment "unwise," and Secretary of State Dean Rusk told the Senate foreign relations committee: "There can be no difference between us . . . on the objective of doing everything that we can to create the right kind of environment for private investment. But I do think that such a [mandatory] provision would create very severe complications in our relations with other governments" (U.S. Senate, 1962, 31).

Thus the traditional roles were reversed, with Congress trying to make policy and the president attempting to obstruct, claiming that new legislation was neither necessary nor desirable. In the end, the executive succeeded in diluting the amendment so that a one-year delay was permitted before aid would have to be suspended. But the nationalizations continued, and many in Congress questioned the administration's commitment. The next year, Hickenlooper and Senator Wayne Morse introduced a more stringent amendment that applied to a much wider category of investment disputes.

Rusk adopted a different strategy to defeat the new amendment. Although he had called the previous year's amendment ill conceived, in 1963 he testified that it "has been a good thing," and he suspended aid to Ceylon for failing to compensate an American oil company. The action served to undercut support for the amendment. By this time the State Department had learned that it would have to defend U.S. businesses overseas to gain congressional approval of the foreign aid bill. In brief, Congress succeeded in pressing a new U.S. interest onto the foreign policy agenda.

U.S. HUMAN RIGHTS POLICY
Through the 1960s the United States gradually lost interest in the Alliance for Progress, and scarce foreign aid resources were diverted to Southeast Asia. Although aid to Latin America declined, Congress's intention to use the aid bill as a vehicle to redirect U.S. foreign policy did not diminish. As presidents changed, Congress seemed to pivot around the new president and propose a new set of priorities. Congress had considered Kennedy insufficiently committed to promoting U.S. business interests; its concerns about Nixon and Ford were that both presidents were uninterested in human rights. Moving hesitantly at first, Congress gradually gained confidence and acted with increasing vigor and determination to compensate for executive uninterest.

American concern for human rights was written in the first ten amendments to the Constitution and extended to the world by the leadership of Eleanor Roosevelt in the United Nations. The most recent incarnation of a U.S. human rights policy began in the early 1970s. Senator Frank Church held hearings in the foreign relations committee on torture and repression in Brazil (U.S. Senate 1971). Distressed over the continuation of U.S. military and economic aid to a regime that routinely tortured and imprisoned its citizens, Church insisted that the Agency for International Development (AID) consider ending its program there. The State Department responded that the United States should not try to impose American standards abroad, but at the same time, AID privately reassessed its program in Brazil and began to reduce it.

To translate a moral impulse into a coherent human rights policy required some intellectual leadership, and that was provided by Congressman Donald Fraser, chairman of a House foreign affairs subcommittee. He organized hearings in his committee that were equivalent to a National Security Council (NSC) interagency policy review and in March 1974 published the conclusions in a report, *Human Rights in the World Community: A Call for U.S. Leadership.* The report contained twenty-nine specific recommendations on ways to incorporate human rights into U.S. foreign policy decision making.[5]

President Richard Nixon devoted little time or attention to Latin America, but one issue that engaged him was the election of a Marxist, Salvador

Allende, as president of Chile in 1970. After failing to prevent Allende from taking power, Nixon approved a policy that contributed to Chile's political polarization and eventually to Allende's overthrow by General Augusto Pinochet. Having ended all aid to Allende, the Nixon administration then started an aid program to the new military regime, despite reports of widespread torture and "disappearances."

The administration's response to the military regime in Chile provided Congress with a concrete case to apply Fraser's recommendations. Led by Congressman Dante Fascell and Senator Edward Kennedy, Congress amended the aid law with a nonbinding sense-of-the-Congress resolution that "the President should deny any economic or military assistance to the government of any foreign country which practices the internment or imprisonment of that country's citizens for political purposes." Instead of reducing or denying aid, the administration asked for an increase, and so the next year, in December 1974, Congress tightened the law, setting a ceiling on economic aid and prohibiting miltitary aid to Chile.

Again, the president ignored Congress's intent and boosted aid to Chile by shifting funds from other projects. Congress took a further step in 1975 by prohibiting aid not just to Chile but to any government that engages in gross violations of human rights "unless such assistance will directly benefit the needy people in such country." The executive, of course, still had the power to judge a country's human rights conditions and the aid program's possible effects, but it was put on notice. As it failed to evince any commitment to implementing the policy, Congress moved step-by-step to deny the executive any discretion. Thus was the policy generalized from the case of Chile to the entire developing world.

The Nixon and Ford administrations wanted to support a government that could "pull Chile together in the long-term" and help it to recover after the anti-American leftist rule of Allende, but it did not want to suggest that it opposed human rights, so it wrapped its true reason in a blanket of other interests. The human rights issue in Chile was "a part of a large relationship," according to the then deputy assistant secretary of state Harry Shlaudeman, "a part which has to be weighed against other parts" (U.S. House 1974, 132–33). Secretary of State Henry Kissinger rejected Congress's signal to reduce aid to Chile on grounds of effectiveness, but he was also arguing prerogative: "We have generally opposed attempts to deal with sensitive international human rights issues through legislation — not because of the moral view expressed, which we share, but because legislation is almost always too inflexible, too public, and too heavy-handed a means to accomplish what it seeks."[6]

Despite this statement, Kissinger requested more aid for Chile, leading some in Congress to believe that his arguments over the means of policy might actually have masked a difference over ends. "Suppose you are in the

Pinochet government," Congressman Donald Fraser asked an administration witness tongue-in-cheek, and despite gross human rights violations, "our Ambassador and AID mission was continuing to negotiate new loans and new assistance. What would be the message you would get?" (U.S. House 1976, 36). That message was different from what Congress wanted the administration to send, and so it limited the executive's discretion; it tied its hands. Don Fraser explained that the restrictions were a result "of growing congressional frustration at the increasing tendency of the executive branch to ignore the statutes enacted by Congress" (U.S. House 1976, 117).

After Carter took office and elevated human rights to be the "soul" of his foreign policy, some congressmen continued to try to expand the policy into other areas, for example, to apply it to the Export-Import Bank, the International Monetary Fund, and GATT. The executive branch under Carter opposed these efforts for the same reasons of prerogative and desire for flexibility that Nixon and Ford had opposed them. At a press conference Carter explained his opposition to the Harkin amendment, which would have required the United States to vote no in the international development banks on loans to countries that violate human rights: "To have a frozen mandatory prohibition against our nation voting for any loan simply removes my ability to bargain with a foreign leader whom we think might be willing to [improve] human rights. . . . We need to have the flexibility" (Carter 1977, 636). Unlike his predecessors or successors, Carter succeeded in stopping the human rights amendments mainly because Congress judged that he would use the flexibility in pursuit of human rights.

Congress began to pass restrictive human rights amendments again after the inauguration of Ronald Reagan, who was more committed to stopping leftist subversion than to curbing human rights violations among "friendly" regimes. The Reagan administration sought large aid packages for the contras and the Salvadoran government, and the Congress repeatedly attached stringent conditions on the use of the aid in order to encourage greater respect for human rights.

THE PANAMA CANAL TREATIES

Although the texture of Carter's policy toward Latin America was formed by human rights, the most controversial political issue he faced was the Panama Canal Treaty. Since the riots in the Panama Canal Zone in January 1964, every U.S. president understood the logic for new canal treaties. The exclusive control by the United States of a ten-mile-wide strip of land through the middle of Panama was an outmoded relic of a bygone era. The longer the United States refused to correct this wrong, the greater the risk to the canal from nationalistic Panamanians, and the more difficult for the United States to build good relationships with the democratic governments in Latin America that identified with Panama's cause. Most U.S. policy makers understood this, but they also recognized that a majority of Americans did not want to give up the canal.

Therefore, treaty negotiations dragged on from 1965. In February 1974 Secretary of State Henry Kissinger negotiated a "Joint Statement of Eight Principles," an outline of a new treaty, with his counterpart, Panamanian foreign minister Juan Tack. The principles called for the termination of perpetual rights by the United States, a gradual transfer of jurisdiction and operation of the canal to Panama, and a new formula for defending the canal. Even before the negotiators set to work to translate these principles into a treaty, the Congress stepped between them. Senator Strom Thurmond of South Carolina introduced a Senate resolution with thirty-four cosponsors (enough to prevent ratification of a treaty) and Congressman Dan Flood and 120 representatives introduced similar resolutions in the House, urging the United States to stop negotiating and "retain continued undiluted sovereignty over the Canal Zone." Thurmond condemned the Kissinger-Tack declaration and argued that it could not be "reconciled with the Senate resolution."[7] The initiatives by Thurmond and Flood effectively precluded any further negotiations until Carter's inauguration.

Despite the political cost, Jimmy Carter decided to give high priority to negotiating a new treaty, for two reasons. First, the administration believed that the canal's security would be jeopardized by delay, since the Panamanian "patience machine," in Omar Torrijos's pungent phrase, "was running out of gas" after thirteen years of fruitless negotiations. Second, because ratification would be politically difficult, the administration decided to try to complete negotiations well in advance of the November 1978 elections.

In 1977 the State and Defense Departments began by negotiating between themselves, but the president directed the negotiators to the real task of brokering an agreement between Panama and the Senate. In July the negotiations bogged down over Panama's insistence on large payments from the United States. As Carter wrote in his memoirs, "Neither I nor Congress would agree to any payments to Panama other than those that could come out of revenues from the Canal itself." Carter realized that he could not ask the Senate to give away the canal and pay Panama at the same time. On 29 July he sent a letter to Torrijos saying that U.S. negotiators were making their last offer, and that time was running out for Senate ratification (J. Carter 1982, 158). Torrijos accepted the economic proposals, and on 7 September 1977, Carter and Torrijos signed two treaties.

The Panama Canal Treaty set a date—the year 2000—when Panama would have complete jurisdiction and operational authority over the canal. From the implementation of the treaty to 2000, the United States would gradually turn over responsibility for the administration, operation, and defense of the canal. The second treaty, on permanent neutrality, guaranteed that the United States would retain the right to defend the canal after the year 2000.

Hearings began in the Senate foreign relations committee on 26 September. Only two genuinely substantive issues were debated: the unilateral right of the United States to defend the canal and the right of American ships to go to "the head of the line" in time of emergency. Although U.S. negotiators believed the treaties dealt adequately with these two issues, key senators disagreed. To resolve the problem, Carter invited Torrijos to the White House on 14 October, and the two agreed to an "Understanding" that removed any ambiguity on these two issues. The majority and minority leaders of the Senate, Robert Byrd and Howard Baker, later introduced this "Understanding" as a treaty amendment.

The Senate ratification debate was second only to that over the Versailles treaty in length, and it was tense and difficult the entire time. On 16 March 1978 the Senate voted first on the Treaty on the Permanent Neutrality of the Panama Canal. One month later, the Panama Canal Treaty passed by the same vote, 68–32.

The Carter administration consulted more regularly and fully with the Senate during the course of the canal treaty negotiations than had ever been done before.[8] As a result of those consultations, the Senate leadership defined the treaties' parameters—requiring that the United States retain the permanent right to unilaterally defend the Canal and not pay Panama.

U.S. POLICY TOWARD NICARAGUA

For a period of fifteen years beginning in 1975, four U.S. presidents struggled to find a policy toward Nicaragua that would facilitate a democratic transition. None succeeded. Ironically, only after President Bush gave up did a democratic solution finally emerge. During this period the issues faced by U.S. policy makers changed quite substantially. From 1975 to 1978 both the Ford and Carter administrations used a combination of carrots and sticks— promises of aid and threats of withdrawal and sanctions—to encourage the Somoza regime to liberalize. Somoza liberalized politics somewhat, but the only change that Nicaraguans wanted was Somoza's departure.

From 1978 to 1979 the Carter administration tried to mediate a democratic transition. Congressional pressures were felt on both sides of the issue: liberals in Congress argued that Carter should push harder to get Somoza to resign, while Somoza's conservative friends insisted that the United States leave him alone, lest the Communists take over. Since the administration's efforts were primarily diplomatic and did not require congressional consent, Congress was never compelled to take a unified position, and the two-sided pressure left the Carter administration the space to pursue the policies it wanted.[9]

After the Sandinistas took power in 1979, Carter decided to try to forget a good relationship by helping the new government. He requested $75 million of aid in November 1979, and Congress approved the program in the summer of 1980, after wrestling with the policy and its implications. The final law carried a laundry list of conditions and limitations on the use of the aid, all of which the Carter administration opposed but was obliged to accept. The key condition was that Carter would have to certify to Congress that Nicaragua was not supporting insurgencies before he disbursed aid. The Carter administration had already pressed this concern in its discussions with the new regime, and there is evidence that the Sandinistas took it into account and modified their support of the Salvadoran guerrillas (FMLN).[10]

Nonetheless, in the light of the congressional mandate, the president sent a State Department representative to Managua in September 1980 to repeat the point with added strength. The Sandinistas pledged not to transfer arms to the FMLN. Documents captured from the FMLN four months later revealed that the second démarche led the Sandinistas to postpone transferring weapons that had been stockpiled and were about to be sent. The Sandinistas kept their word until about November 1980, when, under intensified pressure from Cuba and the FMLN, they finally dispatched the arms, fracturing the tenuous accommodation with the United States.

The Reagan administration came into office believing that the Sandinistas were Communists, opposed to free elections, and intent on aiding guerrillas throughout the region. The administration ended the aid program and then tried to negotiate its security concerns. When those negotiations failed, President Reagan approved a plan in November 1981 to organize, fund, and train a group of Nicaraguans, the contras, to attack the Sandinista government.[11] In March 1982 the contras destroyed two bridges in Nicaragua. The Sandinista government responded by declaring a state of emergency, beginning a process that would polarize politics in Nicaragua and the United States for a decade.

The congressional intelligence committees had initially accepted the contras because the administration claimed that its goal was to interdict arms supplies to Salvadoran rebels. By the end of 1982, however, contra leaders had clearly stated their intention to overthrow the Sandinista government, and Congress began to attach conditions on aid to the contras, insisting that the funds not be used to overthrow the Sandinista government and pressing the administration to negotiate. President Reagan tried to persuade Congress to approve additional aid, but few believed that the administration was genuinely interested in negotiations. Evidence later disclosed during the Iran-contra hearings and Oliver North's trial confirmed that Congress's skepticism was justified. In an NSC meeting on 25 June 1984, Reagan said that the only purpose of mentioning negotiations was to try to convince Congress to give more aid to the contras: "If we are just talking about negotiations with Nicaragua, that is too far-fetched to imagine that a Communist government like that would make any reasonable deal with us, but if it is to get Congress to support the anti-Sandinistas, then that can be helpful."[12]

The 1984 omnibus appropriations bill, signed by Reagan on 12 October 1984, contained a new Boland (II) amendment that prohibited the U.S. government from funding the contras. Boland said that the law "clearly ends U.S. support for the war in Nicaragua" (U.S. Congress 1987b, 41). Though Reagan signed the law, he also told his national security adviser, Robert McFarlane, to "assure the contras of continuing administration support [and]—to help them hold body and soul together—until the time when Congress would again agree to support them" (U.S. Congress 1987b, 4). Oliver North's job was to keep the funds and arms flowing to the contras. His operation began when the law said it should stop, and it continued until aid was approved in the fall of 1986 and his operation was disclosed. Reagan was then compelled to dismiss NSC Adviser John Poindexter and North. The Iran-contra affair that grew out of this scandal undermined Reagan's policy toward Nicaragua and tainted his presidency.

In August 1987 the five presidents of Central America met in Esquipulas, Guatemala, and signed a plan first proposed by Costa Rican president Oscar Arias Sánchez. The plan called for democratization through national reconciliation and an end to outside support for insurgencies. Before that meeting, and afterward, President Reagan requested military aid for the contras from Congress, arguing that only such aid would bring the Sandinistas to the bargaining table. The Central Americans, however, argued that peace would become possible only if the United States rejected military aid to the contras.

Congress had been almost evenly divided on aid to the contras, but the Central American accord decisively shifted the balance in Congress against Reagan's request and in favor of helping to advance the peace plan. It was largely because Congress rejected military but approved humanitarian aid that the Sandinista government decided to negotiate directly with the contras, culminating in a cease-fire agreement signed in Sapoa, Nicaragua, on 23 March 1988.

Reagan's support for the contras and opposition to the peace plans remained unyielding. Every Sandinista misstep was used by the administration to try to pry additional funding out of Congress for the contras. Congress and Central America looked for alternatives, but to the end Ronald Reagan claimed that the contras offered the only path toward democracy in Nicaragua. "I make a solemn vow—as long as there is breath in my body," President Reagan told the hushed delegates at an OAS (Organization of American States) meeting, "I will speak and work, strive and struggle, for the cause of the Nicaraguan freedom fighters."[13]

Even though Congress refused to support the contras, Reagan would not consider the possibility of accommodation with the Sandinistas or with the Democrats in Congress. Most of Congress, however, was tired of fighting this issue. On 18 November 1988 President-elect George Bush went to Capitol Hill to meet with Speaker of the House Jim Wright, who described

Nicaragua as "the most implacable issue of the last eight years, and also the most politically polarizing and personally divisive question on the entire agenda." The president-elect agreed (Wright 1993).

Bush told Wright that he would send his newly designated secretary of state, James A. Baker, to Capitol Hill after the inauguration to work with Wright and the Democratic leadership to try to forge a bipartisan approach to the issue. He was true to his word. On 24 March 1989 the president and the Speaker announced an accord that supported Esquipulas and approved humanitarian aid to the contras, but not military aid. It was a perfect compromise for Bush: he did not have to support the contras, but he also did not have to abandon them.

The bipartisan accord healed the divisions within Congress; it gave some leverage to the Central Americans to obtain Nicaraguan compliance with the accord; and it gave room for the Nicaraguans and for international observers like former U.S. president Jimmy Carter and the Council of Freely Elected Heads of Government, which he chairs, to negotiate the terms of an election that would prove to be the freest and fairest in Nicaraguan history. In the end, the Bush retreat relaxed the pressure on Managua and permitted the development of a political climate that led to the Sandinista defeat at the polls *and* the acceptance by President Daniel Ortega of that defeat. During the election campaign in Nicaragua, the Bush administration was neither able nor interested in reaching an accommodation with the Sandinista government, but when Violeta de Chamorro took power in April 1990, it promised substantial aid.

With regard to U.S. policy toward Central America, Congress's role was that of a balancer rather than an initiator. It compensated for the executive branch's emphasis on a single interest by seeking the neglected interest—the policy niche—and nurturing and supporting it, whether that was security under Carter or human rights and negotiations under Reagan.

THE INVASION OF PANAMA

General Manuel Antonio Noriega, the commander of Panama's Defense Force (PDF), worked closely with Reagan administration officials to support the contras. In early 1988, after U.S. attorneys in Miami and Tampa indicted the general for drug trafficking, the Reagan administration finally changed policies, pressured by an unlikely coalition that included Republican senators Jesse Helms and Alfonse D'Amato and Democratic senators Edward Kennedy and John Kerry. Demanding that Noriega leave office, Reagan decreed an economic embargo and squeezed Panama's economy. Noriega stayed, but the Panamanians suffered. This was the situation that Bush inherited.

Elections scheduled for 7 May 1989 seemed to offer a possible exit. Noriega expected that his presidential candidate would either win or come close enough to winning that he could swing the vote with a small amount of "retail" fraud. The church, however, organized a "quick count" based on a random sample of polling places, and the results showed that Noriega's candidate lost by a 3:1 ratio. Jimmy Carter, who was leading an international delegation to observe the elections, detected and then denounced the fraud and returned to Washington to brief Bush. Carter than sent letters to all the democratic leaders in the hemisphere urging them to call an OAS meeting of foreign ministers to denounce the fraud and encourage respect for the vote. Venezuela took the lead.

On 17 May 1989 the OAS condemned "the grave events and the abuses by General Manuel Antonio Noriega in the crisis and the electoral process in Panama." It dispatched the foreign ministers of Ecuador, Trinidad and Tobago, and Guatemala to try to negotiate a peaceful transfer of power. Noriega blamed the United States and was unresponsive to the OAS mission, which failed to use its potential leverage effectively against the dictator.

On 3 October several PDF officers tried to overthrow Noriega. They held him captive for a few hours while the United States tried to decide whether to support them. Before the question could be answered, Noriega's supporters counterattacked, freed him, and murdered the coup plotters. The confusion surrounding the coup attempt hurt Bush. Congressional Republicans and many Democrats charged him with timidity and indecisiveness, suggesting that a quicker reaction would have displaced Noriega.[14] Bush felt the pressure, though he tried to deny it: "Those doves that now become instant hawks on Capitol Hill; they don't bother me one bit because the American people supported me by over two to one, and I think I sent a strong signal . . . that we are not going to imprudently use the force of the United States."[15]

At the Nineteenth OAS General Assembly in November 1989, the Inter-American Human Rights Commission issued a report calling Noriega's government "devoid of constitutional legitimacy."[16] Several days later, officials in the Bush administration leaked details of a $3 million covert action plan by the United States to unseat Noriega.[17] At the same time, U.S. troops and military equipment were gradually and secretly moved into Panama for possible use.[18] On Friday, 15 December 1989, the Noriega-controlled National Assembly in Panama declared that a "state of war" with the United States existed, and it named Noriega as chief of government. The next day, with tensions running high, the PDF opened fire on a car carrying four U.S. military officers who did not stop at a road block. One officer was killed, a second was injured, and a third who witnessed the event was detained and beaten.

Although this was hardly the first incident against American forces, this one caused Bush to cross his Rubicon. He called it "an enormous outrage" and two days later approved an invasion to be launched at 1 A.M. on

Wednesday, 20 December. At that moment, 10,000 U.S. troops backed by helicopter gunships and fighter-bombers flew into Panama and joined about 13,000 troops already at U.S. bases in the canal area. Their objectives were to capture Noriega, install the Endara government that had been elected on 7 May, and protect American citizens. Although Noriega had often accused the United States of planning an invasion, he was so surprised that he did not even implement his plans to take Americans hostage or harass the U.S. military presence. The United States secured control of the country within five days.

Some days after the invasion, interviews with President Bush and his closest advisers suggested that the pressure he felt after the failed coup of October was an important motive for the invasion: "We suspected that the President felt after the coup that sooner or later we would have to do this," said one senior White House adviser. Another said that Bush felt Noriega "was thumbing his nose at him."[19] Based partly on the fact that both liberals and conservatives in Congress had pleaded for him to take firmer action against Noriega, Bush evidently judged that if the invasion succeeded rapidly, Congress and the people would rally behind him. He was right. The invasion was criticized throughout the world, but at the time it was judged a success in the United States and Panama.[20]

THE BALANCE OF POWER AND THE ROOTS OF CONFLICT

"Since the ending of the Vietnam War," write Thomas M. Franck and Edward Weisband, "more than a President has been deposed—an entire system of power has been overturned." The thesis of their book, *Foreign Policy by Congress*, is that the swing of the pendulum toward congressional dominance that began in the mid-1970s is different from three previous swings in U.S. history. "What we are experiencing is a revolution that will not be unmade" (1979, 3–6). The congressional "revolution" was precipitated by Vietnam, which shattered the foreign policy consensus, and by Watergate, which dethroned the "imperial presidency." But Franck and Weisband argue that the pendulum will not swing back toward the presidency because Congress has institutionalized its new power—by improving its policy capability with more staff and resources and by mandating procedures that require a congressional role in decision making. Moreover, the decentralization of congressional power has had the unintended effect of making it harder for the president to lead. Finally, the two authors argue that Congress's new power permits it to micromanage U.S. foreign policy.

Let us examine each of these assertions and then extract some pertinent propositions from the five cases we have just explored. It is true that Congress has expanded its capabilities. Before 1947, for example, neither the Senate foreign relations committee nor the House foreign affairs committee had a single professional staff member. When the committees needed to write a report on a treaty or a bill, they asked the State Department to do it (Pastor 1980, 16–17). Today, every senator on the committee has at least one foreign affairs adviser.

The assumption of increasing congressional power deserves closer scrutiny. During the last three decades, the increase in the number of staff in Congress combined with the expansion of legislative support systems like the Congressional Research Service and the Congressional Budget Office has provided Congress with the expertise to follow the most complicated issues and to offer specific proposals. Nonetheless, to assess Congress's capabilities, it is not sufficient to compare its current with its past resources. It is also necessary to relate its resources to the magnitude of its contemporary tasks, to the expansion of the executive branch, and to the escalating demands made on legislators by constituents and the media.[21] Total congressional staff has averaged about 1 percent of executive branch personnel throughout the twentieth century. This has remained constant during the last twenty years.[22] It is also worth noting that congressional staff serve 535 times more independently elected officials than do executive branch personnel.

Although the absolute number of congressional amendments or constraints might have increased, so too has the complexity of the legislation; more important, the qualitative relationship between Congress and the president in the area of foreign policy has not changed. The view that a docile Congress followed the president in a blissful spirit of bipartisanship before the Vietnam War is a myth. The Founding Fathers wrote a Constitution that granted a powerful role to Congress in the making of foreign policy, and Congress has rarely been hesitant to use its powers either directly or indirectly, by encouraging the president to use his.

The five cases in the recent history of U.S. policy toward Latin America suggest that Congress's role was important throughout this period, and this seems applicable to other foreign policy areas and across time as well. Congressional pressure played an important role in moving the country into the wars of 1812 and 1898. It restrained the president from getting involved in the two world wars until the moment that U.S. power would prove decisive. Congress alternately goaded and checked the president in Korea and Vietnam. It made the president more cautious about intervening in Lebanon and less cautious about invading Panama.

Those who look back with nostalgia to a bipartisan cold war consensus in the 1950s should look more closely at Eisenhower's struggle with the Bricker amendment. Although Eisenhower was at the peak of his popularity, the Republicans controlled Congress, and the Communist threat appeared to be at its worst, that was the time when the president faced the greatest threat to his prerogative. Republican senator John Bricker of Ohio introduced an amendment in 1953 that would repeal Article 6 of the Constitution (that treaties are the supreme law of the land) and limit the president's authority to negotiate treaties and executive agreements. Eisenhower wrote to his brother that if the amendment passed, it would "cripple the executive power to the point that we would become helpless in world affairs" (Tananbaum 1988, 72). In February 1954, despite Ike's strong opposition, Bricker's amendment came within one vote of gaining the necessary two-thirds of the Senate.

In his book analyzing the Bricker amendment, Duane Tananbaum cogently demonstrates that Eisenhower's approach to Congress and to foreign policy was profoundly affected by this narrow victory and the continuing threat that the amendment might pass. In part to preclude congressional passage of the amendment, Eisenhower agreed not to seek ratification of the Genocide Convention or of the international human rights covenants. He also accepted a bill that required the president to transmit executive agreements to the Senate within thirty days of their execution. Both represented significant abridgements on the executive prerogative which Eisenhower would have resisted under different circumstances.

Also as a result of Bricker's amendment, Eisenhower consulted with Congress more regularly and fully than he probably would have otherwise. In April 1954 congressional opposition to a French request for help in Vietnam was probably decisive in Ike's decision not to intervene, although some now suggest that he used Congress's opposition to buttress his own disinclination to become involved. Ike's early consultations with Congress on a resolution on Formosa in January 1955 and on the Middle East in 1957 permitted him to obtain the support necessary to pursue an effective foreign policy in both places. In short, the halcyon days of bipartisanship in the 1950s were not a result of Congress following the president, but of the president meeting Congress halfway.

It is also worth recalling that the greatest threat to presidential prerogative in the 1950s—the Bricker amendment—occurred when the same party controlled both the White House and Congress. That was also true in the 1930s, when President Roosevelt failed to stop neutrality legislation and was unable to persuade the Senate to permit the United States to join the World Court. Actually, his three Republican predecessors had made similarly unsuccessful efforts vis-à-vis a Republican Senate. All four presidents portrayed these votes as tests of their ability to conduct foreign policy, and it was their own political party—not a divided government—that caused them to fail the test (Olsson 1982).

McCormick and Wittkopf's (1990) analysis of post–World War II voting shows that bipartisanship has been a rare phenomenon. They tested what they called the "Vietnam casualty proposition"—that bipartisanship declined as a result of Vietnam and ideological voting increased—by examining some 2,250 recorded votes on foreign and defense policies since 1947. In only eight of twenty Congresses in the House and twelve of twenty in the Senate did the president receive majority support from both parties on a majority of key issues, and no chronological trend was evident. As regards ideology, the authors found that it "always has been a primary determinant of congressional foreign policy voting," often more important than partisanship (11).

As to another so-called post-Vietnam phenomenon, Louis Fisher wrote, "Micromanagement is a relatively new word to express a very old complaint: intervention by Congress in administrative details." Decrying a problem as old as the Constitution misses the point. "Congress oversteps at times; on other occasions, the executive branch conducts itself in a manner that invites, if not compels, Congress to intervene" (Fisher 1989, 139).

In summary, legislative-executive disagreements preceded Vietnam and the increase of congressional staff and occurred regularly whether both branches were controlled by the same or different political parties. Our review of U.S. foreign policy toward Latin America during the last three decades offers no proof that the secular increase in congressional capabilities has affected either the balance of power between the two branches or the nature of the policy process.

If a cyclical pattern governed, one would have expected the president to have been dominant in the cases of the Alliance for Progress, the contras, and the Panama invasion. It is true that the president initiated all three, but the policy in each of these areas diverged sharply from initial presidential preferences. Had it not been for Congress and interbranch politics, the alliance would have had far more funds on a longer commitment and would have been free of a tie to U.S. foreign investment, the contras would have been flush with money, and Bush might never have invaded Panama.

Similarly, the human rights policy was initiated and the canal treaties were ratified at a time of congressional resurgence, but here again, the more important elements of both policies were the product of interbranch politics. Indeed, our analysis suggests that claims of congressional assertiveness or executive initiative are misleading. The more interesting questions relate to how policy is shaped as a result of the interaction between the two branches and how and why unproductive conflicts between them arise.

Interbranch competition is permanent, sewn into the Constitution, which established two separate institutions—Congress and president—but insisted that they share the powers to declare and make war, to appropriate and spend money, and to make and collect taxes and tariffs. To argue that congressional assertiveness, whether new or old, is the cause of conflict is equivalent to arguing that today's high divorce rate is due to the "new assertiveness" of women. Sometimes Congress and women are culpable; sometimes the president and men are to blame. When one branch trespasses over the constitutional boundary, breaks the rules, or deceives the other, as the Reagan administration did on the contra affair, then the interaction becomes unproductive and foreign policy suffers.

Like divorce from marriage, or war in the international system, inter-branch conflict in U.S. politics can never be ruled out, although the statesman will find ways to pursue his interest short of having to pay the high price of war.

THE IMPACT OF INTERBRANCH POLITICS

The dominant metaphor of a presidentially driven policy is of limited use. Although Congress's hand is not always noticeable, its signature can be identified on virtually every policy. By and large, Congress finds neglected interests and presses a reluctant president to integrate them into his foreign policy. The exchange of signals between the branches produces national policy.

When is the interbranch politics perspective most useful? It depends largely on how foreign policy is defined. Policies can be conceptualized on a continuum, which ranges from executive-dominant policies like diplomacy and intervention at one end to congressional statements and resolutions that affect U.S. relations with other countries at the other. In the middle of the continuum lies the core of U.S. policy, reflected in treaties and laws (especially foreign aid laws) that require the affirmative action of both branches. These are genuine commitments, and interbranch politics is most useful in explaining them.

If the policy is a treaty, such as the one on the Panama Canal, or an aid bill, such as for the Sandinistas, the contras, or the Alliance for Progress, then Congress's role is central, and a national debate is unavoidable. In those cases, the resulting policy is assured of being the product of an interbranch debate. If the policy is diplomacy, as was the case in the Nicaraguan mediation of 1978–79, or an invasion, then the executive branch has considerable room to define its timing and approach. The power of Congress is less visible in executive-dominant policies, but it is always present, because the president understands that to fund his programs, he needs congressional support, and if he ignores Congress on an issue important to its members, then he risks jeopardizing their support on issues important to himself. In the case of the invasion of Panama, bipartisan congressional pressure lowered the cost of invading and increased the political benefits.

Congress-dominant "policies" like resolutions or hearings often have an important effect on foreign countries. For example, Senator Jesse Helms held hearings on Mexico in 1985 that drove the Mexican government to distraction. Resolutions on trade issues also have an impact in Europe and Japan. But the main purpose of these Congress-dominant policies is to send signals to three groups: (*a*) to constituents that their congressman has heard their complaints; (*b*) to the administration to pursue a particular interest more vigorously; and (*c*) to a foreign government to correct a particular problem, whether it is a closed market or a closed political system.

On Central American policy, Congress helped balance U.S. policy and ensure that all interests were represented. Congress kept the ship of state on course, compensating for presidential preferences and adapting to international events. By compelling the president to certify that the Sandinistas were not providing arms to the FMLN, or that the Salvadoran government was investigating the murder of six priests, Congress also provided credible leverage to the president's negotiators.

Congress played the role of initiator on human rights and the executive tried to block the initiative. Congress played a similar role on the Alliance for Progress and investment disputes and, more recently, on drug policy, forcing reluctant administrations to give the issues much higher priority than they would have preferred. Impelled by domestic concerns, Congress pressed an administration that was much more sensitive to international constraints. The interaction was tense but successful in increasing the priority of the issue and the cooperation of other governments.

One of the flaws in theories of foreign policy decision making is that process is too often viewed as somehow disconnected from the debate over interests and ideals. Too many theories assume the foreign policy objective and explore why the executive branch fails to achieve that objective. Unexplored are important questions relating to the objective: is it the correct one? why was it chosen?

The interbranch politics approach suffers from the same defect, but there is a way to remedy it and reconnect policy with process, substance with prerogative, ideals with interests, and public opinion with institutions. The first step is to recognize that there is no ideal foreign policy for any particular problem. Even the most sophisticated computer cannot identify the perfect foreign policy for the United States because the policy is the result of a debate over expected consequences of particular actions in which no side is consistently correct. In an open, pluralistic, decentralized system like that of the United States, the debate occurs in many forums — in newspapers, within the executive branch, within Congress, among interest groups, in academe — but the arena that matters most is between the two branches.

The U.S. system is so open that there is always someone to articulate an idea, interest, or ideal, or, more likely, combine the three into a policy recommendation. If the recommendation is compelling and suits the needs and perspective of the president, then it becomes U.S. policy. If the executive branch proves uninterested or unresponsive, the proposal passes to the second great container, Congress. Given the diversity among members and the need for public recognition, a congressman or senator can always be found to propose a new idea. Whether the proposal gathers a critical mass and becomes law, however, depends on public opinion and on whether the proposal fills a niche in the policy spectrum. These two factors are intimately related: if public opinion supports a proposal, it fills a policy niche. That is how congressional initiatives emerge and pass. They defend a neglected interest or ideal that cannot be excluded from the debate. They balance an administration's policy, or they compensate for its inadequacy.

The executive can try to co-opt, preempt, or resist the initiative. To co-opt or preempt means to absorb the idea into its own policy. To resist means to risk a collision and a self-defeating policy. The existence of the two branches ensures that the policy that evolves from the debate reflects the breadth of U.S. national interests and ideals. The exact permutation depends on the responsiveness of both branches and on the peculiar way in which the two institutions reflect domestic demands and perceive the international landscape.

The executive-dominant model assumes that the optimum foreign policy is the product of a rational choice by the president and his advisers. But such rational choices led to Vietnam, the Bay of Pigs, the Chilean intervention, and Iran-contra, among others. Congress had little or no voice in these debacles, but it did have a compelling voice in the human rights policies, the Panama Canal treaties, and the Bipartisan Accord on Central America, among others — all of which served U.S. interests effectively.

Congress is certainly not the sole repository of wisdom on foreign policy. It has made many mistakes, but as Francis O. Wilcox, who served at different times as a staff director of the Senate foreign relations committee and as an assistant secretary of state, recognized: "If Congress has frequently seemed to be going in one direction and then in another, that is partly because it is a collection of poorly coordinated, strong-minded individuals. But more importantly, it is because that is the way the White House and the Kremlin have moved as well" (Wilcox 1971, 133). The point is not which branch makes better or worse policy, but that the debate between the branches offers the most thorough and systematic mechanism for locating the national interest. Each branch brings its unique perspective and distinct capabilities to the search for the best match between U.S. interests and ideals and geopolitical realities. If each branch modifies its preferences to take into account the other perspective, then the product is a foreign policy that reflects the full interests and aspirations of the nation.

To compensate for the past emphasis on the president's role in foreign policy, there is a growing need for research into the way the two branches interact to make foreign policy. The subjects can be U.S. policy toward regions or countries, or in areas like drugs, terrorism, or development. Future studies can be historical, examining the role of interbranch politics in the Monroe Doctrine, the Open Door policy, or the Korean War, and assess whether patterns have changed significantly.

Hans Morgenthau criticized Congress because it "cannot substitute a foreign policy of its own for the executive's foreign policy of which it disapproves" (1969, 17). In most of the cases examined in this chapter,

Congress did just that, imposing a new set of priorities on a reluctant president. In other words, Congress articulated a new or neglected U.S. national interest and imposed it on the executive branch.

The dominant, executive-based metaphor is clearly inadequate, but it should not be replaced by a congressional model. What is needed is an interbranch politics perspective that investigates both the successes and the collisions in U.S. foreign policy by probing the relationship between the two branches. Such an approach also offers new insights for enhancing the ability of the United States to make effective foreign policy by utilizing each branch's comparative advantage (Pastor 1991).

Chapter Ten

★ ★ ★

DELEGATING
TRADE POLICY

★ ★ ★

I. M. Destler

On 11 October 1962 President John F. Kennedy signed the Trade Expansion Act, authorizing U.S. participation in a global round of tariff negotiations which came to bear his name. On 23 August 1988, almost twenty-six years later, President Ronald Reagan signed the Omnibus Trade and Competitiveness Act authorizing U.S. participation in the multilateral Uruguay Round.

Both laws combined grants of negotiating authority with other changes in U.S. trade law. The timing of both was determined, in part, by the expiration of the old negotiating authority—that of the Reciprocal Trade Agreements Act of 1934, as extended, in June 1962; and the "fast-track" authority under the Trade Act of 1974 for implementing agreements on nontariff barriers, in January 1988. Even the votes on final passage in the House of Representatives were similar: 298–125 for the 1962 law, 290–137 for its 1988 successor.[1]

So what was new? By some measures, a lot. The 1988 law was fifteen times as thick, and took well over twice as long to enact. Unlike the Kennedy measure, moreover, it was the product primarily of congressional initiative. Not only was its initiation shaped by congressional more than executive priorities, but a considerable portion of its 467 pages addressed issues where members of Congress wanted legislation and the administration (for the most part) did not.

Yet once the dust had settled, it was evident that the bottom line had changed much less. Once again, Congress was delegating to the administration effective authority over the *specifics* of U.S. trade policy, particularly on the form and level of import limitation. Once again, Congress forswore direct control over those specifics—through renunciation of the power to amend implementing legislation.[2] Notwithstanding unprecedented trade deficits and growing anxiety about competitive decline, and despite widespread lack of faith in the Reagan administration's trade policy stewardship, the Congress once again passed the initiative on trade policy back to the executive branch: with stiffer guidelines, to be sure, but substantial leeway as well.

Why was this the case? Why did Congress eschew the "dominance" that one influential group of scholars assumes it seeks? Part of the answer, this chapter will argue, is that effective control over policy is much less important for legislators than academic models commonly assume, and less important—in most instances—than it is for senior executive-branch players. But first we need to explore the shape and extent of those changes that have taken place over the last thirty years.

The historical grist for this analysis is provided by the thirty-year period from 1961, the onset of the Kennedy administration, through 1990, the second year of the Bush administration. Bracketing this period were the two bills whose comparison opened this section; in between came one other major authorizing bill, the Trade Act of 1974 for the Tokyo Round; a major bill implementing the results of that round in 1979; and a less comprehensive general trade bill enacted in late 1984. Congress also approved two bilateral free trade agreements: with Israel (1985) and Canada (1988).

Over this same period, a number of protectionist proposals made it partway through the legislative process. The House passed the Mills bill (mandating textile, shoe, and other import quotas) in 1970, and a restrictive omnibus bill (dubbed "ominous" by the Reagan White House) in 1986.[3] The House also voted in 1982 and 1983 for a bill, pressed by the United Auto Workers, to require a high portion of "domestic content" in cars sold within the United States. And Congress addressed numerous proposals for statutory protection of textiles—Hollings amendments passed by the Senate in 1968 and by both houses in 1978; the aforementioned Mills bill; and quota bills vetoed by Presidents Ronald Reagan and George Bush in 1985, 1988, and 1990.

The thirty years concluded with a dramatic failure in trade diplomacy. A December 1990 meeting in Brussels was supposed to bring to its conclusion the Uruguay Round, the broadest effort yet to negotiate reductions in barriers to international commerce, successor to the Kennedy Round of the sixties and the Tokyo Round of the seventies. But this meeting broke up in disagreement over European agricultural import barriers and export subsidies. Efforts to find workable compromises and to conclude the round continued into the fall of 1993, as this chapter goes to press. (Nonetheless, Congress did vote in May 1991 to extend the "fast-track" authority covering the round for two more years, and it extended it further for President Bill Clinton in June 1993.)

The situation in late 1993 was murky, a not abnormal condition for U.S. trade policy. Generating particular controversy was the North American Free Trade Agreement (NAFTA), signed by Bush in 1992 and embraced (with side agreements) by his successor. NAFTA was opposed by a fierce coalition spearheaded by organized labor and Ross Perot; getting it approved by

Congress posed a particularly stern test for Clinton. And NAFTA also posed a stern test for the thesis put forward here. But NAFTA (and the thesis) survived, so the argument advanced here remains relevant. Part 1 of this chapter addresses one central question: what changed between 1960 and 1990 in the process and substance of U.S. trade policy? Part 2 will then ask what this change, or lack thereof, tells us about congressional influence and the interplay between branches.

PART I: WHAT CHANGED BETWEEN 1960 AND 1990?

In 1961 the State Department was still the executive branch agency with primary responsibility for trade policy. But to prepare its comprehensive proposal, the Kennedy administration turned not to George Ball, under secretary of state for economic affairs, but to a White House–based coordinating committee. This model was subsequently incorporated—at congressional insistence—into the 1962 law. Thus was created the president's Special Representative for Trade Negotiations (STR), who headed a small White House staff office that led the U.S. delegation in the Kennedy Round.

In the years since, the office has expanded, its statutory mandate has grown, and its name has been changed—to Office of the United States Trade Representative (USTR). Congressional pressure has been central to this expansion, and key legislators protected the office from Nixon and Reagan administration efforts to reorganize it out of existence. Increasingly, Senate and House trade leaders saw the advantage in having a politically sensitive agency that gave priority to U.S. trade interests and that could take the heat on problems while sharing credit for accomplishments.

Over this same period, Congress deepened its own specialized capacity for trade policy. In 1962 the ways and means committee did not have a single staff member working full-time on trade policy, and it considered all trade legislative matters in full committee.[4] By the time of the 1973–74 trade legislation, it had only one professional trade policy specialist and still no trade subcommittee. Reformers forced the creation of such a subcommittee in 1975, however, and by the late 1980s there were at least five ways and means aides specializing in trade. There was a parallel expansion of staff on the Senate finance committee and on other committees with trade and international economic interests.[5]

These executive and legislative branch changes helped bring about major changes in the process of trade legislation:

The laws became longer.

They took longer to enact.

The Congressional process became more decentralized and complex.

More of the initiative came from Capitol Hill.

Changes in the Legislative Process

Longer Laws. The Trade Expansion Act of 1962 took up 31 statutory pages. The Trade Act of 1974 was triple that length, 98 pages, and the Omnibus Trade and Competitiveness Act of 1988 was almost five times again as long, 467 pages.[6]

One factor in this expansion was the growing complexity of the matters addressed. The Kennedy Round was a relatively straightforward tariff-cutting exercise, whereas subsequent negotiations attacked nontariff barriers incorporated in a broad range of domestic legislation. A related factor was the increasing number of provisions that members of Congress added in committee or on the floor. There was, for example, continuing pressure to amend the "trade remedy" laws to give producers a better shot at obtaining relief from intense import pressure or unfair import competition.[7] And the 1988 law reached well beyond trade policy to encompass a broad range of matters bearing some relation to America's global position: exchange rates, third world debt, foreign corrupt practices, and education for math, science, foreign languages, and basic literacy.[8]

A Longer Road to Enactment. Within five months of Kennedy's message to Congress, ways and means had marked up his bill and the House had voted to enact it; the Senate followed three months later, and the signing ceremony came three weeks after that. In all, eight and a half months had passed. In contrast, it took eight months for the House alone to act on the Nixon trade bill of 1973, and another year for the Senate to follow. In all, the process took twenty-one months. Parallel dates do not exist for the 1988 law, since the administration initially resisted the idea of comprehensive legislation and did not make its own proposal until the congressional process was well advanced. The basic proposal on which the 100th Congress worked was H.R. 3, introduced 3 January 1987, but this was virtually identical to the legislation that had passed the House the year before. So it seems more reasonable to date the beginning to the onset of the House ways and means hearings on 20 March 1986. From this point, it took twenty-nine months and three days for the House-initiated bill to become law. Congressional hearings became more extensive as well.[9]

Why the increased time period? One reason was the broader—and more controversial—content. The 1974 law was delayed for most of a year by the controversy over the Jackson-Vanik amendment linking most-favored-nation status for Eastern bloc nations to their emigration policies. The debate of the late eighties featured many controversial issues, the most visible being the Gephardt amendment penalizing imports from nations running large trade surpluses. Another important factor, however, was the dispersion of power on Capitol Hill.

A More Complex Congressional Process.   Through the sixties and into the seventies, trade policy making on the Hill was dominated by the House ways and means committee and its chairman, Wilbur Mills. By 1973, however, Mills's power was waning and the reform process was waxing. After Mills retired as chairman in 1975, his successor was unable to prevent trade-restrictive proposals from reaching the House floor, as Mills could have done. Meanwhile, on the other side of the Capitol, the Senate finance committee was gaining at least coequal status. By the late seventies, in fact, finance under Russell Long had become the more influential of the two trade committees.

The rise of Dan Rostenkowski to the ways and means chairmanship in 1981 helped right the balance, but by this time that committee was facing competition within the House. A particular rival was the energy and commerce committee, which was able to bring stringent auto import legislation to the floor in 1982 and 1983 under the guise of regulating the "domestic content" of cars manufactured in this country. And the omnibus bill of 1986 to 1988 was a multicommittee product, with Majority Leader—and later Speaker—Jim Wright playing the overall coordinating role. To reconcile the House and Senate versions, a 199-member conference committee was appointed, with 44 senators and 155 representatives. They represented eleven House and nine Senate committees involved in the legislation, and were subdivided into seventeen subconferences responsible for specific titles and sections.

Ways and means still retained primacy over trade in the House, as did finance in the Senate. The committees' roles were strengthened, interestingly, by the innovative "fast-track" procedures adopted in the seventies to buttress the executive branch's credibility in trade negotiations. As noted earlier (see n. 2), these new procedures resulted from change in the target of international trade negotiations: from lowering tariffs to reducing nontariff barriers. On the former, Congress could authorize executive action in advance, by stating in law the percentage of authorized tariff reductions. U.S. negotiators could then bargain credibly with foreign counterparts, for the president could simply proclaim the newly negotiated tariff rates under his delegated authority.

There was no comparable general way to delegate advance authority over nontariff barriers. But in 1974 administration and Senate aides devised a procedural substitute: the promise of quick, up-or-down congressional votes on "the implementing bill submitted by the President" for whatever agreements on nontariff barriers were negotiated, provided that Congress was properly consulted during the negotiations.[10]

As the Tokyo Round agreements were being completed, finance committee senators and their aides let it be known that they wanted to participate in drafting the president's implementing bill. STR Robert Strauss assented, for he needed their backing—and that of their ways and means counterparts—to be confident of winning the up-or-down floor votes on the bill. So in the spring of 1979 the two committees met with Strauss and his aides in separate sessions labeled "nonmarkups," and then together in a "nonconference" to reconcile their differences.[11] The resulting agreement was put in statutory language by the joint efforts of legislative and executive branch lawyers, and modified only slightly by the administration before the president submitted it as his own. Congressional influence on that legislation was therefore substantial, and dominated by the two trade committees (though other committees were engaged on matters within their jurisdictions). For by the terms of the fast-track procedures, no floor amendments were permitted.[12]

This process strengthened what had already become a solid, *cross-branch* alliance between senior USTR officials and the members and staffs of the trade committees. Each was fighting for trade supremacy within its own branch, and each found its ally helpful against its rivals (such as the Treasury and Commerce Departments, or the House committee on energy and commerce).

More Congressional Initiative. The final change in the legislative process was stronger congressional influence over the timing and the substantive agenda. In 1962 the administration dominated both. In 1973–74 it initiated the process and set the basic shape of the legislation, but Congress made major changes. In 1986–88 Congress got the process rolling and determined the basic structure of the law.

The Trade Expansion Act of 1962 was "one of the major legislative efforts of the Kennedy administration" (Sorensen 1965, 410). Designed and sold as a response to the challenge of the new European Community, it combined authorization for negotiating major tariff reductions with a new program of adjustment assistance for workers and firms hurt by rising imports. Congress did, in the words of Robert Pastor (1980, 117), leave "its print and some of its priorities" on the bill.[13] In particular, it forced creation of the STR to lead the negotiations and curbed extension of most-favored-nation treatment to Communist nations. But in comparison with subsequent major trade bills (and also with the more modest trade liberalizing bills of the fifties), the administration prevailed overwhelmingly.

The Nixon administration had similar success in placing trade on the congressional agenda: the ways and means committee devoted most of 1973 to this subject because, and only because, the White House sought authorization to participate in a new multilateral trade round. In its basic structure, moreover, the bill ultimately signed by President Gerald Ford paralleled that sent down by Richard Nixon almost two years earlier.

In substance, however, congressional influence was greater than it had been in 1962. The administration sought general authority to grant most-favored-nation status to any country not receiving it; Congress imposed the Jackson-Vanik condition of open emigration policies, which led the Soviet Union to denounce the bilateral trade agreement signed in 1972. The administration sought modest changes in the laws providing relief from import competition; Congress insisted on going much further, angered in particular by evidence that the Treasury Department had not been enforcing the law that imposed countervailing duties on subsidized imports. Congress also made its mark in placing restrictions on administration authority to grant trade preferences to developing countries and in crafting the "fast-track" procedures discussed above.[14]

Congress had still greater influence in 1986–88. The United States was running unprecedented $100 billion-plus trade deficits. The increased pressure this brought upon members of Congress was compounded by broad dissatisfaction in the business community with the Reagan administration's response. Trade frustration was bipartisan, but Democrats in the House also saw a political opening, an opportunity to label Reagan policies as damaging economically and weak vis-à-vis foreign competitors.

Beginning in 1985, prominent legislators began pressing strong trade restrictive and retaliatory bills. Within a year, the House Democratic leadership began movement on an omnibus measure. Majority Leader Jim Wright pressed and coordinated a process in which multiple committees developed plausibly relevant legislation on issues within their jurisdictions—from conventional trade policy to exchange rates, export controls, international debt, foreign investment, technology development, assistance for agricultural exports, and "education and training for American competitiveness." Separate hearings were held, and separate bills were reported out. Wright then worked with the rules committee in merging them and, in an impressive feat of procedural leadership, achieved House passage in late May by a vote of 295–115. The Senate did not follow that year, however, not because its members were opposed, but because the finance committee was preoccupied with tax reform.

The Reagan White House attacked the House product as "ominous," "rankly political," "pure protectionism." This was an overstatement: "pure protectionism" presumably means direct (and onerous) barriers to imports, and this measure did not restrict imports directly, though its provisions would certainly have complicated foreign access to American markets. The charges reflected the fact that the administration did not want general trade legislation that year. Its fast-track negotiating authority would not expire until January 1988. Moreover, Treasury Secretary James Baker, its dominant international economic policy figure, was orchestrating (and taking credit for) a decline in the value of the dollar, and he wanted time for this to have an impact on the trade balance.

By the time the 100th Congress came to town in January 1987, however, Baker's position had changed. The trade balance was not yet improving, but Democrats had recaptured political control of the Senate, undercutting the administration's procedural leverage, and they had immediately declared trade to be their number one legislative priority. The administration had won international agreement to a new trade round, for which it needed negotiating authority and, specifically, extension of the fast-track procedure. So it declared itself willing to cooperate, and sent up its own draft trade and competitiveness legislation. But Congress paid little attention to the administration bill, for by the time it arrived the House was already reworking its 1986 measure, reintroduced on opening day as H.R. 3.

The substance of H.R. 3 was softened considerably—in the House, in the Senate, and later in conference. Key leaders—finance chairman Lloyd Bentsen in the Senate and ways and means chairman Dan Rostenkowski in the House—wanted a law, not just an electoral issue. So, apparently, did Jim Wright, who was now House Speaker. Moreover, the stock market plunge of October 1987, coming shortly after the formation of the conference committee on H.R. 3, made legislators wary of drastic action that might shake the markets further.[15] So the House-passed Gephardt amendment mandating special import barriers against countries running trade surpluses was replaced by "Super-301," which gave the USTR discretion both in naming "priority foreign countries" for trade negotiations and in setting the U.S. negotiating agenda with these countries. In a delightful illustration of congressional ambivalence, conferees sought to make retaliation against offending foreign practices "mandatory but not compulsory."[16] They also softened a number of Senate-passed provisions, including a ban on imports of the products of the Toshiba Corporation, whose subsidiary had breached national security export controls by selling sensitive technology to the Soviet Union.

The final bill was not so much "protectionist," as often claimed, as aggressive and unilateralist. In many specific provisions it pressed the administration to attack foreign trade barriers. It made retaliation "mandatory but not compulsory" when such efforts proved unavailing. It also, however, included what the administration absolutely required, extension of fast-track authority for the Uruguay Round's implementing legislation.

Changes in Broader Trade Policy Making

Paralleling these changes in the legislative process, and shaped importantly by the laws themselves, were changes in the ongoing conduct of trade policy:

Congressional leverage increased somewhat over ongoing negotiations, as did the role of USTR.

Industry trade grievances won more-sympathetic administrative consideration.

The Negotiating Process. With each multilateral negotiation, Congress imposed somewhat greater requirements for consultation. These extended not just to members and their staffs but to industry representatives as well.

These requirements were reinforced by the shift from tariffs to nontariff barriers. On the former, as in the Kennedy Round, Congress took no action at the end of a round—the president could implement agreements by proclamation. On the latter, Congress had to act, and while the fast-track procedures made expeditious and positive action likely, the vote at the end of the round encouraged the administration to keep in touch, to nurture the political coalition without which there could be no final success. (Of course, members of Congress had multiple agendas, so their direct oversight over the negotiations was in practice intermittent.)

More important was the growing role of Congress's creation, USTR. In the Kennedy Round, it was a small, new office, widely regarded as temporary; by the Tokyo Round, it was established as a permanent agency and *the* central U.S. negotiating arm. It shared power with other executive branch agencies on issues within their spheres, with Agriculture in particular on farm trade, and with Treasury on broad policy leadership. And its anomalous status, as an operating agency within the president's executive office, responsive to Congress as well as to the White House, made for an uneasy existence. Still, USTR's essential role won broad acceptance—by legislators wanting a responsive agent to take the heat on matters they preferred to delegate; by an administration recognizing that sensitivity to congressional politics was a prerequisite for executive flexibility.

Trade Remedy Procedures. Through the 1960s and into the 1970s, industries were typically frustrated in their attempts to win trade relief through administrative procedures. Eligibility criteria for the escape clause were tightly drawn, and imposition of countervailing or antidumping duties was rare. In the seventies, however, Congress changed the rules to make such relief easier to obtain. To some degree, this effort was encouraged by administration officials who saw these procedures as needed safety valves for interests that would otherwise support protectionist legislation. But Congress tilted these processes more in favor of import-impacted petitioners than these officials desired.

The result was more cases—particularly under the laws covering "unfair" foreign practices, subsidies, and dumping—and more granting of relief. In addition, industries like steel and textiles became adept at using these laws to force foreign producers and governments to negotiate "voluntary" export restraints (Destler 1992, chap. 6).

Changes in Policy Substance

In 1960 U.S. merchandise imports totaled $14.8 billion. In 1990 they were $497.7 billion. Adjusted for inflation, this amounted to at least a sevenfold increase, and more than a tripling of imports as a share of GNP: from 2.8 percent in 1960 to 9.1 percent in 1990.[17]

Thus by the most important measure, the actual flow of goods, the U.S. market has become much more open. In terms of legal impediments, official measures affecting imports, the picture is mixed. U.S. tariffs are lower: an average of 12 percent on dutiable imports at the onset of the Kennedy Round and around 5 percent today. But nontariff barriers have spread, particularly in the form of voluntary or negotiated restraints on foreign exports of textiles, steel, and automobiles.[18]

If it is unclear whether U.S. import policy has become more liberal or more protectionist, it *is* clear that export policy has grown more aggressive and unilateralist. In the sixties, U.S. efforts to open up foreign markets were pursued overwhelmingly through multilateral GATT negotiations, aimed at reciprocal steps at market liberalization. In the eighties, this continued to be the preferred approach, but much of our negotiators' energy went into insisting that others open their markets unilaterally, with threats of increased U.S. restrictions if they did not. Moreover, in the Uruguay Round we refused to cut a deal in December 1990 because the European Community resisted agricultural liberalization. In the past we had taken such a no for an answer and settled for liberalization in other areas.

Believing the U.S. market to be more open than others, Congress collectively, and senators and representatives individually, have pushed persistently for such executive branch aggressiveness. USTR has responded, particularly since 1985, making increased use of Section 301 of the Trade Act of 1974, as amended, and most recently employing the "Super-301" provision of the 1988 legislation (Bhagwati and Patrick 1990).

Yet before we conclude that Congress has achieved effective dominance, let us recall certain events of April 1990. By the end of that month, under the "Super-301" provision, USTR Carla Hills was supposed to "identify priority foreign countries" based upon the "number and pervasiveness" of their trade-restrictive practices, and "the level of United States exports" that might result if such practices were removed. The provision was drafted with Japan in mind, and a literal reading of its language would seem to make naming that nation unavoidable. But Hills demurred. She had named Japan in 1989, but since then Tokyo had made concessions on a number of trade issues, and she deemed it wise to reward the Japanese by not repeating the designation. In fact, she named no country at all save India, a minor U.S. trading partner renamed from 1989. Hills declared instead that the primary U.S. trade priority was successful completion of the Uruguay Round. And Congress acquiesced. "In the week before the announcement, members had threatened to scuttle or hold hostage everything from trade agreements with the Soviet Union to the worldwide trade pact being negotiated through the General Agreement on Tariffs and Trade (GATT). . . . But after the announcement, the air seemed to have gone at least temporarily from the balloon" (*Congressional Quarterly*, 5 May 1990, 1333).

Summary
We have analyzed changes in congressional influence over trade policy, taking as our base period the early sixties and the executive-dominated enactment of the Trade Expansion Act of 1962. This ought to maximize the degree of change, for the Kennedy Round period was probably the high point of the twentieth century in presidential trade policy leadership and congressional acquiescence.

We found, over our thirty-year period, a substantial increase in the congressional role. Owing in important part to expanded legislative activity, our trade laws are now longer and more complex. They include many more directives for executive branch officials, and many more constraints on their flexibility. In the mid-eighties, when the U.S. trade imbalance reached historic heights, legislators insisted on enactment of comprehensive legislation and took the lead in fashioning it. Never, since before the Smoot-Hawley Act of 1930, had a major trade law such as this been initiated on Capitol Hill.

And yet, unlike in the period that culminated in Smoot-Hawley, Congress continues to delegate the hard decisions. The year 1990 resembles 1960, not 1930. Congress still eschews making direct, binding, product-specific trade law. It still avoids setting tariff rates, or enacting statutory quotas, just as it has throughout the postwar period. Congressional leaders still cooperate with executive officials in maintaining a system that minimizes the direct impact of legislation on U.S. trade barriers. This system is characterized by:

- delegation to the president of de facto authority to set the level of trade and nontariff barriers, which are arrived at through negotiations with foreign governments;

- use of quasi-judicial procedures for industries claiming injury from imports or unfair foreign trade practices;

- negotiation by the executive of special, "voluntary" export restraint arrangements in cases where a major industry (textiles, steel, autos) is demanding trade relief;

- reliance by both branches on a trade-brokering agency, the Office of the United States Trade Representative, the preferred target of congressional and industry pressure, which takes the heat as it works for compromise on contentious trade matters in U.S. and foreign markets.

Congress controlled trade barriers directly for most of the nation's history. And the Constitution gives it unambiguous authority: no war powers ambiguity here. Moreover, product-specific legislation would allow members to parcel out discrete benefits to constituency interests. But despite record pressure from imports, despite unhappiness with administration policy, despite substantial pressure from constituents, Congress did not seize direct control over American trade policy in the 1980s.

If the breakdown in the Uruguay Round proves permanent, we are likely to see more congressional assertiveness, more pressure for unilateralism. It will become harder to limit such tendencies, for an important counter-weight—the GATT process—will have been weakened. As of this writing, however, Congress still allows presidents and USTRs to tilt U.S. policy toward trade liberalization and market expansion, through multilateral, GATT means wherever possible. It still causes the buck to stop with them. In the concluding section of this paper we explore why.

PART 2: WHY NOT MORE CHANGE? AN EXPLORATION OF WHAT DRIVES CONGRESS

In April 1970 Wilbur Mills introduces a textile quota bill. When the Nixon administration unexpectedly endorses it in June, he welcomes this publicly, but somehow the legislation incorporating it doesn't reach the House floor until mid-November, leaving the Senate insufficient time to give it serious consideration. Early in 1971 Mills encourages and endorses a much more limited Japanese export restraint. Nixon denounces this as inadequate, as does the U.S. textile industry, but it gives Mills an excuse not to press his bill again.

In mid-1978 the author is interviewing one of the Senate's most effective trade policy aides. Asked how he thought senior senators were advising STR Strauss in the Tokyo Round consultations mandated by the Trade Act of 1974, he replied, "I think they say something like this: 'You do what you think is best, Bob, and we'll support you unless you make a bad mistake!'"

In April 1985 the Senate has just passed, 92–0, a Danforth resolution condemning Japanese trade restrictions and calling for retaliation. This measure is nonbinding, but the finance committee then votes in favor of a binding version of the same. The author phones a senior Senate aide to express concern. The response: "You don't understand! The target isn't the Japanese, it's the White House!" (And the binding version never goes to the floor.)

In April 1990, as described above, senators and representatives demand that Japan be named a "priority foreign country," as the language of the 1988 act clearly mandates. Carla Hills does not do so, and Congress quiets down.

In October 1990 the House votes 275–152 to override Bush's veto of textile quota legislation, falling just ten votes short of the two-thirds required. We might conclude that Congress is on the verge of breaking the unwritten, post-Smoot-Hawley rule against statutory restrictions on specific products. But one small problem: motions to override vetoes of similar bills failed by eight votes in August 1986, and by eleven votes in the fall of 1988.

In all five of these episodes—drawn from my ongoing research—we see members of Congress taking activist trade policy postures. In all save the last, these are not everyday members but trade policy specialists, leaders. Yet in each case, they seem somewhat less than hell-bent for direct control over trade policy. In each case, in fact, we see legislators holding back, refraining from full exercise of their constitutional power.

In themselves, these episodes prove nothing. But together they are highly suggestive. If one sets them beside the consistent legislative practice of delegating product-specific trade policy decisions to the president, or the USTR, or the secretary of commerce, or the U.S. International Trade Commission, or (indirectly) to Japan's Ministry of International Trade and Industry, they suggest that senators and representatives may not really want to control trade policy. At least, they do not seem to give it very high priority.

Why might this be the case? They could be afraid of failure—a presidential veto—if they push constituency-specific measures too hard. (But why then do they always seem to fall just a certain number of votes short of overriding such vetoes?)

They could be afraid of success, and the responsibility for consequences that comes with it.

They could believe that statutory trade restrictions are bad policy, but that the threat of Congress imposing them is important to attaining lesser, more-flexible trade actions by the administration.

They could be interested mainly in publicity, visible engagement, posturing to constituents, or participating in some fashion in the trade policy game.

Any or all of these explanations might help us sort out the puzzle that closed part 1 of this chapter. Through the seventies and eighties, we had congressional resurgence, congressional reform, and growing pressure from the business community because of relative U.S. economic decline and the trade imbalance. And through most of the last decade, we had an administration whose macroeconomic policies produced unimaginable trade deficits and whose trade policies were widely disdained. All of these factors ought to have pushed Congress to assume direct control, if such were its bent.

And control is certainly possible. Unlike many other U.S. international transactions, trade can be—and used to be—controlled by general statutory rules labeled tariffs and quotas. It is also, obviously, constitutional for Congress to impose such rules: one of its explicitly enumerated powers is to regulate "commerce with foreign nations." Why then have members of

Congress contented themselves with marginal rather than fundamental trade policy actions?

What follows are some propositions that may be helpful in solving this puzzle. They set forth a view of congressional interests that is in substantial tension with much of the "new institutionalist" literature on Congress. This literature assumes that members' driving motivation is impact on policy. They need backing from constituents, which they purchase through provision of policy payoffs. Legislators are thus, in practice, conduits of pressure from interest groups. Within Congress, the committees and subcommittees most responsive to the dominant constituencies in an issue area come to play the pivotal role, and they use their power to control policy.[19]

This approach, it seems to me, fits trade policy only for the years up through 1930. It strongly resembles the political process that E. E. Schattschneider (1935) discovered in his classic treatment of the enactment of the Smoot-Hawley Act. If Congress were behaving similarly today, we would expect legislators to *enact* textile quotas, adjusting their substance enough to attract an additional ten or so House votes. We would also expect them to *deny* fast-track authority for trade negotiations. Yet Congress has regularly eschewed quotas and extended the fast-track option—most recently in summer 1993.

What follows are six propositions about congressional interests and congressional behavior. They are stated as specific to trade policy, but they may well have broader applicability, so this discussion will be followed by a brief reflection on what might determine their substantive boundaries.

1. On the surface, both Congress and the executive seem to be struggling over policy outcomes, but there is an asymmetry in stakes: executive players give greater priority to controlling trade policy outcomes than do congressional players. However much they may specialize in their substantive work, legislators are—at bottom—generalist politicians. They cannot and do not give anywhere near full-time attention to trade issues. Even for members of the finance and ways and means committees, trade competes with several other major matters within their jurisdictions: taxes, social security, and medicare, for example. USTR officials, in contrast, do spend virtually all their time on trade and judge their own professional success while in office by their trade policy accomplishments.

2. For the generalist politicians who populate Congress, direct control over trade policy is not a necessary means to their broader goal: to maintain and enhance political standing, at home and in Washington. David Mayhew's classic work (1974) depicts members of Congress as single-minded seekers of reelection who pursue public prominence as a means to that end. The above proposition begins with that assumption but

broadens it, drawing on evidence that legislators also tend to be very much concerned about their roles in Washington and how these are regarded by the public and the press (Fenno 1973).

3. For the great majority of members for whom trade is but an occasional concern, it is sufficient to advocate the cause of interests important in one's district, and to strike general trade policy postures that appeal to one's support coalition. For most members in most instances, it is simply not cost-effective to strive for direct personal influence over trade policy outcomes. Mayhew (1974, pt. 1) points to three activities crucial to House members: advertising, position taking, and credit claiming. None of these require actual impact on policy. What the member with limited interest in trade needs, instead, is to take positions responsive to key trade-affected interests in her or his constituency and to sentiment among broader ideological support groups. Interests not important to reelection can be diverted. And in cases where support of legislative protection is demanded (as with members from textile districts), these nonspecialist members need give only their voices and their votes: an industry is unlikely to punish visible advocates of its legislation because others prevent it from becoming law.

4. For legislators on the key trade committees (Senate finance and House ways and means), and the (growing) minority that has singled out trade policy for special attention, controlling policy on core trade matters is neither the only, nor in most cases the best, means of enhancing trade-political standing. The interest of this group in actually legislating on trade will certainly be greater than that of their nonspecialist colleagues. They are "trade policy politicians" in the sense that they build their broader political standing, in part, on trade policy engagement. But even they need not give priority to actual impact on outcomes. They have open to them such time-tested activities as: issue entrepreneurship — speeches, press releases, hearings, travel to the capitals of U.S. trading partners; marginal legislation for credit claiming: the [insert legislator's name] amendment; and major legislative proposals for advertising and position taking which no one expects will become law, such as the domestic content bill for automobiles or the Gephardt amendment.

5. When individual legislators do seek influence over policy, legislation is often not the most effective means to that end. Legislation is only one of several routes open to legislators. Others include lobbying the executive; using legislation as a threat, as Senator John Danforth did with auto quotas in early 1981; and pressuring foreign governments, as illustrated by the same example. Indeed, the executive branch (or international bargaining)

game, where "downtown" officials take the issue-specific heat, may sometimes offer well-connected members of Congress greater opportunity to have an impact than the procedurally cumbersome legislative game.

In a variety of ways, therefore, Senate and House trade specialists can be visible policy players—responding to their constituents, bashing the Japanese, claiming credit for diplomatic or administrative actions taken on their behalf—while retaining their ability to duck blame for unfavorable outcomes.

6. Hence, members of Congress find their interests well served by a system of power sharing that gives them ample opportunity for initiative and visibility but allows the buck to stop elsewhere. Administration leaders, who give greater priority to policy impact, also find their interests better served under this system than in one where specific trade barriers are legislatively determined. They can exploit the leeway the delegation system gives them. Notable is the fact that this system deals with industry pressure by diversion as well as accommodation, through buffering institutions that give legislators ample opportunity either to duck or to assert themselves on trade issues. It is ideal for "blame avoidance" (Weaver 1988, chap. 2). What it reliably provides is not protection for industry, which often finds its claims rejected or deferred, but "protection for Congress" (Destler 1992, chap. 2).

This pattern is obviously not limited to trade policy. One sees it in the legislative veto over international arms sales, a power frequently brandished but never actually employed. It was perhaps present in January 1991, when the Senate and House followed their historic debates over the war in the Persian Gulf with votes authorizing the president to do essentially what he had wanted and intended to do. Weaver (1988) applies a similar behavioral analysis to congressional action to "index" benefits and tax rates, action that by definition reduces legislators' direct power over policy outcomes. And Morris Fiorina (1985) has written along parallel lines about "blame shirking."

Yet on other matters Congress does insist on controlling the details, on making actual policy. Appropriations subcommittees reach deeply into agency operations, particular on defense, as Ralph Carter demonstrates in chapter 7 in this volume. Legislation addresses the specifics of civil rights or criminal law. Congress seeks to control both the amount and the distribution of federal highway funds. Indeed, the same congressional committees that regularly delegate trade authority—House ways and means and Senate finance—insist on detailed control of the tax code.

If Congress seeks to control these not unimportant matters, why does it delegate authority on others? What factors might tilt legislators toward delegation? A full treatment of this issue goes well beyond the scope of this chapter, but it seems useful to suggest several possible relationships. Congress might well be more inclined to delegate to the degree that: (1) the issue falls within the sphere of foreign policy, where many members of Congress believe the president is entitled to greater leeway than in the domestic sphere; (2) the issue is one where a previous exercise of detailed congressional control is widely believed to have brought disastrous consequences; (3) the issue is one where legislators feel caught between their constituencies and their convictions, where they fear that responding to those most active in petitioning them will lead to bad public policy; and (4) the issue is one where successive presidents have adhered to an approach that is generally judged reasonable by the policy community.

Certainly, the second and third propositions apply to trade. The "lesson of Smoot-Hawley" remains a staple of congressional debates. There remains, on many product-specific issues, a "political imbalance" in favor of those seeking trade restrictions (Destler 1992, chap. 1). The fourth proposition is supported by Paul Peterson's comparison between trade and defense in chapter 1: by the mid-1980s the Reagan administration had put together a balanced, mainstream international economic policy, but its defense budgets had lost their "reasonableness" by 1983 at the latest. And the first proposition still applies in part, though legislators regularly insist that trade decisions should be separated from foreign policy and linked instead to economic policy.

In any case, a system of delegating power over trade policy was well established by 1960. Initiated in the wake of Smoot-Hawley, it matured while trade policy receded from public prominence and lost its partisan character. And it survived the trade policy crisis of the 1980s.

There will be occasions, of course, when a critical mass of congressional players become committed to enactment of major trade legislation. This happened in 1986–88. Even in such cases, however, Congress is likely to end up refining at the margins the mechanisms for indirect influence rather than taking direct control of specific product issues or specific bilateral trade relationships.

An overall system where Congress eschews direct responsibility can be attractive to legislators because it gives them greater flexibility in preserving and advancing their careers as politicians while avoiding blame for mistakes. It can be attractive to executive players because they give greater priority to policy outcomes and congressional delegation gives them greater leeway in influencing them. Members of Congress expect executive officials to exploit this leeway and generally find it acceptable when they do so. There has developed, in fact, a symbiotic relationship between the key trade committees and their executive creation, USTR. They reinforce one another within their respective branches. But it is a relationship of mutual, reciprocal influence. USTR is a presidential agent as well as a congressional one.

What, then, is our final conclusion about the balance of influence over trade policy? Essentially, it is that Congress retains ultimate constitutional jurisdiction but continues to delegate responsibility for trade policy specifics, above all for the form and level of import barriers for individual products.

Since 1960, Congress has become much more active and visible on trade issues, asserting its priorities and imposing greater procedural constraints on the U.S. Trade Representative and other executive branch officials. And the NAFTA issue of 1991 to 1993 gave trade a public prominence not seen in many decades, putting acute pressure on members of Congress. But the buck still stops with the president and the USTR. And for reasons set forth in the above propositions, this arrangement still appears to suit Congress very well.

NOTES

★ ★ ★

Chapter One

1. On the growth of executive power during World War I and World War II, see Sundquist 1981, chap. 6.

2. It is possible but, I think, unlikely that small countries have greater latitude on security questions than do large, powerful ones. It could be argued that they can do as they please and "free ride" on the more powerful. But free riders must be acquiescent riders.

3. Some may argue that the United States was particularly constrained by its need to protect the interests of the free world during the cold war. Once the United States spread its economic, military, and nuclear umbrella, it was much more constrained than smaller nations who could "free ride" under U.S. protection. I agree that the cold war constrained U.S. choices, but I do not think it was any more constrained than other countries. Had the United States not fulfilled its responsibilities, the impact would have been more devastating on other nations than on the United States itself. The threat posed by the Soviet Union to the United States was less direct and immediate than its threat to Europe, Asia, and almost any other country one can imagine.

4. The United States may have been the least constrained by the international system in the nineteenth century, when the country was protected from threats from strong European powers by its isolation in the Western Hemisphere. This may account for the perpetuation of a relatively weak presidency throughout the nineteenth century. The Monroe Doctrine can best be understood as an indication that even the weak, legislatively dominated national government of the nineteenth-century United States was prepared to protect its vital interests, should a threat by a major power emerge. The power of the executive branch expanded with the increasing threat to the United States posed by the international system in the twentieth century.

5. For more on the subject of the following paragraphs, see Chubb and Peterson 1989.

6. Perhaps the best discussion of this point is to be found in Key (1949), who argues that it was the absence of parties in the South that perpetuated racial

exclusion and made opposition to dominant economic elites episodic and ineffective.

7. Nor has there been an increase in the overall level of conflictual questioning in armed services, finance, judicial, and agricultural committees (Peterson and Greene 1994).

8. Often congressional opposition is used as a euphemism for a much more broadly based public or political opposition. This is understandable as political rhetoric, but analysts need to keep clear the distinction when assessing the relative power of Congress and the presidency as institutions. If presidents are responding to an assessment of the political situation in the country, and not primarily to congressional critics, then one can hardly attribute power to Congress.

9. But Congress still has the power to ask the executive departments to report implementing decisions to congressional committees for their advance review, a power that is often as effective as the legislative veto (Korn 1993).

10. Detailed discussions of various methodological problems associated with roll-call analysis are contained in the articles included in the collection edited by Shull (1991). Also, see the chapter by Rohde in this volume.

11. This same point was made by Allison (1971) when he said that most international theory assumed the state was a rational, unitary actor (the Model 1 approach, which Allison thought needed to be supplemented by organizational and bargaining theories).

The argument of this chapter is quite the opposite of Allison's. Although Model 1 does not generate the need for the fascinating detail that makes Allison's book a good read, it pretty much explains the origination and resolution of the Cuban missile crisis. Model 1 theory, called here international relations theory, may also explain a good deal of the foreign policy–making process as well. A fuller discussion of the interconnections among the three models can be found in Peterson 1976.

12. Thus, organizational theories of the firm can be reconciled with sophisticated restatements of market theory. On this topic, see Moe 1984, 739–77.

13. But see the interesting theoretical framework proposed by Putnam (1988).

Chapter Two

1. See the 1978 Foreign Intelligence Surveillance Act and 1980s Intelligence Oversight Act. On emergency powers, the International Emergency Economic Powers Act and the National Emergencies Act both built on the Trading with the Enemy Act.

2. As Trimble (1989) put it, by the end of the Reagan administration "many of the congressional triumphs of the 1970s seemed illusory. They did not in practice constrain executive power. The Case Act did not seem to change the use of executive agreements. . . . The National Commitments and War Powers Resolutions did not deter the Executive's use of force" (750).

3. In foreign affairs, two legal advisers to President Bush have argued that "the President possesses a 'general' foreign policy power, which is discretionary, designed to meet the challenges of unforeseen necessities, and thus by nature must be undefinable in its parameters" (Block and Rivkin 1990, 59).

4. Fulbright has since expressed regret about this position.

5. *Regan v. Wald*, 1984, 245, Justice Blackmun dissenting.

6. As the appeals court did in *Beacon Products Corp. v. Reagan*, 1986 (affirmed 1987), upholding the delegation of power in the National Emergencies Act despite the presence of a legislative veto.

7. Koh (1990) argues that the Court has been hamstrung by legislation and that it can and should play a more active role in supporting congressional prerogatives in foreign policy.

8. U.S. Constitution: article 2, section 2, paragraph 1; art. 1, sec. 8, pars. 12, 13, 11; art. 2, sec. 2, par. 2; art. 1, sec. 8, par. 18; and art. 2, sec. 1, par. 1.

9. "A Constitution, to contain an accurate detail of all the subdivisions of which its great powers will admit, and of all the means by which they may be carried into execution, would partake of the prolixity of a legal code, and could scarcely be embraced by the human mind" (Marshall, *McCulloch v. Maryland*, 406).

10. The Congress shall have power "to make all laws which shall be necessary and proper for carrying into execution the foregoing powers, and all other powers vested by this Constitution in the government of the United States, or in any department or officer thereof" (U.S. Constitution, art. 1, sec. 8).

11. In 1832 John Marshall ruled the state of Georgia had no power to enforce its legislation on the lands of the Cherokee Nation within the borders of Georgia. The Cherokee Nation, though not exactly a foreign sovereign, was to be treated as a distinct and independent political community, and its relations with the United States were governed by treaty and not by state law. Existing and future treaties, Marshall wrote, were to be considered "the supreme law of the land." While Marshall's ruling was not enforced, it sent a clear signal that national sovereignty and foreign policy powers could override state authority. See *Worcester v. State of Georgia*, 1832, 559–62. (It was following *Worcester* that President Jackson is rumored to have said of Marshall's decision: "John Marshall has made his decision, now let him enforce it.")

12. See Justice Field's opinions in the *Legal Tender cases*, 1871; and *Chae Chan Ping v. United States* (the Chinese Exclusion case), 1889.

13. James Kerr, 1982, argued that a dissent filed in one of the Insular cases suggested that the Court was applying the Constitution where convenient: "In the political and legal system of the United States it was [now] possible for a territory to be foreign for some purposes yet domestic for others." Kerr 1982, 67.

14. Note well his last line. Even for George Sutherland, the Constitution was not silent or invalid in foreign policy. Where the Constitution spoke, it was to be obeyed: no act of the government could contradict an explicit constitutional prohibition.

15. While the Court will give great latitude in foreign policy cases to Congress and the president acting together, this latitude is not without some limits, particularly when the individual rights of American citizens are at stake. With the glaring exception of *Korematsu v. United States* (the Japanese Internment case) in 1944, the Court has held in a number of cases that the national government cannot strip Americans of their citizenship or livelihood under a foreign policy rationale. Among others, see *United States v. Robel*, 1967; *Trop v. Dulles*, 1957; *Kent v. Dulles*, 1957; *Aptheker v. Secretary of State*, 1967; *United States v. Bishop*, 1977. For a fuller explication, see Silverstein 1991.

16. "Where the heads of departments are the political or confidential agents of the executive, merely to execute the will of the President, or rather to act in cases in which

the executive possesses a constitutional or legal discretion, nothing can be more perfectly clear than that their acts are only politically examinable" (Marshall, *Marbury v. Madison*, 1803, 70).

17. Marshall's argument here foreshadows many of the arguments of the justices in the majority in the Steel Seizure case, *Youngstown Sheet & Tube Co. v. Sawyer*, 1952.

18. Congress had authorized the seizure of vessels bound *to* French ports. Marshall acknowledged that such a law was easily skirted, and that the president's instruction to seize ships bound *to* or *from* French ports was far more likely to interdict the trade Congress sought to block. Although the executive's construction of this law was, Marshall wrote, "much better calculated to give it effect," the executive was nonetheless bound to follow the will and explicit instructions of Congress (*Little v. Barreme*, 178).

19. The case of *Durand v. Hollins*, 1860, is often incorrectly identified as a foundation for broad claims of executive prerogative. *Durand* picked up Marshall's language from *Marbury* while ignoring his recantation in *Little v. Barreme*. *Durand* held that the bombardment of Greytown, Nicaragua, under broad executive orders was constitutional, but, as Glennon (1990) argued, the decision turned on congressional silence in this policy area as well as on Justice Nelson's assumption that the president was acting to save American lives rather than to inflict punishment (Wormuth and Firmage 1989, 41). While such an interpretation lends weight to claims for executive prerogative in the face of congressional silence, it adds nothing to the argument that presidents have plenary power in foreign affairs.

20. One example would be cases where both branches act in concert and the allegation is that they have, together, exceeded the constitutional authority of the national government; a second type would be cases where it is alleged that Congress has unconstitutionally delegated its legitimate authority to the executive. *Curtiss-Wright* would be an example of the later.

21. Justices Clark and Jackson suggested in the Steel Seizure case that had Congress left the field untended, the situation might have been different: the fact that Congress acted was determinative.

22. *Goldwater v. Carter*, 1001, quoting *United States v. Nixon*, 1973, 703, which in turn was quoting *Marbury v. Madison*, 177. This argument was most recently revived in *Dellums v. Bush*, 1990, when fifty-three members of Congress challenged President Bush's authority to engage U.S. troops in combat in Iraq and Saudi Arabia.

23. *Dames & Moore v. Regan*, 1981, 669. Justice Rehnquist noted, however, that "we have in the past found and do today find Justice Jackson's classification of executive actions into three general categories analytically useful" (669).

24. "Before he enter on the Execution of his Office, he shall take the following Oath or Affirmation: 'I do solemnly swear (or affirm) that I will faithfully execute the Office of President of the United States'" (U.S. Constitution, art. 2, sec. 1, par. 8). Also, "he shall take care that the laws be faithfully executed" (art. 2, sec. 3, par. 1).

25. While Attorney General William French Smith argued in 1981 that "in the case of laws that are clearly and indefensibly unconstitutional, the executive can refuse to enforce them and urge invalidation by the courts" (*New York Times*, 30 October 1981, A22), then Assistant Attorney General William Rehnquist said in 1969 that "it seems an anomalous proposition that because the Executive Branch is bound to execute the

laws, it is free to decline to execute them" (quoted in *Lear Seigler*, 1124). As a Supreme Court Justice, Rehnquist has indicated no change of mind (e.g., see *Dames & Moore*, 688).

26. For a fuller review of this phenomenon, see Koh 1990.

27. On rare occasions when both sides have a valid claim, the Court has tried to force an accommodation, as in *United States v. American Telephone and Telegraph Co.* (1977), where a congressional committee demanded records of wiretaps ordered by the executive, but the executive claimed the information was privileged because of national security considerations. Congress argued its constitutional power to investigate trumped the foreign policy claim. The Court held that both sides had enumerated powers at stake and ordered a compromise be struck between them.

28. "The President has entered into binding settlements with foreign nations compromising the claims of U.S. nationals at least 10 times since 1952 without seeking the advice and consent of the Senate" (*American International v. Iran*, 1981, 444).

29. Similarly, the appeals court in *American International* held that "to the extent that denominating the President as the 'sole organ' of the United States in international affairs constitutes a blanket endorsement of plenary Presidential power over any matter extending beyond the borders of this country, we reject that characterization" (*American International*, 438, n. 6).

30. "Every bill which shall have passed the House of Representatives and the Senate, shall, before it becomes a Law, be presented to the President of the United States" (U.S. Constitution, art. 1, sec. 7, par. 2).

31. Robert Dahl flatly rejects this premise: Congress, he wrote, must "see that so far as possible the executive branch has no discretionary power to abuse, however awkward this may make the conduct of foreign affairs" (quoted in Blechman 1990, 13).

32. An excellent account of these powers and their longevity can be found in May 1989.

33. At the time, Block was the senior attorney-adviser, Office of Policy Development, Department of Justice; Rivkin was the legal adviser to the counsel to the president.

34. Recall *Regan v. Wald* and *Dames & Moore v. Regan*, among others.

35. A through review of these successes is well documented in Blechman 1990.

36. Among others, see Mayhew 1974; Fenno 1973.

37. As one judge wrote in 1975: "Whether Congress should devote more effort to defining, limiting or regaining powers previously delegated is not a matter within the jurisdiction of the courts. Whether the pendulum of power should now begin to swing further in the direction of the Congress is a matter of policy, reserved to the people and their elected representatives in the Congress" (*United States v. Yoshida*, 584 n. 37).

Chapter Three

1. For a complete description of the committees examined here, see the Methodological Appendix.

2. For other studies on hearings, see Del Sesto 1980; Payne 1982; and Scicchitano 1986. A reliability check, patterned after Del Sesto, was incorporated into the study as a test for coding accuracy, with a reassuringly high compatibility rate of 97 percent between coders.

3. Respectively, Rep. Robert McClory (U.S. House 1980, 96th Cong., 2d sess., Jan 30 and 31, 1980, 26), and Rep. John M. Ashbrook (U.S. House 1979, 96th Cong., 1st sess., Sept. 20, 1979, 151).

4. Sen. Barry Goldwater (U.S. Senate 1983, 98th Cong., 1st sess., May 16, 1983, 201).

5. Rep. Les Aspin (U.S. House 1977, 95th Cong., 1st and 2d sess., Dec. 27, 1977–April 20, 1978, 47); Sen. Frank Church (U.S. Senate 1975, 94th Cong., 1st sess., Sept. 23–25, 1975, 61).

6. Church (U.S. Senate 1975, 94th Cong., 1st sess., Sept. 23–25, 1975, 59); Rep. Morgan F. Murphy (U.S. House 1975, pt 2, 94th Cong., 1st sess., Sept. 12, 1975, 664).

7. Respectively, the Aspin subcommittee (see U.S. House 1977, 95th Cong., 1st and 2d sess., Dec. 27, 1977–April 20, 1978), the Bayh committee (see U.S. Senate 1980, 96th Cong., 2d sess., Feb. 21–Apr. 16, 1980), and the Boland committee (see U.S. House 1983, 98th Cong., 2d sess., Sept. 20–22, 1983).

8. In 1992 Gates succeeded on an unprecedented second try for the DCI position.

9. The exceptional hardball displayed by GOP overseers in 1987–88 resulted chiefly from the lengthy critical questioning advanced by three Republican senators especially outraged by the Iran-contra scandal: William S. Cohen (Maine), Arlen Specter, and Paul S. Trible, Jr. (Va.).

10. On this phenomenon, see Johnson, Gellner, and Kuzensky 1992.

11. The measures are drawn from Johnson, 1989c, 323; and Kegley and Wittkopf, 1982, p. 58.

12. George J. Tenat, interview with the author, Washington, D.C., 14 December 1990.

13. Interview with the author, 12 December 1990.

14. Interview with the author, 13 December 1990.

15. See, e.g., testimony of Rep. Henry J. Hyde in U.S. House 1987, 200.

16. This language is from the Intelligence Oversight Act of 1991.

17. For one of many statements confirming the trustworthiness of the intelligence committees, see U.S. Congress 1987, 144.

18. Author's interview with CIA official, Langley, Va., 26 March 1991.

19. See Johnson 1992. The series of amendments offered by Congressman Boland in the mid-1980s placed increasingly restrictive limits on CIA covert action in Nicaragua.

20. Webster interview with the author, Langley, Va., 2 May 1991.

21. Casey's informal remarks were presented at a conference on intelligence at CIA headquarters in Langley, 12 June 1984. Richard Helms, who served as DCI from 1967 to 1973, has also frequently expressed his dismay over the growth of congressional participation in intelligence matters (interview with the author, Washington, D.C., 12 Dec. 1990). He would be happier if, like a crab, intelligence oversight could go backward—though he is resigned to the view that the earlier era of benign neglect is unlikely to revisit Capitol Hill anytime soon.

22. See n. 13.

23. See n. 14. This was perhaps true for a time; but William Colby (interview with the author, Washington, D.C., 22 Jan. 1991), among others, now dismisses the Freedom of Information Act as an important check on the CIA: recent amendments to

the law have exempted the Agency from handing over operational files—and rightly so, in Colby's view, to ensure the protection of sources and methods. These are precisely the files, however, where mischief is most likely to be found.

24. In an interview in *U.S. News & World Report*, 16 May 1977.

Chapter Four

1. In Roger Davidson's words: "On Capitol Hill, the center stage of policy making is held by the committees and subcommittees. They are the political nerve ends, the gatherers of information, the sifters of alternatives, the refiners of legislative detail. 'It is not far from the truth to say,' wrote Woodrow Wilson in 1885, 'that Congress in session is Congress on public exhibition, whilst Congress in its committee-rooms is Congress at work'" (1981, 99).

2. For all the study of congressional behavior, the systematic study of hearings is a virtually uncharted area. Among works that have given some attention to hearings, see, in addition to the chapter by Loch Johnson in this volume, Davidson and Hardy 1987; Walker 1977.

3. We have been made aware of the possibility that the transcripts of hearings are occasionally edited before publication, possibly biasing our results. Yet it is not clear that the frequency or intention of this editing has changed over time. In addition, the published hearing, even if edited, is itself an important political document indicative of interbranch relations. We thus have no reason to believe that there is a systematic bias.

4. Controlling for the controversial nature of an issue when attempting to ascertain the assertiveness of a question may simply be controlling for the very thing one is trying to explain. Thus, in our main analysis in table 1, we do not include our indicator of controversy: the length of the hearing in which the question was asked. However, in unreported analyses, we controlled for the controversial nature of the issue under discussion, and, by and large, there is very little change in the size of the coefficients.

5. In order to allow for easier interpretation of the interaction term (threat by hawkishness) the threat and hawkishness variables were centered around their mean.

6. The data on the percentage of GNP allocated for defense expenditures and the congressional changes in the president's budget are taken from the chapter by Ralph Carter in this volume.

7. The coefficients for divided government fall short of significance at the $p < .1$ level. But this is after controlling for the party affiliation of the questioner, which masks the total impact of divided government. Thus the effect of divided government measured here is the effect of party control of a committee independent of the number of seats it holds. When the party affiliation of the questioner is excluded from the analysis (not shown) and the full impact of divided government is assessed, the coefficient shows a stronger, more significant influence of divided government on the level of conflict.

8. The level of conflict in the Senate is higher, but the size of the relationship between chamber and conflict falls just short of being significant at the .1 level.

9. See also *Federalist Papers* No. 55, p. 342; No. 59, p. 360; and No. 63, pp. 382–84.

Chapter Five

1. These votes can be found in *Congressional Quarterly Weekly Report*, respectively, 12 January 1991, 136, and 20 April 1991, 1014.

2. LeLoup and Shull (1979) used "box-score" data to show that presidential success in foreign and defense policies converged to the level for domestic policies in the period 1965–75. Sigelman (1979) employed roll-call votes on important measures (called "key votes") and concluded that there was no evidence of greater presidential success on foreign and defense policy, either in earlier or later years.

3. Because of the small number of cases, there is no temporal breakdown on these data, so there is no indication of a time trend in regard to important votes.

4. The data employed here were collected for another project that dealt only with the House of Representatives (see Rohde 1991), and equivalent data are not now available for the Senate. Thus the discussion and analysis in this paper will be confined to the House. Presidential positions, issues, and types of votes were coded from the descriptions published by Congressional Quarterly, Inc., and these were merged with other data on roll calls made available by the ICPSR.

5. Another provision of the Legislative Reorganization Act that made record votes on amendments (and on other questions) more feasible was the adoption of the House's electronic voting system, which went into operation in 1973. This substantially reduced the amount of time it took to complete a record vote. For a discussion of the consequences of these provisions, see Smith 1989, esp. 16–35.

6. Among presidential-position votes, most of the procedural votes are accounted for by motions to recommit and votes on the passage of special rules (measures that set the terms for floor debate on individual bills).

7. Of course, many defense issues involve matters of foreign policy, so more-accurate labels might be "defense policy" and "nondefense foreign policy." Such usage would be unnecessarily awkward, however, especially since that distinction is what the conventional labels have always connoted. Defense policy includes weapons procurement, war powers, defense organization, and military security issues (like foreign military aid), but not things like military construction and veterans' benefits, which are classified as domestic issues. Foreign policy includes issues like nonmilitary foreign aid and foreign trade matters. Thus the distinction between the two hinges on military versus nonmilitary matters.

8. For more general discussions of the reforms see Smith and Deering 1990; Rieselbach 1986; and Rohde 1991.

9. For an excellent brief discussion of this era, see Cooper and Brady 1981. Since 1955 Democrats have been the majority party in the House, as they have been, except for four years (1949–51, 1953–55), since 1933. It will simplify both the theoretical discussion and the presentation of data if I confine myself to that time period. We lose little empirical coverage by this, since the presidential-position data on roll calls only begin with 1953.

10. Sinclair (1982) offers a detailed account of these divisions and their development over time.

11. For example, Secretary of State Dulles argued in 1958 against proposed foreign aid cuts, saying the failure to channel funds to important areas "would almost serve as notice that we would have to take some losses" to communism. Quoted in Rourke 1983, 181.

12. Between 1953 and 1988, 96.6 percent of all the bills and joint resolutions (i.e., not just those on which the president took a position) that received a roll-call vote on initial regular passage received majority support. (Since many bills are adopted by voice vote, the actual rate of passage is even higher.) Since we will employ this subset of votes below, I should be clear here on its definition. "Initial" passage excludes votes on conference reports or veto overrides. This limits consideration to the House's judgment on content before disagreements with the Senate have been bargained away. "Regular" passage excludes passage by suspension of the rules. Because of the two-thirds majority requirement for passage, these would require separate analysis. "Bills and joint resolutions" exclude simple and concurrent resolutions, which don't involve presidential approval. Similarly, I exclude those few joint resolutions that involve passage of constitutional amendments. With that one exception, bills and joint resolutions are equivalent, and for convenience I will refer to the set simply as "bills."

13. Of course, the nature of committees and the degree of presidential-congressional conflict would vary substantially across domestic issues. However, space limits do not permit drawing those distinctions here, so we can regard the domestic policy category as just an aggregate baseline against which to compare defense and foreign policy issues.

14. Viewed from this vantage point, we can see how sole concentration on conflictual roll-call votes could mislead us about the amount of presidential sucess in foreign and defense policy, both over time and relative to domestic issues. Let us consider two time periods. In the first period, Congress gives the president exactly what he wants on most bills, so in those cases there is either no roll call or roll calls are all virtually unanimous. Still, there is disagreement in a few cases, and the president's position loses on a couple of votes. Then in the second period, for whatever reason, disagreement sharply increases on these issues. There are *many* conflictual roll calls on alternatives opposed to the president's position, and the number (but not the proportion) on which his preferred side loses increases. Clearly, interbranch conflict on foreign and defense policy is up in the second period, and presidential success is down. However, a focus on just the conflictual roll calls would lead to the opposite conclusion. Conflictual roll-call data permit us to compare the patterns of conflict over time *on those votes where there is conflict*. Those data alone do not tell us about the frequency of conflict, or how often Congress accedes unanimously to the president's wishes. Yet this is important information for evaluating changing patterns of presidential success and support.

15. This led Sen. Mark Hatfield (R-Ore.) to say at the time that the program had become "food for war." See *Congressional Quarterly Weekly Report*, 1 September 1990; 2767.

16. For a discussion of the impact of membership change and reform on this committee, see Ornstein and Rohde 1977.

17. For a very useful account of Carter's relationships with Congress see Jones 1988b.

18. In an extreme example, when Carter's ambassador to the United Nations, Andrew Young, said to a French newspaper that there were political prisoners in the United States as well as abroad, a resolution of impeachment was introduced in the House. Majority Leader James Wright (D-Tex.) moved to table the resolution. He

was opposed by only fifteen conservative Democrats, but a majority of Republicans voted no.

19. For discussions of Reagan's agenda see Light 1983; ix–xi; Jones 1988a.

20. The electoral roots of the changing issue alignments among representatives are discussed in Rohde 1988; Rohde 1991, chap. 3. Essentially the argument is that conservative (and mostly southern) Democratic voters reacted negatively to the domestic and defense policies of the party in the 1960s and 1970s and began moving to the Republican party. Also, in the South the Voting Rights Act enfranchised blacks, who mostly joined the Democrats. These two trends, coupled with the effects of court-mandated redistricting, substantially liberalized the constituencies of southern Democrats, made Democratic constituencies in the North and South more like one another, and made both more divergent from the constituencies of Republican representatives.

21. For example, Cox and McCubbins's (1993, chap. 7) analysis shows that the positions of Armed Services Democrats were usually significantly more conservative than those of all House Democrats from the 92d Congress through the 100th.

22. See Rohde 1991, 72–75.

23. These votes are not only the most theoretically relevant but also the most frequent. Of the 2,726 presidential-position votes between 1955 and 1988, 881 (31.1%) were on initial passage, and 707 (25.9%) were on first-degree amendments. The next most frequently occurring vote was on recommittal motions, which accounted for slightly less than 9% of the total.

24. Most of the roll-call studies on the two-presidencies hypothesis have used an 80 percent majority break point to exclude roll calls. However, majorities of this size can still entail a great deal of disagreement when considered from a partisan or ideological point of view. For example, in a Congress like the 95th (1977–79, when the Democrats had a 292–143 majority), if all the Democrats voted together on a roll call, with an 80 percent overall majority the Republicans could be voting 61 to 39 percent *against* (if all members voted). This is hardly a nonconflictual vote from a partisan perspective. Thus the 90 percent cutoff would seem a better criterion for consensual support for a bill. In the example, the maximum Republican split would be 70 to 30 percent in favor.

25. The figure for Kennedy-Johnson is inflated by Johnson's success in the 89th Congress, after the landslide victory in 1964. Less explicable is the fact that the proportion of consensual votes was also high in the 90th Congress, when the Republicans were significantly stronger. This appears to be due to a lot of roll calls on "little," noncontroversial bills.

26. The analysis deals only with first-degree amendments because the inferences that can be drawn from them are different from those regarding second-degree amendments (i.e., amendments to amendments). As Smith points out (1989, 183–87), primary amendments are efforts to change committe bills (expressing at least some dissatisfaction with them), while secondary amendments may be used by bill supporters to protect the original bill's content as far as possible. Thus in regard to secondary amendments we could not infer any disagreement with the bill.

Since it will be necessary in some instances to restrict attention to nonconsensual votes, it would seem preferable to do so for the entire analysis of amendments to keep the data comparable at all points. This excludes only nineteen (3.1%) of the cases.

27. The difference between the two Reagan terms seems to be due mostly to the difference in the kinds of bills involved. Seven of the amendments he favored in his second term involved changes to the Democratic trade bill or attempts to pass humanitarian aid for the Nicaraguan contras. Neither of these issues were involved on first-term amendments.

28. These defense amendments reflected Carter's different priorities, as noted earlier. For example, he supported deleting funds for an additional nuclear carrier and adding funds for a cruise missile–carrying aircraft.

29. It is for this measure that the exclusion of consensual votes is necessary. The difference between which group favors an amendment or bill has little potential meaning when the overall rate of support is 99 percent. By excluding consensual votes we guarantee that there is at least a minimal amount of underlying disagreement. Of course, it is still possible that the difference between the two groups will be very small, but that is true of any categorical measure. An alternative classification scheme would be to categorize each amendment by the party of the sponsor. This could be misleading, however. Frequently an amendment's proponents perceive it to be in their interest to give the appearance of bipartisanship by getting a sponsor from the other party.

30. The overwhelming majority of the Republican-favored amendments involved cuts in (or restrictions on) foreign aid to international agencies, conflict over our changing relationship with Taiwan, or attacks on the implementation of the Panama Canal Treaty.

31. The evidence from recommittal votes also illustrates the difference between the Reagan adaminstration and those before. Motions to recommit seek to send bills back to the committee of origin, either to kill the bill or to make a specific changes in it. The motion is the province of the minority party, so it is rare for Democratic presidents to support one. In the Eisenhower and in the Nixon-Ford administrations, only 10 percent or less of the motions to recommit favored by the president involved foreign or defense policy bills. Under Reagan, on the other hand, 67 percent (eight of twelve) involved such bills. In fact, Reagan supported *every one* of the motions to recommit that were offered on those types of bills; previous Republican presidents didn't even support half of them.

32. For defense bills, 50 percent were Democrat favored. The proportion of bills on which the president supported passage was also 50 percent. Indeed they were the same bills: seven bills were Democrat favored and the president opposed them; seven were Republican favored and he supported them.

33. The reader will notice that I have presented no evidence regarding the proportion of bills on which a majority supported the president's position. This is because, as noted above, almost all bills that come to a vote pass. Thus the president's rate of success at this stage is almost entirely a function of how often he favors or opposes passage. When he supported passage he almost always won, and when he was opposed he almost always lost.

34. One prominent proponent of this view has been James L. Sundquist. For a recent statement, see Sundquist 1988.

35. For discussions of the relationship between divided government and electoral choice see Fiorina 1989; and Jacobson 1990.

36. While this analysis has focused on the House, it is appropriate to discuss briefly the generalizability of the findings to the Senate. Support for presidential decisions in the Senate should also be dependent on the degree of preference overlap based in electoral coalitions and on particular institutional arrangements. Moreover, the kinds of political trends discussed here should have reduced the presidential advantage on foreign and defense policy in the Senate as well. Beyond these generalizations, we cannot say much more without a separate analysis at least as detailed as this one. That is because the political coalitions of senators can be very different from those of representatives, potentially resulting in a very different pattern of preferences in the Senate compared to the House. In addition, institutional patterns are different in the Senate, with, for example, very different committee-floor and member-leadership relationships. (For a discussion of these issues related to the degree of partisanship in each institution, see Rohde 1992.) These factors could result in very different expectations regarding changing patterns of presidential-Senate agreement and conflict.

Chapter Six

1. Unless otherwise noted, references to foreign policy include defense and national security policy as well.

2. Unless otherwise indicated, "leaders" refers to the top four elected party leaders, one for each party in each house. The role of congressional party leaders in the foreign and defense policy arena often has been explained by two norms, institutional deference and committee deference. Congress's proper role was to defer to the president on matters of foreign policy and national security. And leaders' proper role was to defer to specialists on the foreign and defense policy committees. In the 1950s leaders Lyndon Johnson and Sam Rayburn frequently articulated these norms, and, at the time, scholarly observers accepted their interpretations. Wildavsky concluded that congressmen "are ordinarily not serious competitors with the President because they follow a self-denying ordinance. They do not think it is their job to determine the nation's defense policy" (1966, 10). In my view, few of the strategic choices on the major policies are best viewed as the product of habit or prescriptive norms, although leaders often find it useful to invoke established practice and high principle when explaining their own behavior.

3. On leadership goals, see Sinclair 1983, 1–3; Smith 1993.

4. Of course, the status quo in nondomestic policies is not always easily manipulated by the president. Congress has sought greater control of the policy status quo in many areas by moving to annual authorizations and requiring more advance notice and disclosure from the executive branch. But presidential flexibility in managing foreign policy in the face of unpredictable international conditions is a necessity that limits the extent to which Congress can give itself a permanent strategic advantage vis-à-vis the president without undermining the probability of achieving its own foreign policy goals.

5. Attributing shifts in relative power is a tricky business. At root, the problem is inferring congressional compliance with presidential preferences when the level of agreement between presidents and Congress varies. Ideally, presidents' and Congress's policy preferences would be measured independently of their observed behav-

ior. Lacking direct measures of preferences, we cannot distinguish deference from genuine agreement. Nor can we measure the effect of institutional or procedural developments controlling for the effects of changes in preferences. Nevertheless, the proponents of the resurgent Congress thesis make the credible claim, based on evidence beyond legislative success rates, that congressional preferences changed in ways that produced a new strategic situation in the late 1960s and thereafter. See Rourke 1983.

6. The Speaker is excluded because he seldom votes.

7. Very similar results are obtained when attention is limited to the very most contested and "key" votes, as identified by Congressional Quarterly (data not shown). I thank Professors Jon Bond and Richard Fleisher for sharing their data with me.

8. I thank Stephen Hess, Steven Roberts, and Martin Tolchin for pointing out that in the last five years or so the *Times* has reduced the number of stories providing daily updates on developments and substituted fewer but larger stories. This would reduce the number of stories mentioning congressional leaders.

9. See *President Eisenhower's Meetings with Legislative Leaders*, taken from a file at the Eisenhower Library, which includes memoranda on Eisenhower's formal meetings with leaders drafted by a professional historian, L. Arthur Minnich, who served as assistant staff secretary. Burns notes that weekly meetings with one's own party leaders had become an "institution" by the time Eisenhower was president (1963, 255).

10. According to Eisenhower, inviting more than just the top two Republican leaders of each house was an innovation necessary for providing an early warning system. Truman apparently invited only the "Big Four" (Greenstein 1982, 112).

11. On Rayburn, see Steinberg 1975, 318–21.

12. Some observers attribute at least part of the responsibility for the cooling of Eisenhower's feelings about Johnson and Rayburn to the absence of John Foster Dulles in the last two years of Eisenhower's presidency. Dulles, as secretary of state, courted Congress and organized many of the bipartisan leadership meetings. It also has been noted that Senator Walter George's departure from the Senate and the chairmanship of the Committee on Foreign Relations at the end of 1956 eliminated a moderating influence on Johnson.

13. John Erlichman reports that the Republican leaders "rarely were given a chance to say anything" at the weekly breakfast sessions. See Erlichman 1982, 204.

14. Scott's relations with the Nixon administration also may have suffered because Scott appears to have believed that a key White House aide worked against his election as Republican floor leader.

15. Mansfield claims that he encouraged Nixon to pursue his China initiatives at these meetings.

16. In the case of the *Mayaguez* incident, Ford briefed congressional leaders after issuing orders for the use of force to free the captured Marines. See Ford 1979, 280–81, 283.

17. Several instances are noted in Carter 1982.

18. Several sources were searched for evidence on leaders' activity: *Congressional Quarterly Weekly Report*, the *New York Times*, several book-length treatments of congressional foreign policy activity (most useful is John Rourke's extensive book on

Congress and foreign policy, *Congress and the Presidency in U.S. Foreign Policymaking*), and leaders' and presidents' biographies. The search was restricted to the fifteen or sixteen top foreign and defense policy issues for the Congresses examined. The top issues were selected on the basis of the subjects most frequently discussed in the *Department of State Bulletin* and the subjects highlighted in the *CQ Almanac*, an annual review of Congress and public policy. This approach is necessarily biased against the inclusion of issues that did not become public. For example, in 1956 congressional leaders' opposition to a loan to Egypt for construction of the Aswan dam helped to convince President Eisenhower not to formally request legislation from Congress. And in 1963 and 1964 congressional leaders' views played a role in President Johnson's decision not to pursue a multinational nuclear force with NATO allies, but the issue was not subject to much public discussion and it is not addressed in the *Department of State Bulletin*.

Chapter Seven

1. The turning point in the Vietnam War, in terms of its impact on U.S. politics, was the Communist Tet Offensive of February 1968. For additional consideration of pre- and post-Tet changes in congressional foreign policy behavior, see R. G. Carter 1986.

2. This term comes from Blechman 1990b.

3. In 1954 Frederic R. Coudert (R-N.Y.) offered an amendment to the FY1955 defense appropriations bill barring the use of any money to send U.S. troops into combat without congressional consent. He said he wanted to prevent future Koreas and keep the United States out of Indochina. President Eisenhower said the amendment would inhibit the flexibility of the commander-in-chief, and it was defeated overwhelmingly on the House floor. For more on this and the other specific congressional actions cited hereafter, see the appropriate year's *Congressional Quarterly Almanac*.

4. Not surprisingly, during the 1980s Reagan was consistently able to get the Republican Senate to restore part of what the Democratic House deleted from his requests. Yet the lack of a similar structural situation (i.e., "split control") in the pre-Vietnam period precludes any comparison of pre- and post-Vietnam differences.

Chapter Eight

1. Tower, Nunn, Cohen, and Warner were mainstays of the Senate armed services committee, often with collateral service on the select committee on intelligence. Aspin, as chairman of House armed services, and Fascell, as chairman of House foreign affairs, were central to that body's actions on national security issues, as was Cheney in his service as minority whip and a ranking member of the intelligence committee.

2. Finney (1987) provides a concise historical perspective. The ABM plans of both the Johnson and Nixon years involved the use of large nuclear warheads over the United States, unlike the conventional Patriot missiles employed against shorter-range offensive missiles in the 1991 Gulf War. The limited success of the Patriots against crude threats would have been a catastrophic failure if the attacking missiles carried nuclear weapons. The Gulf War experience both revived interest in defenses against accidents or limited attacks by third world countries and demonstrated the implausibility of effective defenses against large-scale attacks.

3. *Strategic Arms Limitation Talks* includes the full record of the SALT I debate. See also Platt 1978, 9–36.

4. See also U.S. Senate 1979.

5. Reagan voiced initial inclinations on this subject in campaign interviews (Scheer 1982).

6. Yankelovich and Harman 1988, 78–79. The authors interpret poll findings not so much as "firm support for a policy of freezing weapons development" as a "symbolic way of saying 'Enough is enough.'"

7. Gore's involvement in these questions grew out of work on the House intelligence committee; Dicks was a rising member of the defense appropriations subcommittee. Frye 1983–84.

8. In later years Congress confined the MX deployment to fifty missiles in silos, while development of Midgetman moved forward slowly. The 1992 START II agreement in principle projected the elimination of land-based MIRV systems.

9. A status report on these issues is in Aspin 1991.

10. Few documents are available regarding the work of the Senate Observer Group; a number are collected in *Congressional Record*, 13 June 1985, S 8157–8170.

11. Remarks by Max Kampelman, former head of the U.S. delegation to the Negotiations on Nuclear and Space Arms, in "Executive-Congressional Relations" 1991, 18.

12. Six weeks earlier fifty-two senators, including fourteen Republicans, had written the president to urge continued compliance with the SALT II ceilings; *Congressional Record*, 10 April 1986, p. S4026; see also Krepon 1989, 243–53. A *Washington Post*–ABC News poll, taken shortly after Reagan's announcement, found 61 percent of the respondents favoring retention of SALT II limits until a new agreement was concluded, with only 29 percent supporting the president's view; see Barry Sussman's report of the survey, *Washington Post*, 25 June 1986, A16. The United States in fact exceeded the SALT II limits in November 1986, when the deployment of a modified B-52 broke the ceiling on the number of permitted MIRV missile launchers and cruise missile–equipped bombers.

13. In addition to Stuetzle et al. 1987, see Garthoff 1987; and the exceptionally valuable retrospective commentaries in University of Pennsylvania Law Review 1989.

14. See Nunn's statement in U.S. Senate 1987, 54–78.

15. The inflamed controversy over the ABM Treaty is not representative of Judge Sofaer's important work as a scholar and public servant. Fairness requires one to note his major study of war powers (1976), and the firm stance he took against those in the Reagan administration who were prepared to submit clearly misleading testimony during the Iran-contra episode.

16. Fulbright's testimony in U.S. Senate 1987, 26–31.

Chapter Nine

1. De Tocqueville (1945, 240–45) argued that the Constitution's grant of substantial foreign policy powers to Congress made the U.S. government "decidedly inferior to other governments" in this area. Kennan (1951, 66–67) viewed the democratic foreign policy–making process as prehistoric.

2. I have addressed the question of the causes of the disagreement between Congress and the president on Iran-contra in Pastor, 1993.

3. For a fuller development of the interbranch politics approach, see Pastor 1980, esp. 49–62, 345–53; Pastor 1992, chap. 6.

4. Metternich was troubled by the idealistic side of the doctrine, which he saw as fomenting revolution: "In fostering revolutions wherever they show themselves, in regretting those which have failed, in extending a helping hand to those which seem to prosper, [the United States] lends new strength to the apostles of sedition, and reanimates the courage of every conspirator" (qtd. in Perkins 1927, 167).

5. For two descriptions of the emergence and evolution of the human rights policy, see Schoultz 1981; and Pastor 1980, 301–21.

6. Quoted in "U.S. Policy on Rights Backed by Kissinger," *New York Times*, 20 October 1976.

7. For a discussion of Congress's role in precluding negotiations, see Pastor 1975.

8. Howard Baker, then Senate minority leader and member of the foreign relations committee, announced at the opening of the hearings that the U.S. negotiators "did much more [in consulting with the Senate] than anybody I have ever known has done" (95th Congress, 1st Session, U.S. Senate 1977, 87–88).

9. Bauer, Pool, and Dexter (1972) have explained how countervailing pressures permit Congressmen the space to vote for their own preferences in U.S. trade policy. For a detailed description of U.S. policy toward Nicaragua, see Pastor 1987.

10. For a discussion of U.S. efforts to preclude Sandinista support for Salvadoran rebels and the Sandinista response to these efforts, see Pastor 1987, 202–07, 216–28.

11. This section is based on Pastor 1987; Gutman 1988; the Iran-contra reports of Congress; and an interview with Thomas Enders, Ditchley Park, England, 20 May 1989.

12. This and other excerpts of the document were reprinted during the North trial in the *New York Times*, 14 April 1989, 9. In the full minutes that have been declassified, Robert McFarlane criticizes Nicaragua and other "Marxist-Leninist regimes" for using negotiations as "tactical exercises," though that is precisely the way Reagan said the United States should think about neogtiations with Nicaragua (10).

13. Reagan's address was reprinted in the *New York Times*, 8 October 1987, 8.

14. See, e.g., "Panama Crisis: Disarray Hindered White House," *New York Times*, 8 October 1989, 1, 6; "Amateur Hour," *Newsweek*, 16 October 1989, 26–31.

15. Bush's interview with Latin American press, 25 October 1989, Washington, D.C., 10, reprinted in *Public Papers of the Presidents*, George Bush, 1989, Vol. II, 1393.

16. Paul Lewis, "OAS Deems Rule by Noriega Illegal: Group Deplores Panamanian and Accuses His Regime of Rights Violations," *New York Times*, 14 November 1989.

17. Michael Wines, "U.S. Plans New Effort to Oust Noriega," *New York Times*, 17 November 1989, A3.

18. Michael R. Gordon, "U.S. Drafted Invasion Plan Weeks Ago," *New York Times*, 24 December 1989, 1, 5.

19. Maureen Dowd, "Doing the Inevitable: Bush Reportedly Felt that Noriega 'Was Thumbing His Nose at Him,'" *New York Times*, 24 December 1989, 5; R. W. Apple, Jr., "Bush's Obsession: President Says Noriega's Hold on Power Has Left Him 'Extraordinarily Frustrated,'" *New York Times*, 26 December 1989, 5.

20. A CBS news poll in Panama in early January found that 92 percent of Panamanian adults approved of the sending of troops, and 76 percent wished the United States had sent them during the coup in October. The invasion was also approved by the American people: 74 percent said it was justified, and only 7 percent thought the United States should not have taken such action. More significantly, the invasion measurably improved Bush's overall ratings, lifting him up to where 76 percent approved of the job he was doing, a higher level at that point in his term than any president had had since John F. Kennedy. See two articles in the *New York Times*: Michael R. Kagay, "Panamanians Strongly Back U.S. Move," 6 January 1990, 7; Michael Oreskes, "Approval of Bush, Aided by Panama, Hits 76% in Poll: A Rarely Achieved Level," 19 January 1990, 1, 11.

21. The Congressional Management Foundation estimated that the volume of mail received by congressional offices increased by 2,000 percent since 1970. Most members receive between 500 and 1,000 letters a week. Cited in "New Lawmakers Find Winning Was Easy Part," *New York Times*, 6 January 1991, 11.

22. For statistics from 1970 to 1987, see U.S. Bureau of the Census 1989, table 514, p. 319; for statistics going further back, see Bureau of the Census 1975, 1102–3.

Chapter Ten

1. The latter was the vote, actually, not on the bill Reagan signed but rather on H.R. 3, which he vetoed because of an extraneous provision requiring advance notification of workers in certain instances of plant closings. Shortly thereafter, a new bill (H.R. 4848) was introduced—H.R. 3 minus this and another offending provisions. H.R. 4848 was passed quickly by both houses and signed into law. The main legislative action took place on H.R. 3, however, and that will be the basis for the temporal comparisons in this paper.

2. Through a special procedural commitment known as the "fast-track" rules, Congress has bound itself since 1974 to an up or down vote, within a 60-to-90-day time period, on legislation submitted by the president to implement international trade agreements whose negotiation Congress has authorized. In the 1934–74 period, delegation of trade power was accomplished simply by authorizing the president to negotiate reductions in tariffs and implement the new rates by presidential order. But more-recent trade negotiations have centered on nontariff barriers. Agreements on these must be implemented by changes in U.S. law which are wide-ranging and hence impossible for Congress to authorize specifically in advance.

3. This included the widely publicized Gephardt amendment, which would have imposed special import barriers on the products of nations which ran large trade surpluses globally and vis-à-vis the United States.

4. The nonlegislative subcommittee on foreign trade, chaired by Hale Boggs, had one professional staff aide in the late 1950s.

5. This expansion reflected a rise in congressional assertiveness vis-à-vis the executive, but even more a rise in competition *within* Congress: decentralization of power within committees, and dispersal of power across committees.

6. The 1962 law ran from 76 STAT. 872 to 76 STAT. 903; the 1974 law from 88 STAT. 1978 to 88 STAT. 2076; and the 1988 law from 102 STAT. 1107 to 102 STAT. 1574. The Trade Agreements Act of 1979 implementing the Tokyo Round accords took up 173 statutory pages, 93 STAT. 144 to 93 STAT. 317.

7. Amending these laws was not, in most instances, necessary for U.S. participation in the international negotiations, but it was typically a quid pro quo imposed by congressional champions of these laws. Susan Schwab, long a senior Senate aide on trade policy and director-general of the U.S. and Foreign Commercial Service in the Bush administration, has summarized the contents of comprehensive trade legislation as $(X - Y) + Z$, where X is the negotiating authority sought by the administration, Y is the limits and conditions Congress places on that authority, and Z is the ancillary trade provisions legislators are able to attach. These Z provisions are constrained, in turn, by the threat of presidential veto. For her comprehensive analysis of the enactment of the 1988 trade bill, see Schwab 1993.

8. Roughly half of the law's pages covered matters under the jurisdiction of committees other than those with primary trade responsibility, House ways and means and Senate finance.

9. For the Trade Expansion Act of 1962, Ways and Means held twenty-one days of hearings, with testimony and supporting materials totaling 4,217 pages. For the Trade Act of 1974, the committee held twenty-four days of hearings totaling 5,317 pages. There was no single set of hearings on what became the 1988 legislation: a (possibly incomplete) count of general ways and means trade hearings in 1986 and 1987 comes to nineteen days and 4,100 pages. But ten other House committees were also involved, and an incomplete count of their hearings in 1986 and early 1987 includes energy and commerce (nine days, 1181 pages); foreign affairs (seventeen days, over 1,215 pages); banking (one day, 483 pages); small business (three days, 680 pages); merchant marine and fisheries (one day, 358 pages); science, space, and technology (three days, 1,170 pages); and armed services (two days, 82 pages). In addition, several of these committees held broad hearings in 1985 anticipating and preparing the ground for omnibus legislation.

10. The time period for applying this procedure was extended for eight more years in 1979, and the procedure was authorized—with additional wrinkles—for bilateral free trade agreements in 1984, and for the Uruguay Round talks in 1988. Congress extended the procedure for two additional years in May 1991.

11. A "markup" is a committee meeting that drafts or amends legislation, with the aim of reporting it to the floor. A conference is the meeting that reconciles differences in the versions of a bill enacted by the House and Senate. Technically, these spring 1979 meetings were neither, because Congress was not yet formally considering the legislation but simply advising the executive branch on what the president should propose. In practice, however, the meetings performed similar functions: hence the "nonmarkup" and "nonconference" labels.

12. For more detail, see Cassidy 1981; Destler and Graham 1980.

13. For summaries of that legialtive process, see Pastor 1980, 105–17; Preeg 1970, 44–53.

14. In the drafting of the Trade Agreements Act of 1979 to implement the Tokyo Round agreements, senators and representatives insisted on another major revision of the countervailing duties and antidumping laws. On that and subsequent implementation, see Destler 1992, chap. 6. On the executive-congressional politics of 1973–74, see Destler 1980, chaps. 9–11; and Pastor 1980, chap. 5.

15. The Smoot-Hawley precedent had fresh relevance, since its enactment in

1930—after the crash of 1929—is generally credited with deepening the Great Depression.

16. This phrase originated at a hearing of the Senate committee on finance, in an exchange between Senator Bob Packwood and former STR Robert Strauss. It was widely repeated by senators and aides as the bill made its way into law (Bello and Holmer 1990, 59).

17. A particularly useful measure of the impact of imports on U.S. producers is their ratio (adjusted for inflation) to total U.S. goods production. In 1970 imports were 14.6 percent of U.S. output of goods, measured in constant (1982) dollars. In 1989 they were 26.9 percent. This meant broader choices for American consumers, but greater pressure on U.S. firms that made competing products.

18. In a paper assessing the 1980–89 period, I conclude—citing comprehensive analyses—that the increase in U.S. market restrictiveness was, at most, "marginal" (see Destler 1991). In a stimulating article, Douglas Nelson (1989) argues that, in its action on the trade remedy laws, Congress has responded to a political imbalance (in favor of protectionism) similar to the imbalance that existed before 1930, but that, simultaneously, the executive branch has gained control over "liberalization policy" through multilateral negotiations (and the president's foreign policy power). This combination has led, he asserts, to a "discontinuous downward shift in the level of protection . . . followed by a continuing rise in the level of protection [through the trade remedy procedures]" (93).

19. For examples of the "new institutionalist" approach, see Shepsle and Weingast 1984, 1987; McCubbins, Noll, and Weingast 1989; and McCubbins and Schwartz 1984. All are sophisticated in their treatment of congressional motivation, and the "fire alarm" concept of legislative oversight highlighted by McCubbins and Schwartz is certainly applicable to trade policy making. But all assume that the goal of legislators' policy-related activity is to have an impact on policy outcomes, on what government actually does. For a useful, restrained application of this approach to trade policy, see O'Halloran 1990.

★ ★ ★
REFERENCES
★ ★ ★

Aberbach, Joel. 1990. *Keeping a Watchful Eye: The Politics of Congressional Oversight*. Washington, D.C.: Brookings Institution.

Allison, Graham. 1971. *Essence of Decision*. Boston: Little, Brown.

Ambrose, Stephen. 1984. *Eisenhower: The President*. New York: Simon & Shuster.

Art, R. J. 1985. "Congress and the Defense Budget: Enhancing Policy Oversight." In *Reorganizing America's Defense*, edited by R. J. Art, V. Davis, and S. P. Huntington. Washington, D.C.: Pergamon-Brassey's International Defense Publishers.

Aspin, Les. 1991. "Missile Defenses and the ABM Treaty: Moving Toward a Consensus." Remarks before the American Defense Preparedness Association, 27 June.

Bach, Stanley, and Steven Smith. 1989. *Managing Uncertainty*. Washington, D.C.: Brookings Institution.

Baker, Ross K. 1990. "Mike Mansfield and the Birth of the Modern Senate." Paper presented at the Everett McKinley Dirksen Center Symposium on Senate Leadership, Washington, D.C., 17 May.

Bauer, Raymond, Ithiel de Sola Pool, and Lewis A. Dexter. 1972. *American Business and Public Policy*. Chicago: Aldine-Atherton.

Bax, F. 1977. "The Legislative-Executive Relationship in Foreign Policy." *Orbis* 20:881–904.

Bello, Judith Hippler, and Alan F. Holmer. 1990. "The Heart of the 1988 Trade Act: A Legislative History of the Amendments to Section 301." In *Aggressive Unilateralism: America's 301 Trade Policy and the World Trading System*, edited by Jagdish Bhagwati and Hugh T. Patrick, 49–89. Ann Arbor: University of Michigan Press.

Bernstein, Robert A., and William W. Anthony. 1974. "The ABM Issue in the Senate, 1968–70: The Importance of Ideology." *American Political Science Review* 68:1198–1206.

Berry, Jeffrey M., Kent E. Portney, and Ken Thomson. 1992. *The Politics of Urban Democracy*. Washington, D.C.: Brookings Institution.

Bhagwati, Jagdish, and Hugh T. Patrick. 1990. *Aggressive Unilateralism: America's 301 Trade Policy and the World Trading System*. Ann Arbor: University of Michigan Press.

Blechman, Barry. 1990a. "The New Congressional Role in Arms Control." In *A Question of Balance: The President, the Congress, and Foreign Policy*, edited by Thomas E. Mann. Washington, D.C.: Brookings Institution.

———. 1990b. *The Politics of National Security: Congress and U.S. Defense Policy*. New York: Twentieth Century Fund/Oxford University Press.

Bledsoe, R. 1983. "Congressional Committees and the Defense Budget: By the Numbers." Unpublished paper prepared for the Roosevelt Center for the Study of Public Policy, Washington, D.C.

Block, Lawrence J., and David B. Rivkin, Jr. 1990. "The Constitution Still in Danger: An Exchange." *New York Review of Books*, 16 August, 50.

Bond, Jon R., and Richard Fleisher. 1990. *The President in the Legislative Arena*, Chicago: University of Chicago Press.

Bumpers, Dale, John Chafee, and Patrick Leahy. 1987. "Salvaging SALT: The New Congressional Compromise." *Arms Control Today* 17, no. 10 (December): 3–6.

Burns, James MacGregor. 1963. *The Deadlock of Democracy: Four-Party Politics in America*. Englewood Cliffs, N.J.: Prentice-Hall.

Caldwell, Dan. 1991. *The Dynamics of Domestic Politics and Arms Control: The SALT II Ratification Debate*. Columbia: University of South Carolina Press.

Carroll, H. N. 1958. *The House of Representatives and Foreign Affairs*. Pittsburgh: University of Pittsburgh Press.

Carter, Jimmy. 1977. *Public Papers of the Presidents of the United States: Jimmy Carter*. Vol. 1. Washington, D.C.: Government Printing Office.

———. 1982. *Keeping Faith: Memoirs of a President*. New York: Bantam Books.

Carter, Ralph G. 1986. "Congressional Foreign Policy Behavior: Persistent Patterns of the Postwar Period." *Presidential Studies Quarterly* 16:329–59.

Cassidy, Robert C., Jr. 1981. "Negotiating about Negotiations." In *The Tethered Presidency*, edited by Thomas M. Franck, 264–82. New York: New York University Press.

Chubb, John E., and Paul E. Peterson. 1989. "American Political Institutions and the Problem of Governance." In *Can the Government Govern?* edited by Chubb and Peterson, 1–30. Washington, D.C.: Brookings Institution.

Cohen, Julius. 1952. "Hearing on a Bill: Legislative Folklore?" *Minnesota Law Review* 37:38–39.

Coleman, James. 1957. *Community Conflict*. New York: Free Press.

Congressional Quarterly, Inc. 1946–90. *Congressional Quarterly Almanacs*. Washington, D.C.: Congressional Quarterly News Features.

Cooper, Joseph, and David Brady. 1981. "Institutional Context and Leadership Style: The House from Cannon to Rayburn." *American Politican Science Review* 75:411–25.

Cox, Gary W., and Mathew D. McCubbins. 1993. *Legislative Leviathan: Party Government in the House*. Berkeley and Los Angeles: University of California Press.

Dahl, Robert. 1964. *Congress and American Foreign Policy*. New York: W. W. Norton.

Davidson, Roger H. 1981. "Subcommittee Government: New Channels for Policy Making." In *The New Congress*, edited by Thomas E. Mann and Norman J. Ornstein. Washington, D.C.: American Enterprise Institute.

———. 1985. "Senate Leaders: Janitors for an Untidy Chamber?" In *Congress Reconsidered*, edited by Dodd and Oppenheimer. 3rd ed. Washington, D.C.: Congressional Quarterly Press.

Davidson, Roger H., and Carol Hardy. 1987. "Indicators of Senate (House) Activity and Workload." *Congressional Reference Service Report(s) for Congress*. Washington, D.C.: Congressional Reference Service.

Davidson, Roger H., and Walter J. Oleszek. 1981. *Congress and Its Members*. Washington, D.C.: Congressional Quarterly Press.

Del Sesto, Steven L. 1980. "Nuclear Reactor Safety and the Role of the Congressman: A Content Analysis of Congressional Hearings." *Journal of Politics* 42:226–41.

Destler, I. M. 1992. *American Trade Politics*. 2d ed. Washington, D.C.: Institute for International Economics; New York: Twentieth Century Fund.

———. 1980. *Making Foreign Economic Policy*. Washington, D.C.: Brookings Institution.

———. 1991. "U.S. Trade Policy-making in the Eighties." In *Politics and Economics in the Eighties*, edited by Alberto Alesina and Geoffrey Carliner, 251–81. Chicago: University of Chicago Press, for the National Bureau of Economic Research.

Destler, I. M. and Thomas R. Graham. 1980. "United States Congress and the Tokyo Round: Lessons of a Success Story." *World Economy* (June): 53–70.

Donovan, Robert J. 1956. *Eisenhower: The Inside Story*. New York: Harper & Brothers.

Eagleton, Thomas. 1974. *War and Presidential Power: A Chronicle of Congressional Surrender*. New York: Liveright.

Edwards, George C., III. 1989. *At the Margin: Presidential Leadership in Congress*. New Haven, Conn.: Yale University Press.

———. 1991. "The Two Presidencies: A Reevaluation." In *The Two Presidencies: A Quarter Century Assessment*, edited by Steven A. Shull, 101–16. Chicago: Nelson-Hall.

Edwards, John. 1982. *Superweapon: The Making of the MX*. New York: Norton.

Erlichman, John. 1982. *Witness to Power*. New York: Simon & Shuster.

Evangelista, Matthew. 1989. "Issue Area and Foreign Policy Revisited." *International Organization* 43, no. 1 (Winter): 147–71.

Evans, Rowland, and Robert Novak. 1966. *Lyndon B. Johnson and the Exercise of Power*. New York: New American Library.

———. 1971. *Nixon in the White House: The Frustration of Power*. New York: Random House.

"Executive-Congressional Relations and the Treaty Ratification Process." 1991. Report of a conference cosponsored by the Woodrow Wilson International Center for Scholars and the Henry L. Stimson Center. Washington, D.C., 17–18 January.

Fenno, Richard F., Jr. 1966. *The Power of the Purse*. Boston: Little, Brown.

———. 1973. *Congressmen in Committees*. Boston: Little, Brown.

———. 1990. *Watching Politicians: Essays on Participant Observation*. Berkeley: University of California, Institute of Governmental Studies.

Finney, John W. 1987. "A Historical Perspective." In *The ABM Treaty: To Defend or Not to Defend?* edited by Walther Stützle, Bhupendra Jasani, and Regina Cowen, 29–44. New York: Oxford University Press.

Fiorina, Morris P. 1985. "Group Concentration and the Delegation of Legislative Authority." In *Regulatory Policy and the Social Sciences*, edited by Roger G. Noll. Berkeley and Los Angeles: University of California Press.

———. 1989. "An Era of Divided Government." Manuscript.

Fisher, Louis. 1989. "Micromanagement by Congress: Reality and Mythology." In *The Fettered Presidency: Legal Constraints on the Executive Branch*, edited by L. Gordon Crovitz and Jeremy A. Rabkin. Washington, D.C.: American Enterprise Institute.

Fleisher, Richard. 1985. "Economic Benefit, Ideology, and Senate Voting of the B-1 Bomber." *American Politics Quarterly* 13:200–11.

Foote, Joe S. 1990. *Television Access and Political Power: The Network, the Presidency and the "Loyal Opposition."* New York: Praeger.

Ford, Gerald R. 1979. *A Time to Heal*. New York: Harper & Row.

Fossedal, Gregory. 1987. "NSC Minutes Show President Leaning to SDI Deployment." *Washington Times*, 6 February, 1.

Franck, Thomas M., and Edward Weisband. 1979. *Foreign Policy by Congress*. New York: Oxford University Press.

Frye, Alton. 1975. *A Responsible Congress: The Politics of National Security*. New York: McGraw-Hill.

———. 1983–84. "Strategic Build-Down: A Context for Restraint." *Foreign Affairs* 62, no. 2 (Winter):293–317.

———. 1986. "The MX and Strategic Policy." In *Making Government Work: From White House to Congress*, edited by Robert E. Hunter, Wayne L. Berman, and John F. Kennedy, 152–78. Boulder, Colo.: Westview Press.

———. 1987. "North's Abuse of Precedents." *Wall Street Journal*, 24 July, 16.

Frye, Alton, and William D. Rogers. 1979. "Linkage Begins at Home." *Foreign Policy* 35 (Summer): 49–67.

Fukuyama, Francis. 1992. *The End of History and the Last Man*. New York: Free Press.

Fulbright, William F. 1961. "American Foreign Policy in the 20th Century under an 18th-Century Constitution." *Cornell Law Quarterly* 47:1–13.

Garthoff, Raymond L. 1987. *Policy versus the Law: The Reinterpretation of the ABM Treaty*. Washington, D.C.: Brookings Institution.

George, Alexander L. 1979. "Case Studies and Theory Development: The Method of Structured, Focused Comparison." In *Diplomacy: New Approaches in History, Theory, and Policy*, edited by Paul Gordon Lauren. New York: Free Press.

Glennon, Michael J. 1990. *Constitutional Diplomacy*. Foreword by William F. Fulbright. Princeton, N.J.: Princeton University Press.

Goerevitch, Peter. 1978. "The Second Image Reversed: The International Sources of Domestic Politics." *International Organization* 32 (Autumn): 881–912.

Greenstein, Fred I. 1982. *Hidden Hand Presidency: Eisenhower as Leader*. New York: Basic Books.

Gutman, Roy. 1988. *Banana Diplomacy: The Making of American Policy in Nicaragua, 1981–1987*. New York: Simon & Schuster.

Haass, Richard. 1979. "The Role of Congress in American Security Policy." *Adelphi Papers*, no. 153.

Hamilton, Alexander, James Madison, and John Jay. 1961. *The Federalist Papers*. Edited by Clinton Rossiter, New York: Mentor.

Handberg, R., and R. Bledsoe. 1979. "Shifting Patterns in the American Military Budget Process: An Overview." *Journal of Strategic Studies* 2:348–61.

Harvard Law Review. 1983. "The International Emergency Economic Powers Act: A Congressional Attempt to Control Presidential Emergency Power." *Harvard Law Review* 96:1102–20.

Heclo, Hugh. 1977. *A Government of Strangers*. Washington, D.C.: Brookings Institution.

Huntington, Samuel P. 1957. *The Soldier and the State*. Cambridge, Mass.: Harvard University Press, Belknap Press.

———. 1961. *The Common Defense*. New York: Columbia University Press.

———. 1989. "American Ideals versus American Institutions." Reprinted in *American Foreign Policy: Theoretical Essays*, edited by G. John Ikenberry. Boston: Scott, Foresman.

Jacobson, Gary C. 1990. *The Electoral Origins of Divided Government: Competition in U.S. House Elections, 1946–1988*. Boulder, Colo.: Westview Press.

Jentleson, Bruce W. 1990. "American Diplomacy: Around the World and along Pennsylvania Avenue." In *A Question of Balance: The President, the Congress, and Foreign Policy*, edited by Thomas Mann, 146–200. Washington, D.C.: Brookings Institution.

Johnson, Loch K. 1980. "The U.S. Congress and the CIA: Monitoring the Dark Side of Government." *Legislative Studies Quarterly* 5:477–500.

———. 1988. *A Season of Inquiry: Congress and Intelligence*. Chicago: Dorsey.

———. 1989a. *America's Secret Power: The CIA in a Democratic Society*. New York: Oxford University Press.

———. 1989b. "Controlling the CIA: A Critique of Current Safeguards." *Harvard Journal of Law & Public Policy* 12:371–96.

———. 1989c. "Strategic Intelligence: An American Perspective." *International Journal of Intelligence and Counterintelligence* 3:299–332.

———. 1992. "On Drawing a Bright Line for Covert Operations." *American Journal of International Law* 86:284–309.

———. 1992–93. "Smart Intelligence." *Foreign Policy* 89:53–70.

Johnson, Loch K., Erna Gellner, and John C. Kuzenski. 1992. "The Study of Congressional Investigations: Research Strategies." *Congress & the Presidency* 19:138–56.

Jones, Charles O. 1981. "Congress and the Presidency." In *The New Congress*, edited by Thomas E. Mann and Norman J. Ornstein. Washington, D.C.: American Enterprise Institute.

———. 1983. "Presidential Negotiation with Congress." In *Both Ends of the Avenue:*

The Presidency, the Executive Branch and Congress in the 1980s, edited by Anthony King. Washington, D.C.: American Enterprise Institute.

———. 1988a. "Ronald Reagan and the U.S. Congress: Visible-Hand Politics." In *The Reagan Legacy*, edited by Jones, 30–59. Chatham, N.J.: Chatham House.

———. 1988b. *The Trusteeship Presidency: Jimmy Carter and the United States Congress*. Baton Rouge: Louisiana State University Press.

Kaiser, Fred. 1977. "Oversight of Foreign Policy: The U.S. House Committee on International Relations." *Legislative Studies Quarterly* 2:255–80.

Kanter, Arnold. 1972. "Congress and the Defense Budget: 1960–1970." *American Political Science Review* 66:129–43.

Katzenstein, Peter J. 1983. "The Small European States in the International Economy: Economic Dependence and Corporatist Politics." In *The Antinomies of Interdependence: National Welfare and the International Division of Labor*, edited by John G. Ruggie, 91–130. New York: Columbia University Press.

Kegley, Charles W., Jr., and Eugene Wittkopf. 1982. *American Foreign Policy: Pattern and Process*. 2d ed. New York: St. Martin's Press.

Keller, Bill. 1981. "Special-Interest Lobbyists Cultivate the 'Grass Roots.'" *Congressional Quarterly Weekly Report*, 12 September, 1741.

Kennan, George F. 1951. *American Diplomacy, 1900–1950*. Chicago: University of Chicago Press.

Keohane, Robert. 1984. *After Hegemony: Cooperation and Discord in the World Political Economy*. Princeton, N.J.: Princeton University Press.

Kerr, James. 1982. *The Insular Cases: The Role of the Judiciary in American Expansion*. New York: Kennikat.

Key, V. O. 1949. *Southern Politics*. New York: Random House.

Koh, Harold. 1990. *The National Security Constitution: Sharing Power after the Iran-Contra Affair*. New Haven, Conn.: Yale University Press.

Korb, L. J. 1973. "Congressional Impact on Defense Spending, 1962–1973: The Programmatic and Fiscal Hypotheses." *Naval War College Review* 26, no. 3 (November–December): 49–61.

Korn, Jessica. 1993. "Separation of Powers in Practice: The Limits of the Legislative Veto and the Impact of *Chadha*." Ph. D. diss., Department of Government, Harvard University.

Kornhauser, William. 1959. *The Politics of Mass Society*. New York: Free Press.

Krasner, Stephen D. 1978. *Defending the National Interest: Raw Materials Investments and U.S. Foreign Policy*. Princeton, N.J.: Princeton University Press.

Kravitz, Walter. 1977. "Relations between the Senate and the House of Representatives: The Party Leadership." In *Policymaking Role of Leadership in the Senate*, by Commission on the Operation of the Senate. Washington, D.C.: Government Printing Office.

Krepon, Michael. 1989. *Arms Control in the Reagan Administration*. Lanham, M.D.: University Press of America.

Kurth, James. 1989. "A Widening Gyre: The Logic of American Weapons Procurement." Reprinted in *American Foreign Policy: Theoretical Essays*, edited by G. John Ikenberry, 14–37. Boston: Scott, Foresman.

LaFeber, Walter. 1987. "The Constitution and United States Foreign Policy." In *The*

Constitution and American Life, edited by David Thelen. Ithaca, N.Y.: Cornell University Press.

Laurance, Edward J. 1976. "The Changing Role of Congress in Defense Policy-Making." *Journal of Conflict Resolution* 20:213–53.

LeLoup, Lance T., and Stephen A. Shull. 1979. "Congress versus the Executive: The 'Two Presidencies' Reconsidered." *Social Science Quarterly* 59:704–19.

Light, Paul. 1983. *The President's Agenda*. Baltimore: Johns Hopkins University Press.

Lindsay, James M. 1990. "Parochialism, Policy, and Constituency Constraints: Congressional Voting on Strategic Weapons Systems." *American Journal of Political Science* 34:36–60.

Lobel, Jules. 1986. "Covert War and Congressional Authority: Hidden War and Forgotten Power." *University of Pennsylvania Law Review* 134 (June): 1035.

Lowi, Theodore. 1964. "American Business, Public Policy, Case Studies and Political Theory." *World Politics* 16:676–715.

MacNeil, Neil. 1966. *Dirksen: Portrait of a Public Man*. New York: World Publishing Co.

Mann, Thomas E. 1990a. "Making Foreign Policy: President and Congress." In *A Question of Balance: The President, the Congress, and Foreign Policy*, edited by Mann. Washington, D.C.: The Brookings Institution.

———. ed. 1990b. *A Question of Balance: The President, the Congress, and Foreign Policy*. Washington, D.C.: Brookings Institution.

Mansfield, Harvey C., Jr. 1989. *Taming the Prince: The Ambivalence of Modern Executive Power*. New York: Free Press.

May, Christopher. 1989. *In the Name of War: Judicial Review and the War Powers since 1918*. Cambridge, Mass.: Harvard University Press.

Mayhew, David. 1974. *Congress: The Electoral Connection*. New Haven, Conn.: Yale University Press.

———. 1992. *Divided We Govern*. New Haven, Conn.: Yale University Press.

McCormick, James, and Eugene R. Wittkopf. 1990. "Bush and Bipartisanship: The Past as Prologue." *Washington Quarterly* 13 (Winter): 5–16.

McCubbins, Mathew, Roger Noll, and Barry Weingast. 1989. "Structure and Process, Politics and Policy: Administrative Arrangements and the Political Control of Agencies." *Virginia Law Review* 75, no. 2 (March): 431–82.

McCubbins, Mathew, and Thomas Schwartz. 1984. "Congressional Oversight Overlooked: Police Patrols versus Fire Alarms." *American Journal of Political Science* 28 (February): 165–79.

McNaugher, Thomas L. 1989. *New Weapons, Old Politics*. Washington, D.C.: Brookings Institution.

Mearscheimer, John J. 1990. "Back to the Future: Instability in Europe after the Cold War." *International Security* 15, no. 1 (Summer): 5–56.

Meier, Kenneth J., and J. R. Van Lohuizen. 1978. "Interest Groups in the Appropriations Process." *Social Science Quarterly* 59:210–17.

Moe, Terry. 1984. "The New Economics of Organization." *American Journal of Political Science* 28 (November): 739–77.

Morgenthau, Hans J. [1946] 1966. *Politics among Nations*. 4th edition. New York: Knopf.

————. 1969. "Congress and Foreign Policy." *New Republic* 160, 14 June.

Nelson, Douglas. 1989. "Domestic Political Preconditions of US Trade Policy: Liberal Structure and Protectionist Dynamics." *Journal of Public Policy* 9, no. 1: 83–108.

Newhouse, John. 1989. *Cold Dawn: The Story of Salt.* New York: Holt, Rinehart & Winston.

Nolan, Janne E. 1989. *Guardians of the Arsenal: The Politics of Nuclear Strategy.* New York: Basic Books.

————. 1991. "The INF Treaty Ratification Debate." Paper prepared for a conference co-sponsored by the Woodrow Wilson International Center for Scholars and the Henry L. Stimson Center, Washington, D.C., 17–18 January.

O'Donnell, Guillermo. 1973. *Modernization and Bureaucratic Authoritarianism.* Politics of Modernization Series, no. 9. Berkeley: University of California, Institute for International Studies.

Ogul, Morris S. 1976. *Congress Oversees the Bureaucracy: Studies in Legislative Supervision.* Pittsburgh: University of Pittsburgh Press.

Ogul, Morris S., and Bert A. Rockman. 1990. "Overseeing Oversight: New Departures and Old Problems." *Legislative Studies Quarterly* 15:5–24.

O'Halloran, Sharyn. 1990. "Congress, the President, and U.S. Trade Policy: Process and Policy Outcomes." Paper presented at the Annual Meeting of the American Political Science Association, San Francisco, 1 September.

Oldfield, Duane M., and Aaron Wildavsky. 1989. "Reconsidering the Two Presidencies." In *The Two Presidencies: A Quarter Century Assessment*, edited by Steve A. Shull, 181–90. Chicago: Nelson-Hall.

Olsson, Christer. 1982. *Congress and the Making of United States Foreign Policy, 1933–40.* Lund Studies in International History. Stockholm, Sweden: Esselte Studium.

O'Neill, Thomas P., Jr., with William Novack. 1987. *Man of the House.* New York: Random House.

Ornstein, Norman J., Thomas E. Mann, and Michael J. Malbin. 1990. *Vital Statistics on Congress, 1989–1990.* Washington, D.C.: Congressional Quarterly Press.

Ornstein, Norman J., and David W. Rohde. 1977. "Shifting Forces, Changing Rules and Political Outcomes: The Impact of Congressional Change on Four House Committees." In *New Perspectives on the House of Representatives*, edited by Robert Peabody and Nelson Polsby, 186–269. 3d ed. Chicago: Rand McNally.

Parry, Robert, and Peter Kornbluh. 1988. "Iran-Contra's Untold Story." *Foreign Policy* 7:3–30.

Pastor, Robert A. 1975. "Coping with Congress's Foreign Policy." *Foreign Service Journal* 52, no. 12: 15–18, 23.

————. 1980. *Congress and the Politics of U.S. Foreign Economic Policy.* Berkeley and Los Angeles: University of California Press.

————. 1987. *Condemned to Repetition: The United States and Nicaragua.* Princeton, N.J.: Princeton University Press.

————. 1991. "Congress and U.S. Foreign Policy: Comparative Advantage of Disadvantage?" *Washington Quarterly* 14, no. 4 (Fall): 101–14.

————. 1992. *Whirlpool: U.S. Foreign Policy toward Latin America and the Caribbean.* Princeton, N.J.: Princeton University Press.

———. 1993. "The War between the Branches: Explaining U.S. Policy toward Nicaragua, 1979–89." In *Public Opinion and U.S. Foreign Policy*, edited by Richard Sobel. Lanham, Md.: Rowman & Littlefield.

Payne, James L. 1982. "The Rise of Lone Wolf Questioning in House Committee Hearings." *Polity* 14:626–40.

Peabody, Robert L. 1976. *Leadership in Congress*. Boston: Little, Brown.

———. 1981. "Senate Party Leadership: From the 1950s to the 1980s." In *Understanding Congressional Leadership*, edited by Frank H. Mackaman. Washington, D.C.: Congressional Quarterly Press.

Peppers, Donald A. 1991. "The 'Two Presidencies' Thesis: Eight Years Later." In *The Two Presidencies: A Quarter Century Assessment*, edited by Steve A. Shull, 26–35. Chicago: Nelson-Hall.

Perkins, Dexter. 1927. *The Monroe Doctrine, 1823–1826*. Cambridge, Mass.: Harvard University Press.

Peterson, Paul E. 1976. *School Politics Chicago Style*. Chicago: University of Chicago Press.

———. 1981. *City Limits*. Chicago: University of Chicago Press.

Peterson, Paul E., and Jay P. Greene. 1994. "Why Executive-Legislative Conflict in the United States is Dwindling." *British Journal of Political Science* 24:33–35.

Peterson, Paul E., and Mark C. Rom. 1988. "Lower Taxes, More Spending and Budget Deficits." In *The Reagan Legacy*, edited by Charles O. Jones, 213–40. Chatham, N.J.: Chatham House.

Platt, Alan. 1978. *The U.S. Senate and Strategic Arms Policy, 1969–1977*. Boulder, Colo.: Westview Press.

Preeg, Ernest H. 1970. *Traders and Diplomats: An Analysis of the Kennedy Round of Negotiations under the General Agreement on Tariffs and Trade*. Washington, D.C.: Brookings Institution.

President Eisenhower's Meetings with Legislative Leaders, 1953–1961. 1986. Frederick, Md.: University Publications of America.

"Presidential Job Ratings." 1991. *Cook Political Report*, 29 October: 33.

Putnam, Robert. 1988. "Diplomacy and Domestic Politics: The Logic of Two-Level Games." *International Organization* 42, no. 3 (Summer): 427–60.

Rae, Nicole C. 1989. *The Decline and Fall of Liberal Republicans from 1952 to the Present*. New York: Oxford University Press.

Ransom, Harry Howe. 1975. "Secret Intelligence Agencies and Congress." *Society* 12:33–38.

———. 1987. "The Politicization of Intelligence." In *Intelligence and Intelligence Policy in a Democratic Society*, edited by Stephen J. Cimbala, 25–46. Dobbs Ferry, N.Y.: Transnational Publishers.

Reed, J. W. 1984. "Congress and the Politics of Defense Reform." In *The Defense Reform Debate*, edited by A. A. Clark, et al. Baltimore: Johns Hopkins University Press.

Reichley, James. 1985. "The Rise of National Parties." In *The New Direction in American Politics*, edited by John Chubb and Paul E. Peterson, 175–202. Washington, D.C.: Brookings Institution.

Report of the President's Commission on Strategic Forces. 1983. N.p. April.

Rieselbach, Leroy. 1986. *Congressional Reform*. Washington, D.C.: Congressional Quarterly Press.

Ripley, Randall B. 1967. *Party Leaders in the House of Representatives*. Washington, D.C.: Brookings Institution.

———. 1969a. *Majority Party Leadership in Congress*. Boston: Little, Brown.

———. 1969b. *Power in the Senate*. New York: St. Martin's Press.

Ripley, Randall B., and James Lindsay. *Congress Resurgent: Foreign and Defense Policy on Capitol Hill*. Ann Arbor: University of Michigan Press, 1993.

Rohde, David W. 1988. "Variations in Partisanship in the House of Representatives, 1953–1988: Southern Democrats, Realignment and Agenda Change." Paper presented at the Annual Meeting of the American Political Science Association, Atlanta, Georgia.

———. 1990. " 'The Reports of My Death Are Greatly Exaggerated': Parties and Party Voting in the House of Representatives." Manuscript.

———. 1991. *Parties and Leaders in the Postreform House*. Chicago: University of Chicago Press.

———. 1992. "Electoral Forces, Political Agendas, and Partisanship in the House and Senate." In *The Postreform Congress*, edited by Roger Davidson, 27–47. New York: St. Martin's Press.

———. 1993. "Partisanship, Leadership, and Congressional Assertiveness in Foreign and Defense Policy." In *The Politics of American Foreign Policy*, edited by David Deese. New York: St. Martin's Press.

Rostow, Eugene. 1989. "President, Prime Minister or Constitutional Monarch?" *American Journal of International Law* 83 (October): 740.

Rourke, John. 1983. *Congress and the Presidency in U.S. Foreign Policymaking: A Study of Interaction and Influence, 1945–82*. Boulder, Colo.: Westview Press.

Russett, B. M. 1970. *What Price Vigilance?* New Haven, Conn.: Yale University Press.

———. 1990. *Controlling the Sword: The Democratic Governance of National Security*. Cambridge, Mass.: Harvard University Press.

Schattschneider, E. E. 1935. *Politics, Pressures, and the Tariff*. New York: Prentice-Hall.

Scheer, Robert. 1982. *With Enough Shovels: Reagan, Bush, and Nuclear War*. New York: Random House.

Schlesinger, Arthur M., Jr. 1973. *The Imperial Presidency*. Boston: Houghton Mifflin.

Schlozman, Kay, and John Tierney. 1986. *Organized Interests and American Democracy*. New York: Harper & Row.

Schoultz, Lars. 1981. *Human Rights and United States Policy toward Latin America*. Princeton, N.J.: Princeton University Press.

Schwab, Susan C. 1993. "The Omnibus Trade and Competitiveness Act of 1988: The End of an Era in U.S. Trade Policy?" Ph.D. diss., School of Business and Public Management, George Washington University.

Scicchitano, Michael J. 1986. "Congressional Oversight: The Case of the Clean Air Act." *Legislative Studies Quarterly* 11:393–407.

Shepsle, Kenneth A. 1989. "The Changing Textbook Congress." In *Can the Government Govern?*, edited by John E. Chubb and Paul E. Peterson, 238–66. Washington, D.C.: Brookings Institution.

Shepsle, Kenneth A., and Barry R. Weingast. 1984. "Legislative Politics and Budget Outcomes." In *Federal Budget Policy in the 1980s*, edited by G. Mills and J. Palmer, 343–67. Washington, D.C.: Urban Institute.

————. 1987. "The Institutional Foundations of Committee Power." *American Political Science Review* 81, no. 1 (March): 85–104.

Shull, Steve A., ed. 1991. *The Two Presidencies: A Quarter Century Assessment.* Chicago: Nelson-Hall.

Sigelman, Lee. 1991. "A Reassessment of the Two Presidencies Thesis." In *The Two Presidencies: A Quarter Century Assessment*, edited by Steve A. Shull, 63–72. Chicago: Nelson-Hall.

Silverstein, Gordon. 1991. "Constitutional Constraints? How Constitutonal Interpretation Shapes American Foreign Policy." Ph.D. diss., Harvard University.

Sinclair, Barbara. 1982. *Congressional Realignment, 1925–1978.* Austin: University of Texas Press.

————. 1983. *Majority Leadership in the U.S. House.* Baltimore: Johns Hopkins University Press.

Smist, Frank J., Jr. 1990. *Congress Oversees the United States Intelligence Community.* Knoxville: University of Tennessee Press.

Smith, Steven S. 1989. *Call to Order.* Washington, D.C.: Brookings Institution.

————. 1993. "Forces of Change in Senate Party Leadership." In *Congress Reconsidered*, edited by Lawrence C. Dodd and Bruce I. Oppenheimer, 261–63. 5th ed. Washington, D.C.: Congressional Quarterly Press.

Smith, Steven S., and Christopher Deering. 1990. *Committees in Congress.* 2d ed. Washington, D.C.: Congressional Quarterly Press.

Sofaer, Abraham. 1976. *War, Foreign Affairs and Constitutional Power: The Origins.* Cambridge, Mass.: Ballinger.

Sorensen, Theodore C. 1965. *Kennedy.* New York: Harper & Row.

Steinberg, Alfred. 1975. *Sam Rayburn: A Biography.* New York: Hawthorn Books.

Stockman, David A. 1986. *The Triumph of Politics: Why the Reagan Revolution Failed.* New York: Harper & Row.

Strategic Arms Limitation Talks (SALT): Legislative History of the Jackson Amendment, 1972. 1972. Offset and released by Senator Henry M. Jackson.

Stützle, Walther, Bhupendra Jasani, and Regina Cowen, eds. 1987. *The ABM Treaty: To Defend or Not to Defend?* New York: Oxford University Press.

Sundquist, James L. 1981. *The Decline and Resurgence of Congress.* Washington, D.C.: Brookings Institution.

————. 1987. *The Case for Constitutional Reform.* Washington, D.C.: Brookings Institution.

————. 1988. "Needed: A Political Theory for the New Era of Coalition Government in the United States." *Political Science Quarterly* 103:613–35.

Sutherland, George. 1919. *Constitutional Powers and World Affairs.* New York: Columbia University Press.

Talbott, Strobe. 1984. *Deadly Gambits.* New York: Knopf.

Tananbaum, Duane. 1988. *The Bricker Amendment Controversy: A Test of Eisenhower's Political Leadership.* Ithaca, N.Y.: Cornell University Press.

Tocqueville, Alexis de. 1945. *Democracy in America.* Vol. 1. New York: Vintage Books.

Trimble, Phillip. 1989. "The President's Foreign Affairs Power." *American Journal of International Law* 83 (October): 750.

Truman, David B. 1959. *The Congressional Party: A Case Study*. New York: John Wiley & Sons.

U.S. Bureau of the Census. 1975. *Historical Statistics of the United States: Colonial Times to 1970, Part 2*. Washington, D.C.: Government Printing Office.

———. 1989. *Statistical Abstract of the United States*. Washington, D.C.: Government Printing Office.

U.S. Congress. 1987a. Senate Select Committee on Secret Military Assistance to Iran and the Nicaraguan Opposition, and House Select Committee to Investigate Covert Arms Transactions with Iran. *Joint Hearings on the Iran-Contra Investigation*. 100th Congress, 1st sess. August.

———. 1987b. *Report of the Congressional Committees Investigating the Iran-Contra Affair*. 100th Congress, 1st sess. November.

U.S. House. 1974. Committee on International Relations. *Hearings on Human Rights in Chile*. 93d Cong., 2d sess. June.

———. 1975. Permanent Select Committee on Intelligence. *Hearings on U.S. Intelligence Agencies and Activities*. Part 1: *Intelligence Costs and Fiscal Procedures*. Part 2: The *Performances of the Intelligence Community*. 94th Cong., 1st sess. August–September.

———. 1976. Committee on International Relations. *Hearings on Chile, the Status of Human Rights and Its Relationship to U.S. Economic Assistance Programs*. 94th Cong., 2d sess. April–May.

———. 1977. Permanent Select Committee on Intelligence. Subcommittee on Oversight. *Hearings on the CIA and the Media*. 95th Cong., 1st sess. December.

———. 1978. Permanent Select Committee on Intelligence. *Hearings on Disclosure of Funds for Intelligence Activities*. 95th Cong., 2d sess. January.

———. 1979. Permanent Select Committee on Intelligence. Subcommittee on Legislation. *Hearings on Graymail Legislation*. 96th Cong., 1st sess. September.

———. 1980. Permanent Select Committee on Intelligence. Subcommittee on Legislation. *Hearings on Proposals to Criminalize the Unauthorized Disclosure of the Identities of Undercover United States Intelligence Officers and Agents*. 96th Cong., 2d sess. 30 January.

———. 1983. Permanent Select Committee on Intelligence. *Hearings on Congressional Oversight of Covert Activities*. 98th Cong., 2d sess. 20–22 September.

———. 1985. Committee on Foreign Affairs. Subcommittee on Arms Control, International Security and Science. *Hearing on ABM Treaty Interpretation Dispute*. 99th Cong., 1st sess. 22 October.

———. 1987. Permanent Select Committee on Intelligence. Subcommittee on Legislation. *Hearings on H.R. 1013, H.R. 1317, and Other Proposals Which Address the Issue of Affording Prior Notice of Covert Actions to the Congress*. 100th Cong., 1st sess. April–June.

U.S. Senate. 1962. Committee on Foreign Relations. *Hearings on Foreign Assistance Act. 1962*. 87th Cong., 2d sess.

———. 1971. Committee on Foreign Relations. Subcommittee on Western Hemisphere Affairs. *Hearings on United States Policies and Programs in Brazil*. 92d Cong., 1st sess. 4, 5, 11 May.

_____. 1975. Select Committee to Study Governmental Operations with Respect to Intelligence Activities. *Hearings on the Huston Plan*. 94th Cong., 1st sess. September.

_____. 1977. Committee on Foreign Relations. *Hearings on Panama Canal Treaties, Part 1*. 95th Cong., 1st sess. September–October.

_____. 1979. *The Salt II Treaty*. Exec. Rept. No. 96-14. 96th Cong., 1st sess. 19 November.

_____. 1980. Select Committee on Intelligence. *Hearings on the National Intelligence Act of 1980*. 96th Cong., 2d sess. 21 February–16 April.

_____. 1983. Select Committee on Intelligence. *Hearings on S.1324, an Amendment to the National Security Act of 1947*. 98th Cong., 1st sess. June.

_____. 1987. Committee on Foreign Relations. *Hearings on the ABM Treaty and the Constitution*. 100th Cong., 1st sess. 11 March.

U.S. Superintendent of Documents. 1989. *Historical Tables, Budget of the United States Government, Fiscal Year 1990*. Washington, D.C.: Government Printing Office.

_____. 1990. *Budget of the United States Government, Fiscal Year 1991*. Washington, D.C.: Government Printing Office.

_____. 1991. *Budget of the United States Government, Fiscal Year 1992*. Washington, D.C.: Government Printing Office.

_____. 1991. *Historical Tables, Budget of the United States Government, Fiscal Year 1992*. Washington, D.C.: Office of Management and Budget/U.S. Government Printing Office.

University of Miami Law Review. 1988. "Symposium: Foreign Affairs and the Constitution: The Roles of Congress, the President, and the Courts." *University of Miami Law Review* 43 (November).

University of Pennsylvania Law Review. 1989. "Arms Control Treaty Reinterpretation." *University of Pennsylvania Law Review* 137, no. 5 (May): 1353–1588.

Walker, Jack L. 1977. "Setting the Agenda in the U.S. Senate: A Theory of Problem Selection." *British Journal of Political Science* 7:423–47.

Waltz, Kenneth N. 1979. *Theory of International Politics*. New York: McGraw Hill.

Warburg, Gerald. 1989. *Conflict and Consensus: The Struggle between Congress and the President over Foreign Policymaking*. New York: Ballinger.

Weaver, R. Kent. 1988. *Automatic Government: The Politics of Indexation*. Washington, D.C.: Brookings Institution.

Wilcox, Francis Orlando. 1971. *Congress, the Executive, and Foreign Policy*. New York: Harper & Row.

Wildavsky, Aaron. 1966. "The Two Presidencies." *Transaction* 4 (December): 7–14. Reprinted in Wildavsky 1975. 448–61.

_____, ed. 1975. *Perspectives on the Presidency*. Boston: Little, Brown.

_____. 1988. *The New Politics of the Budgetary Process*. Glenview, Ill.: Scott, Foresman.

_____. [1966] 1991. "The Two Presidencies." In *The Two Presidencies: A Quarter Century Assessment*, edited by Steven A. Shull, 11–25. Chicago: Nelson-Hall.

Wilson, James Q., ed. 1980. *The Politics of Regulation*. New York: Basic Books.

Wilson, Woodrow. [1885] 1956. *Congressional Government: A Study in American Politics*. New York: Meridian.

Wormuth, Francis, and Edwin Firmage. 1989. *To Chain the Dog of War*. 2d ed. Urbana: University of Illinois Press.

Wright, Jim. 1993. *Worth It All: My War over Peace*. New York: Maxwell MacMillan.

Yankelovich, Daniel, and Sidney Harman. 1988. *Starting with the People*. Boston: Houghton Mifflin.

★ ★ ★

THE CONTRIBUTORS

★ ★ ★

Ralph G. Carter, former President of the Foreign Policy Analysis Section of the International Studies Association, is Associate Professor and Chair of the Political Science Department at Texas Christian University. His most recent publication, with John T. Rourke and Mark A. Boyer, is *Making American Foreign Policy* (Dushkin Publishing Group, 1994).

I. M. (Mac) Destler is Professor at the School of Public Affairs, University of Maryland, and Director of its Center for International and Security Studies at Maryland (CISSM). He is also Visiting Fellow at the Institute for International Economics, publisher of his recently revised *American Trade Politics*.

Alton Frye is National Director and Senior Vice-President of the Council on Foreign Relations, which he has also served as Washington Director and President. A frequent contributor to *Foreign Affairs* and *Foreign Policy*, he was a member of the recent National Academy of Public Administration panel that published *Beyond Distrust: Building Bridges Between Congress and the Executive* (1992).

Jay P. Greene is an Assistant Professor of Political Science at the University of Houston. His dissertation at Harvard University examines presidential-congressional relations.

Loch K. Johnson is a Regents Professor at the University of Georgia and author of *America's Secret Power: The CIA in a Democratic Society* (Oxford University Press); *America As a World Power*, 2d ed. (McGraw-Hill); and, with Charles S. Bullock III, *Runoff Elections in the United States* (University of North Carolina Press).

Robert A. Pastor is Professor of Political Science at Emory University and Director of the Latin American Program at Emory's Carter Center. He is the author of nine books, including *Congress and the Politics of U.S. Foreign Economic Policy* (University of California Press) and *Whirlpool: U.S. Foreign Policy Toward Latin America and the Caribbean* (Princeton University Press). Director of Latin American Affairs on the National Security Council from 1977 to 1981, Pastor has organized election observation missions to eight countries in the Americas, including Nicaragua, Panama, and Mexico.

Paul E. Peterson is Henry Lee Shattuck Professor of Government and Director of the Center for American Political Studies at Harvard University. Recent publications include a volume, edited with John Chubb, *Can the Government Govern?* and, with Mark C. Rom, *Welfare Magnets: A New Case for a National Standard*, both published by Brookings.

David W. Rohde is Manning J. Dauer Eminent Scholar in Political Science at the University of Florida. Recent publications include *Parties and Leaders in the Postreform House* (University of Chicago Press) and, with Paul R. Abramson and John H. Aldrich, *Change and Continuity in the 1992 Elections* (CQ Press).

Gordon Silverstein is Assistant Professor of Government at Dartmouth College. Publications include *Imbalance of Powers? How Constitutional Interpretation Shapes American Foreign Policy* (forthcoming).

Steven S. Smith is Professor of Political Science at the University of Minnesota. Recent publications include *Committees in Congress* (CQ Press) and *Managing Uncertainty in the House of Representatives* and *Call to Order: Floor Politics in the House and Senate*, both published by Brookings.

★ ★ ★

INDEX

★ ★ ★

Select Committee on Intelligence, Senate. *See* Intelligence committees, congressional

Select Committee on Secret Military Assistance to Iran and the Nicaraguan Opposition, Senate. *See* Inouye-Hamilton committees

Select Committee to Study Government Operations with Respect to Intelligence Activities, Senate. *See* Church committee

Senate, U.S.: and Gulf of Tonkin Resolution, 76; and House contrasted, 79–80, 89–90, 133, 154, 258n.36; leadership of, 129 (*see also* Baker, Howard; Byrd, Robert; Cohen, William S.; Dirksen, Everett; Fulbright, J. William; George, Walter; Jackson, Henry; Johnson, Lyndon; Knowland, William; Mansfield, Mike; Nunn, Sam; Scott, Hugh; Taft, Robert; Tower, John; Warner, John); and Persian Gulf Resolution, 76; powers of, 133 (*see also* Filibuster; Treaties, Senate and); presidential support in, 258n.36; responsibilities of, 79, 89

Senate Arms Control Observer Group. *See* Arms

Serbs, vs. Croats, 3

Ships, USN: congressional authorization of, 176; fast deployment logistics, 168. *See also* Carriers; Submarines

Shultz, George, 190, 191, 197, 200

Silos, missile, 182, 186, 261n.8. *See also* Multiple protective shelter (MPS) system

Slavery, in U.S., 208

Smith, William French, 250n.25

Smoot-Hawley Act, 78, 238, 241, 244, 264–65n.15

Social security, congressional focus on, 241

Sofaer, Abraham, 196–98, 261n.15

Somoza Debayle, Anastasio, 215

Sorenson, Theodore C., 59

South Africa, Republic of, 3

South America. *See* Brazil; Chile

South Vietnam, 110, 169. *See also* Vietnam War

Soviet Union: and arms control, 3, 77, 168; Carter and, 12, 110; cold war stance of, 247n.3; Congress and, 59, 148; crumbling of, 3, 12, 13, 18, 91; and Cuba, 204; expansionism of, 6; missiles of, 183; U.S. and, 3, 24, 91, 176, 178, 183–201, 209, 237 (*see also* Cold war; Soviet Union, Congress and); U.S. fear of, 88, 91, 92, 185 (*see also* Anticommunism; Cold war); and Vietnam, 77; and world trade, 233, 237. *See also* Brezhnev, Leonid; Communism; Gorbachev, Mikhail; Moscow summit; Sputnik

Spanish-American War, 27, 205, 208, 221

Speaker of the House of Representatives: and foreign policy, 153, 154; and media, 140; power of, 106–107, 132; vote of, 259n.6

Special interests. *See* Interest groups

Special Representative for Trade Negotiations (STR), president's, 230

Specter, Arlen, 59, 252n.9

Speeches, congressional, 242

Sputnik, 74, 162, 176, 178

Staffs, congressional, 74, 172, 220–21, 223

Stalin, Joseph, 202

START, 13, 168, 187, 190, 200

START II, 261n.8

"Star Wars." *See* Strategic Defense Initiative

State Department, U.S.: communists in, 8, 91

Steel industry, U.S.: import threat to, 236–38; Truman and, 31–32, 37

Steel Seizure case. See *Youngstown Sheet & Tube Co. v. Sawyer*

Stevens, Ted, 190

Stock market, plunge of, 235, 265n.15

Ways and means committee, House, 230–33, 235, 242, 243, 264nn.8,9
Weapons. *See* Arms; Chemical weapons; Nuclear weapons; Weapons systems
Weapons systems, U.S., 168, 171. *See also* ABM system; DIVAD; MIRV; Missiles; MX system; Safeguard ABM system; Strategic Defense Initiative
Webster, William H., 71
Weinberger, Caspar, 186
Whales, protection of, 40–41
Whigs, U.S., 8
White, Byron, 41
Wilcox, Francis O., 226
Wildavsky, Aaron, 14–16, 20, 101–103, 258n.2
Wiley, Alexander (U.S. senator), 43
Wilson, Woodrow, 8, 207

Wiretaps: CIA and, 65; president-authorized, 251n.27
Wofford, Harris, 3–4
Worcester v. State of Georgia, 249n.11
World Bank, 13
World Court, 222
World War I, 28, 221
World War II, 31, 221
Wright, Jim, 140–44, 217–18, 232, 234, 235, 255–56n.18

Yalta Conference, 147
Yeltsin, Boris, 202
Young, Andrew, 255n.18
Youngstown Sheet & Tube Co. v. Sawyer, 250n.17
Yugoslavia, 3

Zablocki, Clement J., 56